Starting a Business on a Shoestring

Michel Syrett and
Chris Dunn

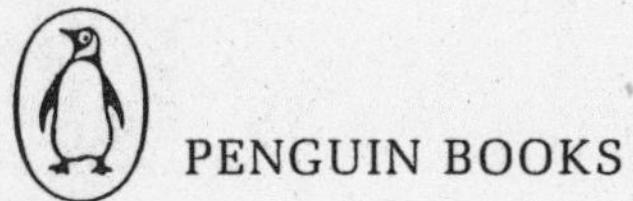
PENGUIN BOOKS

PENGUIN BOOKS

Published by the Penguin Group
27 Wrights Lane, London W8 5TZ, England
Viking Penguin Inc., 40 West 23rd Street, New York, New York 10010, USA
Penguin Books Australia Ltd, Ringwood, Victoria, Australia
Penguin Books Canada Ltd, 2801 John Street, Markham, Ontario, Canada L3R 1B4
Penguin Books (NZ) Ltd, 182–190 Wairau Road, Auckland 10, New Zealand

Penguin Books Ltd, Registered Offices: Harmondsworth, Middlesex, England

First published 1988

Filmset in Linotron 202 Melior
Typeset, printed and bound in Great Britain by
Hazell Watson and Viney Limited
Member of BPCC plc
Aylesbury Bucks

PENGUIN
SELF-
STARTERS

Starting a Business on a Shoestring

Michel Syrett started his journalistic career as an entertainment reviewer on a series of community-based weekly newspapers. His interest in employment and vocational guidance stemmed from his appointment as editor of the weekly recruitment magazine *Jobs Weekly*. He went on to become managing editor of Newpoint Ltd before establishing his own consultancy in 1981. In the past seven years he has written on a wide range of careers and management topics, most frequently for *The Times* and the *Sunday Times*. In addition to his freelance writing, he is also Associate Director of Training and Development Publications Ltd and editor of the quarterly management review *Manpower Policy and Practice*. In writing this book, he draws on his own experience as a successful consultant and on his close association with TDP. Other books by Michel Syrett include *How to Survive Unemployment* (with Robert Nathan); *Graduate Careers in Accountancy*; *Employing Job Sharers, Part-Time and Temporary Staff*: *Temporary Work Today* and *Goodbye Nine-to-Five*.

Chris Dunn BSc (Hons), MIPM, held senior line management and staff personnel posts for over eleven years, including key management posts within Rank Xerox Limited. In 1984 he founded (with his partner Barry Spence) two sister businesses, Training and Development Associates (TDA), providing training consultancy support, and Training and Development Publications (TDP), which specializes in developing and publishing open learning programmes, including *Making Redundancy Work for You*, *A Guide to Creative Job Search* and *Changing Direction*. In co-writing this book, he has been able to combine his professional skills as a counsellor with his personal experiences of funding and building up a small business, particularly with regard to the marketing and selling aspects required. In 1986 TDA and TDP became part of Rex Stewart and Associates, a well-established advertising group.

SERIES EDITORS: Stephen Coote and Bryan Loughrey

Contents

To J, with love

Preface

One in nine working people are now self-employed or run their own business – over four times the number that existed in 1979. In terms of advice, financial assistance, regional and local support and general business opportunity, there has never been a better time to consider starting your own enterprise. The encouragement of small business has been a cornerstone of the present Government's economic policy and this has resulted in a comprehensive range of special schemes designed to provide self-employed people with aid and support including tax incentives, training courses, less red tape, more advice through the Small Firms Service and better finance through the Enterprise Allowance Scheme, the Loan Guarantee Scheme and the Business Development Scheme. Nor has the range of support been confined to central government initiatives. Through the highly successful Enterprise Agency movement and through such locally based organizations as the Industrial and Commercial Finance Corporation, the Action Resource Centre and Urban and Economic Development Ltd, small-scale entrepreneurs can turn to a very wide range of support to help them start and develop their business ideas.

Yet for all this and despite the undoubted enthusiasm of the people who start up on their own, VAT statistics suggest that at least 26 per cent of all small businesses fail within the first two years of trading. Of the ones that survive, less than 25 per cent (Midland Bank estimates) succeed in providing their proprietors with a high standard of living. Recession, insufficient faith by the bank, sheer bad luck and other external factors have clearly played a part in producing this worrying statistic. But in most cases businesses fail because the demand for their services or products is insufficient, they lack the right financial resources, they are badly managed, or simply because the proprietor lacks the right temperament and cannot cope with the strain or responsibility.

The purpose of this book is therefore neither to encourage readers nor to deter them from starting their own business. It aims to help you take your own decision. This should be based on a balanced assessment of your own suitability to be an entrepreneur and an accurate judgement of the market potential of your product or service. To this end, the book provides a comprehensive series of self-assessment exercises, supported by basic information and advice on every aspect of business start-up.

But we also wished to provide an inside look at the personal experiences of people in small businesses and the challenges, problems and encouragement they encountered. We have done this through the case-studies used throughout the text to illustrate specific learning points. Their stories provide a human perspective of what it is like to be self-employed. Their numbers include school-leavers, college graduates, housewives, pensioners and the formerly unemployed, with businesses ranging from a local supplier of picnic hampers to a national manufacturer of Christmas crackers. All started out with less than £5,000 as business capital and many with significantly less.

In order to get their businesses off the ground, most had to accept greatly reduced standards of living. They had to work every evening and over most weekends, sacrificing their social lives, giving up annual holidays and depriving themselves of much that they would previously have believed essential to their lifestyle. A few (like David Hollis on page 64) have been rewarded with rapid financial expansion. Others (like Marion Carter on page 114) miscalculated the effort and financial resources needed and were obliged to give up. The majority make enough to meet their financial needs, but not much more. For all the pain and heartache, few regret the experience and most relish the greater control that running their own enterprise has enabled them to exercise over their lives.

Cautionary advice notwithstanding, we hope that, as a result of using the book, you will feel sufficiently confident of your abilities and the market potential of your business idea to go ahead with your plans. But even if you finish the text feeling that it would be unwise to proceed any further, the greater knowledge of your skills and abilities that you should have picked up will prove very useful in your personal and professional life. Good luck!

Chris Dunn
Michel Syrett
January 1988

Acknowledgements

No book is accomplished single-handedly. We would like to thank the many individuals and organizations who contributed material and ideas to the text. In particular we are grateful to:

Helen Steadman, for preparing the appendices to this book with such attention to detail;

Training and Development Publications Limited, for allowing us to adapt the existing exercises on which Chapter 3 is based;

Chris George, of the accountancy firm Styles & George, for helping us to compile the sections in Chapters 7 and 8 on 'writing a business plan' and 'reviewing business development';

Helen Steadman, Ann Hills, Melanie Wood and Kieran Duignan, for their help in putting together the many case-studies which appear throughout the book;

Rank Xerox UK Limited, for their permission to adapt and use the management skills profile included in Chapter 3;

the Manpower Services Commission, for their permission to use extracts from *Business Success Through People* (a small-business kit designed as part of the Adult Training strategy);

Vicky Hibbert, for correcting our appalling grammar;

Veronica Jones, of Veronica Jones Associates, for word-processing the original manuscript (and for contributing her own story).

Finally, we would like to thank the many small-business people we approached in the course of researching this book. The text which follows is, to a large extent, a reflection of their own experiences, views and solutions.

How to use this book

Different people choose to start their own business for different reasons. Some spot the market potential for a business idea and *then* consider the personal and financial implications. Others develop the urge to set up on their own without any particular business in mind and *then* look around for a business idea to provide an outlet for their independent feelings.

Although this book follows a logical sequence, each section is self-contained, allowing you to 'dip' into the text in whatever order best meets your needs. Precisely how you use it will depend on how much consideration you have already given to the process of starting your own business. You may, for example, already have a concrete idea of the skills needed and have already chosen a suitable product or service you can offer. Alternatively, you may have picked up this book in a totally open frame of mind.

If you have already given a lot of thought to the process of starting a business, you may have covered many of the points raised in the book, so you will be able to work quickly through the sections. You can use the exercises and case-studies to clarify, evaluate and summarize your ideas. If you have not had the opportunity to consider the possibility of self-employment, you should spend more time and work your way through stage by stage.

One final point. The book makes numerous references to the role of partners. This can prove confusing since the word 'partner' could denote the person with whom you share your life (such as a spouse or lover) or a business partner. Both have equally important roles to play – indeed they can sometimes be one and the same person. To help distinguish between the two, wherever possible we have used the description 'personal partner' and 'business partner'.

1 Preparation and Planning

1 *Why Self-employment?*

You have probably picked up this book because you are considering, or have already decided to start, a small business of your own. As you think about the implications, you may worry about the financial commitment and the degree of financial insecurity that this major decision in your life will bring. You may also be insecure about your ability to cope with the personal challenges involved; about whether you really have the skills, knowledge and experience required.

This book can help you. The various exercises, case-studies and information will enable you to:

- assess and identify the skills, knowledge and experience you will need to start a small business;
- work out which skills you have, analyse and categorize your experience so that you can choose the most suitable product(s) or service(s) to form the basis of your enterprise;
- assess the potential market for your products or services and whether the demand will prove sufficient to ensure a regular flow of business;
- identify and obtain the moral support you will need;
- calculate accurately the kind and extent of the finance you will require;
- search out all the possible sources of financial support, including many of the more unusual that are not always considered by traditional guides;

- plan the launch and development of your enterprise in a systematic and logical manner.

In providing this kind of support, the book has four main messages:

- That the independence and fulfilment of running your own enterprise is not just for a privileged few. A staggering one in ten of the working population are now self-employed, and they represent people from all ages, backgrounds and occupations – including school-leavers, graduates, housewives and pensioners.
- That many small businesses do not need extensive financial support, involving complicated and heavy commitments to lending institutions. Many of the businesses now emerging are small-scale enterprises, run from home and financed in a simple and cost-effective fashion.
- That, in many ways, there has never been a better time to start a small business – hopeful entrepreneurs can turn to a range of financial, advisory and support systems that continue to grow year by year.
- That, despite these encouraging trends, *less than 25 per cent* of new businesses succeed in providing a high standard of living for their proprietors and at least 26 per cent cease trading within two years of their establishment. This figure is based on VAT returns. It incorporates the many people who leave self-employment for reasons other than business failure, but it does *not* include the many business failures that occur among enterprises which do not register for VAT. Why do so many small businesses fail? In most cases it is because:

  - there is not sufficient demand for their services or products
  - the business lacks sufficient resources
  - the business is badly managed
  - the proprietor does not have the right temperament and cannot cope with the strain or responsibility.

All these potential issues should therefore be confronted before you take the first step towards starting up on your own.

The main purpose of this book, therefore, is to consider *whether* and *how* you should start your own enterprise. Before you turn to the process of self-assessment and practical planning this will entail, it is worth taking a closer look at the growing economic 'club' you are thinking of entering, and finding out:

- Why people start their own business.
- What kind of people are involved.
- What kind of support they can expect to receive.

Making the choice

Why do people start their own business? The reasons vary from individual to individual, but some of the more commonly expressed reasons include:

- A desire to express their skills, creativity and individuality in a way not open to them in their present employment.
- Because the prospects of promotion or advancement in their present occupation/profession are very limited.
- Because the prospects offered by self-employment are greater than those offered by an employed position. This particularly applies to:
  - school-leavers or graduates leaving full-time education
  - people unexpectedly made redundant
  - women returning to their careers after bringing up a family
  - people forced to retire early.

These reasons were highlighted in a recent Small Firms Survey undertaken by the Institute of Manpower Studies (see Table 1.1, below).

Table 1.1 **Main reasons for setting up in busines**

Reason	Percentage of total
Saw market need/had good idea/desire for profit	12
Unemployment or threatened unemployment	15
Desire for independence from employer	13
Connections with family or friends	12
Knowledge of, or interest in, trade	13
Long-standing ambition to own business	4
'Opportunity arose'/other reason	6
Took over established firm	8
Previously in business	7
Long-established firm	10
(No information given)	
Total	100

Source: IMS Small Firms Survey, 1986

The important thing to note is that, in most successful business start-ups, two important factors had to be present:

- the ability to spot a market opportunity;
- (equally important) the individual's 'readiness' to take advantage of that opportunity.

Case-study 1.1: Diana Breeden

The importance of being ready was vividly expressed by Diana Breeden, who started a successful marketing consultancy for the textile industry in 1984.

'The origins of my business go back to the point when, ten years ago, I was offered a post in a textile agency. Initially I was pressured to take on secretarial duties, but I was adamant that I didn't want to do so. Gradually, I took on an increasing responsibility for co-ordinating the marketing consultancy side of the business. The agency acted as a "go-between" for producers of textile cloth and potential purchasers/manufacturers. The job entailed tripping backwards and forwards between producers and purchasers. It involved a great deal of travel, enabled me to build up considerable communication and financial research skills, as well as giving me very good contacts in the industry.

'The next critical stage in my move towards self-employment

was when I married. My employer suggested that I could do the work at home. This was perfectly feasible, since I tended to work alone, without being involved in daily contact with anyone from the agency – all I needed was a desk and a telephone. This gave me the confidence to work on my own, and regulate my own activities.

'The event that forced me to take the idea of "going it alone" seriously was when a close contact offered me a new job. I started to consider my prospects at the agency. By now I had built up considerable experience in the field of marketing textiles. I didn't see the managing director for weeks on end, I was handling a very large budget, and he had complete trust in me. I had the skills I needed, the business contacts and the confidence. In addition, the prospects at the agency were now limited. I wasn't going anywhere and nothing was moving.

'The offer of a new job didn't appeal either – by now I was thirty and was finding it a difficult age to face. I kept asking myself, "Is this really what you want to do for the rest of your life?" Very troubled, I went shopping at Selfridges and wandered aimlessly around the store for over two hours – God knows what the commissionaires must have thought. By the time I walked out, I had made up my mind not to accept the new job but to set up my own consultancy. My decision was helped by the fact that, unable to recruit me as a permanent employee, my contacts offered me a freelance contract to undertake the same work.

'I think that you have to wait until you are ready. If someone had suggested the idea of self-employment earlier in my career, I would have recoiled in horror, because at that time it was too much for me to cope with. But if you have the ability, you get around to taking the step in your own time.'

Learning points

Diana's account of her path to self-employment illustrates a number of points:

- The decision to start a business rarely comes in a blinding flash. The seeds may be laid early on in life, but circumstances may lead to their fruition taking years, sometimes decades.

- The decision, when it comes, is often a logical step. Diana built up the skills, the knowledge and the experience, and eventually found the right way to develop them.
- The circumstances must, however, be right. The offer of a new job triggered Diana's mind at exactly the right time in her career – when she was thirty and open to the prospect. Had the opportunity come earlier in her life, she may not have been able to take advantage of it.

Opportunity and readiness must therefore overlap.

Everybody's doing it – some examples

Diana is not alone in her decision. A very wide range of people have decided to start their own business in recent years. Below are just a few examples, some of which appear in greater detail later in the book. All were started with less than £5,000 capital. See if one or more echoes your own feelings.

- A seventeen-year-old school-leaver without any previous work experience started a pet food delivery service to local residents who found it difficult to shop for heavy tins in high-street supermarkets. He decided to start his own business 'because I was young and had no commitments'.
- A Cambridge graduate, with help from the Graduate Enterprise Programme (see page 260), set up a small business selling novelty soaps and toiletries. The manufacturing, packaging and distribution are done by sub-contractors – so all that is required for the business is an office, a telephone and a good deal of entrepreneurial flair.
- Three partners from Ravensbourne College of Art set up a clothing company, designing and manufacturing upmarket sweaters. This year they exhibited at Olympia and now have £15,000 worth of orders from the United States.

- Having been made redundant three times, a twenty-one-year-old mechanic set up a business servicing and maintaining Fiat vehicles. Since starting the company in 1983, he has tripled the workspace he has access to and taken on an apprentice under a government training scheme. 'I keep my prices low, have a tidy, well-organized workshop, and enjoy giving good service to my customers,' he explained.
- A secretary in her late twenties decided to escape from a nine-to-five office routine by becoming a freelance translator and interpreter. 'No one told me that the world could be a different shape,' she said. (Further details – page 57.)
- A journalist in her early twenties, fed up with working for managers she didn't respect, teamed up with her boyfriend to publish her own journal. With the exception of printing, the enterprise is entirely home-based. It was self-sufficient within eight months, and she was voted publishing entrepreneur of the year in 1984. (Further details – page 142.)
- A pensioner, financially secure but bored with life, drew on his amateur knowledge of Eskimo dog breeds to start a puppy breeding kennels. Originally based at home, he has just moved into purpose-built premises. 'Age is no barrier to commercial success if you are fit and healthy,' he said.
- A female manager, in her thirties, made redundant from her job with an overseas property development company, set up her own word-processing and printing company. 'I don't fit easily into conventional working teams,' she commented. 'My husband and I sacrificed everything to get the business started. We've had no guaranteed weekends or evenings for nearly three years, and no spending money for just as long. But it has been worth it.' (Further details – page 39.)
- A fourteen-year-old schoolboy started a business making and selling Christmas crackers to earn extra pocket money. Now twenty-three, he employs six full-time staff

and around thirty homeworkers, supplying crackers to well-known stores such as Habitat, Heals, Harrods, Paperchase and Rymans. 'Looking back at my first customer (who bought 150 boxes), he didn't just buy them for commercial reasons – I think he was fascinated by what I was doing!' (Further details – page 64.)

- A former air hostess now runs a £200,000-a-year turnover, supplying picnic hampers to 'the beau monde . . . and others'. The business was started without any outside financial grants and expanded through the clever use of local press publicity. (Further details – page 71.)
- A female production manager in a company publishing children's books set up her own business, providing commercial companies with creative marketing support. The business was initially funded by a part-time secretarial job with a local helicopter marketing company. 'One minute I was working for myself and wearing all the hats – the next, I was working for someone else and only wearing one.' (Further details – page 136.)
- A fifty-two-year-old manager was made redundant after twenty years with the same company. He used his redundancy settlement to set himself up as a management consultant. 'I'm not making a fortune, but I am doing all right,' he commented. (Further details – page 140.)

Prospects and support

The wide variety of people deciding to start their own business is reflected in government statistics.

In Case-study 1.2, you will find a statistical breakdown of the current growth of small business in Great Britain. From it, you will see that a number of important trends have emerged:

- The number of people choosing self-employment to develop their careers is rising every year.
- Although a substantial majority of self-employed people

are men (75 per cent), the number of women starting their own business is rising three times as fast.

- The substantial majority of new businesses are in professional and managerial occupations.
- Over half of those people choosing self-employment decide to do something completely different from what they were employed to do in previous jobs.
- Over 60 per cent of self-employed people do not employ anyone, and more than half of them are probably small and home-based.
- Nearly half of 'new' work is being taken up by self-employed people.
- Nevertheless, the mortality rate of new businesses is alarmingly high, with at least 26 per cent ceasing to trade within two years of being established.

Table 1.2 **Occupation of small entrepreneurs: 1985**

Occupation	1985 %
Managers and administrators	25
Engineers, scientists, technologists	2
Other professions	3
Technicians and draftsmen	1
Craftsmen	18
Operatives	22
Support services	14
Personal services	8
Others	7
Total	100

Source: IMS Small Firms Survey

Case-study 1.2: The self-employed in the mid-1980s

Today, about 95 per cent of all businesses in the UK are small firms. They employ over a quarter of the total workforce and generate 20 per cent of the gross national product. As John Cope, Minister of State at the Department of Employment with special responsibility for Small Firms, recently commented: 'Nowhere is enterprise more evident than in the small business sector which has grown tremendously in recent years.'

Between 1979 and 1986, the number of people entering self-employment rose by over about 40 per cent, at a time when numbers in conventional employment fell by about 7 per cent. In 1986 there were about 2½ million self-employed people – one in nine of the whole working population.

The range of occupations they have is very broad (see Table 1.2, above). A staggering 806,000 are managers; 361,000 are in the professions; 545,000 are in craft occupations, and about 50,000 perform clerical services.

Another interesting trend is the steady rise of women entrepreneurs. In 1981 there were 1.64 million self-employed men in Britain, but only 417,000 self-employed women. By 1986 the number of self-employed men had risen by 18 per cent to 1.94 million, 14 per cent of all employed men; while for women there was a more dramatic increase of 51 per cent, taking female self-employment to 631,000, or 6 per cent of all employed women.

One reason for this is that women tend to be concentrated among professionals in education and health services, in clerical and related occupations and in cleaning and hairdressing – all occupations where the growth in self-employment has been strongest.

Between spring 1985 and spring 1986, over 400,000 people joined the ranks of the self-employed. Of these, 45 per cent had been employees a year earlier, while a further 19 per cent were unemployed. 37 per cent of all self-employed people in 1986 had employees of their own.

Many people changed their occupations when becoming self-employed. Over half (55 per cent) of those who had previously been employees changed occupations when working for themselves, with more than 36 per cent making a major career change.

Despite all the optimism, however, 'death' rates among young and very small firms are alarmingly high. At least 26 per cent of all new firms cease trading within two years. In addition, of those firms established after 1980, something like three-fifths have failed to grow or take on additional staff. Nevertheless, a substantial proportion of new work being created is for the self-employed. Of the

*1,044,000 new jobs created between March 1983 and September 1986, a staggering 445,000 were for self-employed people.**

There are three main reasons why self-employment and business start-ups have proved so popular in the 1980s:

- changing patterns of work;
- the impact of new technology;
- political and community initiatives.

Changing patterns of work

The recession changed the very narrow attitude that employers were taking towards working hours in the 1960s and 1970s. It prompted them to take a far closer look at the specific costs of employing full-time staff, not only in terms of the actual salary they paid or the fringe benefits they offered, but also in terms of the hidden costs of employment, such as the expense and time involved in recruiting staff; the cost of office space and equipment; the cost of salary administration and National Insurance payments; and the cost of employing staff in permament positions at times when business was quiet.

Many have come to the conclusion that it is often cheaper to 'contract out' to outside consultants, freelancers, sub-contractors and outside businesses many of the business activities they had previously handled in-house. This has accounted for the big increase in self-employed managerial and professional work. The availability of this kind of work is also likely to increase. A survey of 300 companies by the CBI in 1984 found that nearly a third expected the amount of work they would contract out to increase.

Case-study 1.3: Networking at Rank Xerox

A good example of why employers are contracting out a wider

* These statistics are drawn from reports published by the Department of Employment, the Department of Trade and Industry and the Institute of Manpower Studies between 1983 and 1987.

variety of work is given by the networking schemes set up by Rank Xerox in 1981.

Under the scheme, selected and carefully trained volunteers were invited to leave the parent company and establish their own businesses as consultants. They were to be based at home or in community offices and connected to Rank Xerox through a microcomputer under the contract offered to other organizations. The payment provided under the contract is a fee for work completed, not pay for days worked. The networkers also receive a discount on the microcomputers and other machinery, help with furnishings and setting up, and tax advice.

The corporation started the scheme for two major reasons:

- *Cost – they estimated that salaries accounted for less than a third of the total cost of employing someone, with the cost of office facilities accounting for another third. So an employee earning £10,000 p.a. was actually costing the company around £27,000 p.a. Rank Xerox hope to save £5 million a year through using the networkers.*
- *Motivation – Rank Xerox found that a growing number of their employees wanted to assume a greater degree of control over the way their work is organized. Once they were made independent from the parent company, their productivity increased and so did their motivation.*

By July 1984, there were 48 networkers, and their numbers have steadily risen, by about one or two each month. They provide a very wide range of services, including marketing, market research, business planning, operational research, financial control, taxation advice, management services, technical service engineering, systems analysis, programming, security, training and personnel.

A crucial factor in the scheme's success has been the creation by the networkers of a small business support association. Called Xanadu, it was originally formed as a loosely knit self-help organization but has now become a self-financing profit-making company with its own elected board of directors.

Its strength, however, still lies in the independence of its individual business members. It exists to:

- *create market awareness;*
- *provide information about business opportunities and sources of legal and professional advice;*
- *give proper counselling, advice and training to members in running their own business;*
- *provide a link with Rank Xerox from which both members and Rank Xerox can benefit.*

The link with Rank Xerox remains important, especially in the early stages of each consultancy's existence. Xerox does not stipulate that all the person's work be performed outside the corporation's premises – only that most of it is, so that what remains does not need expensive permanent office space. The company has found that the presence of the networker in the central office for half a day a week (or one day a fortnight) allows enough time to review the consultancy's progress and gives the person concerned the chance to remain involved in the social life of the company.

Undoubtedly Xanadu's greatest achievement has been the provision of continuous business support to its members through centres at Heathrow and London. The full range of services offered by the centres includes word-processing, use of a telex/telecopier, photocopying, printing, general clerical assistance, micro-bureau services, the use of a private or open office, mailshots, an accommodation address, and the use of a conference room, a well-stocked library, telex and overhead projectors. All of these services are offered at a considerable discount to members of Xanadu. Even more importantly, the support centres provide members with the opportunity to take and exchange ideas, with the sense of belonging which most small-business people sacrifice when they choose to go it alone.

The impact of new technology

New technology now makes it possible for many functions previously handled inside large companies to be done at home or in a small locally based operation. It also makes small businesses far more self-sufficient. Word processors save valuable hours of secretarial and administrative work and, used in combination with cheaper and more effective photocopiers, enable small businesses to produce cost-effective presentation material, sales literature and other published matter. Teletext, Prestel and other computerized information services allow cheap but comprehensive information to be transmitted directly into the home or work base. Sophisticated answerphone services enable business people on their own to keep in touch with their offices while visiting clients or suppliers. Open learning systems, using interactive text, video and audio tapes, permit self-employed people to learn new skills and knowledge at home that previously could have been acquired only through formal courses. Cellular telephones, electronic mail systems, interactive video and broadcasting, cable television and cheaper telex systems will serve to increase the scope for cheaper, more cost-effective small businesses.

Political and community initiatives

The encouragement of small business has been a cornerstone of government policy during the early 1980s. Government policy directed towards increasing the incentives and reducing the difficulties faced by small businesses has played a large part in encouraging people to 'go it alone'. Government policy has helped small businesses in several major ways.

Finance

The availability of finance for small firms has been improved by the following schemes (with varying degrees of success).

Loan Guarantee Scheme. The Loan Guarantee Scheme was started in 1981. It aims to provide finance for viable businesses that fail to get alternative backing under their own steam. Individual term loans up to £75,000 are made available for between two and seven years, with a government guarantee on 70 per cent of each loan. Small businesses in most sectors are eligible. The Loan Guarantee Scheme has had a chequered history, primarily because banks' confidence in the government's guarantee has not always been forthcoming, and the failure rate of businesses set up under the scheme has been alarmingly high. Nevertheless, the 1986 Budget extended the scheme for a further three years and reduced the cost to borrowers by halving the premium on loans.

The Enterprise Allowance Scheme. Started in 1982, this scheme encourages unemployed people to start their own businesses. It pays to successful applicants an allowance of £40 per week for up to a year. The Enterprise Allowance Scheme has proved immensely popular. More than 200,000 people have already started up businesses with its help. Greater emphasis is now placed on providing participants with better advice, counselling and training.

The Business Expansion Scheme. Started in 1983, the Business Expansion Scheme provides income-tax relief on new equity investment in unquoted companies. The scheme was extended in the 1986 Budget and targeted more precisely towards genuinely risky enterprises.

The Venture Capital Scheme More suitable for rapidly expanding enterprises, the Venture Capital Scheme encourages the provision of finance by enabling individuals and investment companies to claim income or corporation tax relief on losses incurred on the disposal of new shares issued by unquoted trading companies.

Premises

The English Industrial Estates Corporation (EIEC) concentrates on providing premises for small businesses (up to 2,500 sq. ft). Special rental and tenancy agreements have been devised to meet the needs of small businesses and entrepreneurs. EIEC works with a number of public-sector bodies, most notably the Department of Trade and Industry, the Development Commission, universities and the Scottish and Welsh Development Agencies.

Training

The government, through the Manpower Services Commission, has provided training courses for the self-employed and small-business people since 1977, but since 1984 the volume and range of this training has been greatly increased to give over 50,000 places on courses during 1986/7. For people wishing to start their own business, there are the Business Enterprise and New Enterprise Programmes. For graduates, there are the Graduate Enterprise Programme and the Graduate Gateway Programme. Details of all of these can be found in Appendix IV (see page 259).

Innovation

The Small Firms Merit Award for Research and Technology (SMART), started in 1986, aims to encourage small firms and potential entrepreneurs to submit highly innovative ideas that cannot attract existing sources of funding. This competitive scheme was being run by the Department of Trade and Industry on a one-year trial basis in biotechnology and instrumentation at the time of writing.

Taxation

The ability of individuals to start and develop businesses has been improved by a wide range of tax changes. Capital Gains Tax exemption limits have been increased to £6,300. Retirement reliefs have been extended to cover retirement at 60, retirement through ill-health and the disposal of shares in family holding companies of trading groups. Tax relief has also been introduced to help people to incorporate their business. Losses on loans made for business purposes can also now be offset against Capital Gains Tax.

Income tax relief is available on personal borrowing raised to make investments in partnerships, close companies, co-operatives and employee buy-outs. Relief is also available for interest on loans to partners buying plant and machinery for use in their business.

In addition, losses incurred in any of the first four years of trading by a new business carried on by an individual can qualify for special income tax relief. This can be obtained against earnings during a three-year period before the new trade started. Expenses incurred in the process of setting up a business are also now deductible from subsequent trading profits so long as the expenditure is undertaken in the three years.

Finally, changes to National Insurance contributions were made in October 1985. These introduced graduated contribution rates for both employers' and employees' contributions, with the rates being lower than employees' earnings. Since the staff of small firms tend to be in lower-paid occupations, this has partially benefited small businesses.

Advice

The Small Firms Service (SFSO) has been greatly expanded since 1979. The Service provides wide-ranging information and advice for people wishing to start up a business. Particular developments have been more Small Firm Centres and counselling teams, a new range of fact sheets and a computerized information service. Since 1985 the Service has also concentrated on providing specialist counselling and supplementing the work of Local Enterprise Agencies (see below).

Other government-supported advisory services include:

Local Enterprise Agencies These are independent organizations supported by local businesses which provide help and advice to small firms. They can also arrange or provide suitable start-up capital or loans.

Rural Development Commission (formerly CoSIRA). This organization operates a network of thirty-two offices providing rural small businesses with advice on local opportunities and conditions; business management, marketing and technical advice; training in the right skills and financial services.

Business and Technical Advisory Services (BTAS). This organization, run by the Department of Trade and Industry, provides subsidized consultancy services for small and medium-sized firms on productivity, design and quality assurance. In September 1986 its services were extended to include marketing advice.

Finally, the Business Improvement Services package of schemes run by the Department of Trade and Industry aims to help small firms in areas affected by job losses in particular industries – steel, textiles, shipbuilding, deep sea fishing and tin-mining. Grants are available for consultancy advice on marketing, financial management, the application of computers and licensing.

This is just a summary of the services available to people wishing to start small businesses. Further details of most of the schemes or organizations listed above can be found in the Appendix (see pages 235–72).

Other Measures

Government policies have already lifted many administrative burdens from small businesses through wider access to planning permission, simpler and more flexible building regulations and less complicated tax procedures. The 1981 Companies Act, for example, reduced the amount of detailed financial information small companies need to file with the Registrar of Companies and simplified the arrangements for approval of company names.

The government has also announced its intention to relax the rules governing the amount of information small companies have to disclose in their accounts within the constraints of European law and the needs of the Inland Revenue.

Learning points

What conclusions should you draw from the information set out above? How should it affect the way in which you choose to set up your business, your choice of product or service and your assessment of your suitability as an entrepreneur? Consider the following learning points.

- Do not be deterred if you do not see yourself as the stereotypical entrepreneur. Small-business people today come from all ages, backgrounds and occupations. They include women of all ages, pensioners (over 100,000 self-employed people are over age sixty-five), graduates and school-leavers.

- Do not be overawed by the potential complications involved. Many successful businesses are small, home-based and simple to establish.
- Do not be afraid to choose an idea unrelated to your previous occupation. Over 50 per cent of people starting their own business change their occupation in doing so.
- Despite all the enthusiasm and encouragement of government, industry and enterprise agencies, at least 26 per cent of all firms cease trading within two years of their establishment. The risks of starting your own business are therefore as great as ever. When considering your options, therefore, make sure that you take into account:
  - the market potential of your product or service. Who is going to buy it? Why are people going to buy it? Where are they going to buy it? When are they going to buy it? How much of it are they going to buy?
  - the views of your family, spouse and dependants. Their support will be vital if your business is to succeed;
  - your own suitability. Are you really sure you will have the stamina and possess the right underlying skills to succeed?
  - the need for the right financial support and day-to-day administration. More small businesses fail through poor financial administration than for any other reason;
  - all the sources of support available to you.

These points will be explored in greater depth during the next two sections of the book.

2 Assessing Yourself

One vital factor in the success of any business is the ability of the founder(s) to cope with challenges, problems and sacrifices which are inevitable in such a dramatic change in their lives. It is worth remembering that, for many people, starting a new business involves:

- a drop in their standard of living in the early stages of the enterprise (and sometimes for a period of years);
- no holidays and few weekends or evenings that are totally free from work;
- social isolation;
- immense self-discipline and a capacity to work long hours for little immediate return.

It is also worth remembering that all those you share your day-to-day life with (marriage partners, lovers, children and other dependants) will be equally affected and may have to share many of the same challenges and sacrifices.

It is therefore important that, from the outset, you are confident in your ability to make the business work and that you and all those affected by your lifestyle are willing to accept the sacrifices involved as a necessary price of success.

On the assumption that your interest in starting a business is more than a passing one, you need to find out:

- what personal skills, knowledge and experience are required;
- what characteristics you have which will help or hinder your chances of success;
- what sacrifices you will have to make and whether or not you are prepared to pay the price.

You should also have a clear view of what you personally want to achieve in starting your own business.

This chapter explores these questions and issues from a wide range of viewpoints and situations. Inevitably the focus is on you, your personality, motivation, values, needs, skills and personal objectives. As you progress through the text, at regular intervals you will be encouraged to consider the personal implications. Checklists and exercises are offered as a means to structuring your thoughts. It can also be invaluable to share your ideas with others, particularly those who have been through this thought-process.

The questions explored are not designed to turn you on to or away from the decision to start a small business; they are designed to help you consider matters with your eyes open and to assess the personal risks and opportunities potentially facing you if you choose the small-business route.

Exercise 2.1: The secret of success: an initial reaction (1)

The Oxford Dictionary describes an entrepreneur as: (1) 'A person who organizes and manages a commercial undertaking, especially one involving commercial risks'; (2) 'A contractor acting as intermediary'.

Taking this basic definition, there are four main elements involved:

- The ability to recognize and take advantage of business opportunities.
- The ability to take risks – but to distinguish between those that are acceptable and those that are unacceptable.
- The ability to organize the resources needed to take advantage of the opportunity.
- The ability to combine the resources and the opportunity in order to make a reasonable profit.

Leaving aside the obvious need to have a business idea and the issue of what entry route you might be starting from (for example, starting a business out of a hobby or identifying a market opportunity), does this general description excite or discourage you?

At this stage it might be useful to note down your response to each of these four roles and the factors behind it on a separate sheet of paper.

The four roles of the entrepreneur

- Opportunity taker
- Risk taker
- Organizer of resources
- Creator of profit

Exercise 2.2: The secret of success: an initial reaction (2)

The leading management writer Robert Heller recently defined nine necessary qualities to ensure business success. Do you possess those qualities? Tick the appropriate response.

1. A high level of drive and energy. YES NO
2. Enough self-confidence to take carefully calculated, moderate risks. YES NO
3. A clear idea of money as a way of keeping score and as a means of generating still more money. YES NO
4. The ability to get other people to work with you and for you productively. YES NO
5. High, but realistic, achievable objectives. YES NO
6. A belief that you can control your own lifestyle. YES NO
7. A readiness to learn from your own mistakes and failures. YES NO
8. A long-term picture of the future of your business. YES NO
9. An ability to compete with self-imposed standards. YES NO

Once again, test your initial reaction to these ideas of running your own business by totalling how many of these qualities you feel you possess.

Assessing your business potential: an introduction

Bearing in mind the issues and thoughts raised by Exercises 2.1 and 2.2, you now need to relate these to your own skills, knowledge and personal circumstances.

The exercises below are designed to help you assess your abilities and circumstances in relation to three critical areas:

- your personal values and motivation;
- your family's viewpoint;
- your business skills.

In answering the questions, it is important that you be honest about your reactions. If you are in any doubt about your abilities or feel you may need additional skills to improve your chances of success, it is better to be aware of this at a time when you are not over-committed and are able to take actions to compensate for the problem.

The role of a supporter and partner

Your assessment of your abilities and business potential will benefit from a second opinion. The exercises allow for responses from two other participants:

A partner/relative. This should be the person who is likely to be most affected personally by your decision to start a business and to whom you are more likely to turn for support. Depending on your circumstances, it could be your marriage partner, the person with whom you share your life, a parent or other older relative, or a grown-up child.

A 'supporter'. Although the responses of your partner/relative are very important, their second opinion will be affected by their emotional feelings for you. You should therefore complete the exercises with the additional opinion of an objective 'supporter'. The supporter you choose should be a close friend who knows you and your personal circumstances sufficiently well to be able to judge the accuracy of your own responses to the questions. Ideally, he/she should also have some knowledge of your working life and career. A former or present colleague at work with whom you also have a friendship would make an ideal supporter.

In addition to providing responses to the specific questions in the exercises, the role of your supporter could also be extended as follows: first, to lend an ear, to listen to your ideas, conclusions and plans; secondly, to help you establish the practicality of your plans and ideas by asking questions and testing theories; thirdly, to help you by developing your plans with suggestions and advice, and by providing encouragement.

Supporters should not be too critical. They should not promote their own ideas at the expense of yours. In the final stages of every decision, it should be you who makes the choice.

If, having considered carefully, you cannot identify someone whom you would choose to be a supporter, this will not detract from the value of the material in this book. However, the opportunity to talk things through with someone objective can be very helpful and should be taken whenever possible.

Evaluating the responses

The printed exercises which follow should be copied on separate sheets of paper by you and any partner/relatives and/or supporters whom you have asked to help. Many of the questions allow for three basic responses: 'Yes', 'No' and 'Not Sure'. Where appropriate, responses to the same questions should be made by both partner/relatives and supporters to check whether your assessment of your abilities and suitability is sufficiently accurate. Particular attention should be paid to questions which provoke a 'No' or 'Not Sure' response made by *any* of the participants in the exercise. These should be noted and discussed. Only when there is a 'Yes' response from *all* the participants should you pass straight on to the next question. At the end of each set of questions, a summary of the issues raised by the responses should be made, on separate sheets of paper, by you, partner/relatives and supporters. These should then be discussed and kept for use in Exercise 2.6 on page 45.

The questions make a number of assumptions:

- that you have a personal partner (someone with whom you share your life);
- that you may have dependants;
- that you have had some form of previous work experience.

If this is not the case, simply ignore those questions which obviously do not relate to your circumstances.

Exercise 2.3: Your personal values and motivation

The questions below cover your reasons for starting a small business and the personal values you will bring to it. The questions should also be answered by your partner/relative and supporter. Remember, however, that their responses to the questions should relate to *your* (not *their*) suitability as a self-employed person.

Your competitiveness

- Do you enjoy competitive situations? YES NO NOT SURE
- Are you effective in competitive situations? YES NO NOT SURE

Your motivation

- Are you ambitious? YES NO
- Have you considered what you want to achieve from business success (rating: 1 is low, 5 is high)
  - financial reward 1 2 3 4 5
  - status 1 2 3 4 5
  - independence 1 2 3 4 5
  - influence 1 2 3 4 5
- Are you sufficiently sure of your ability to succeed to risk

your standard of living and that of your dependants to achieve it? YES NO NOT SURE

Your work rate

- Are you used to working long hours? YES NO NOT SURE
- Are you prepared to work long hours in the future, even to the extent of sacrificing:

  – social life YES NO NOT SURE

  – annual holidays YES NO NOT SURE

  – weekends YES NO NOT SURE

  – leisure pursuits YES NO NOT SURE

Your health

- Is it medically safe for your body to be placed under regular stress? YES NO NOT SURE
- Are you fit enough to cope with a heavy workload over a prolonged period? YES NO NOT SURE
- Will you be able to cope with the medical stress involved? YES NO NOT SURE
- If you are unsure as to any of these questions, have you consulted your doctor or taken other professional advice? YES NO

Your commitment

- Do you get easily discouraged? YES NO NOT SURE
- Do you become easily bored? YES NO NOT SURE
- Once you start a project, do you generally see it through on time? YES NO NOT SURE

Your ability to organize your own work

- Are you personally well organized? YES NO NOT SURE
- Are you good at identifying priorities? YES NO NOT SURE
- Are you good at fixing high but realistic and achievable objectives? YES NO NOT SURE
- Do you work to fixed deadlines? YES NO NOT SURE

- Without the direct supervision of somebody else, would you be able to undertake a regular amount of work each day and to a regular, self-imposed standard?

YES NO NOT SURE

General reactions to Exercise 2.3

Having completed all the questions and fully discussed those which provoked a 'No' or 'Not Sure' response from any participant, all participants should summarize the issues they feel were raised by the exercise on separate sheets of paper. These should then be compared, discussed and kept for use in Exercise 2.6 on page 45.

Exercise 2.4: Considering your family

Your family's reaction could play a crucial role in the success of your putative venture. Their support and encouragement will be vital if you are to cope with the challenges of the difficult early years.

Consider the following questions with the member of your family on whose support you will most rely. It could be a marriage partner, a parent or even a son or daughter, depending on your individual circumstances. (In the course of discussing the issues raised, you should also take into account the feelings of all those family members who are directly dependent on your income and lifestyle.)

Ignore those questions which are obviously not relevant to your personal circumstances. Once again, summarize your reactions and those of your family on separate sheets of paper, for comparison, discussion and further use in Exercise 2.6 on page 45.

- Does your family/partner agree with your decision to start your own business?
- Do they understand and feel committed or excited by the business idea (if you have already formulated it – see Chapter 3)?

- Do they accept that you will have to work long hours, possibly involving evenings and weekends?
- Do they accept that their standard of living may drop as a result?
- Are they prepared to sacrifice:
  – family holidays
  – joint leisure pursuits
  – joint social entertaining
- Would they be prepared to see the home mortgaged to fund the business in a crisis?
- If they do not do so already and are able to, would they be willing to go out to work to help fund the business?
- Are they willing and able to be actively involved in the business? What skills can they offer?

Considering your family – some guidelines

Discussing developments with your family at regular intervals will not only help to keep them in the picture; it can also be a useful opportunity to assess ideas, test your own thoughts out and also to consider how your lifestyle will change.

If you are going into business with a partner, it can be important to get on with each other's family units. This is even more important if a husband-and-wife or other personal partnership is involved in the same business.

Meeting socially, talking to one another about general matters and specific views on the business – how it will work, how people see it progressing, what people want to get out of it and how they see their personal contribution, etc. – all of this can help to ensure that the 'team' shares the same objectives and that, if there are fundamental differences, they can be identified early on rather than letting them deteriorate. It is worth remembering that relationships often change dramatically under business stress.

Finally, if you can involve your personal partner or family actively in the business, the motivation and challenge can be shared to a far greater extent than if you leave them on the sidelines. The reasons for the hard work will become that much more apparent and the triumphs and failures be shared with greater insight.

The extent to which you can involve your partner/family in the business will depend on their circumstances, skills and motivation. The two case-studies that follow illustrate the different degrees of shared involvement which two couples developed. They illustrate the benefits, but also the personal hardships, which starting a business can bring to the family.

Case-study 2.1: Veronica and Nigel Jones

Veronica Jones runs a word-processing, copying and printing service for local businesses in West London. The business was developed from a simple typing service which she started after the overseas property development operation she was working for ceased trading in 1983.

'The business was originally started to carry on the idea of an overseas property service on my own,' she explained. 'When I was made redundant, the owner gave me an electronic typewriter as compensation, and the typing service was supposed to supplement the income I would receive from the property side of the business. However, I quickly discovered that I was meeting much nicer people through the typing service and there was a far more regular stream of business.'

Although she had taken a typing course when a teenager, Veronica had no training in word processing and printing, and she developed these sides of the business from on-the-job experience. A critical factor in the success of the business has been the commitment of her husband, Nigel, and their joint willingness to make quite considerable sacrifices in order to make the business work.

'For 2½ years, we didn't have any spending money,' she continued. 'We were worried sick. Nigel was earning enough to pay the mortgage, and without his financial support I don't know how I would have managed. The business initially brought in very little money and I had to channel what little it did back into the enterprise.'

Veronica also stressed the strains that running the business brought to their domestic arrangements. 'In the three years I have been involved in the enterprise, we have had no guaranteed week-

ends together and have found it almost impossible to make any evening arrangements. Sometimes Nigel comes home after his own work and I have to say, "Look, I'm terribly busy. I can't walk the dog, I can't cook the supper, I can't do the washing-up, and I haven't had the time to do the ironing," and he winds up having to do it all himself.'

Veronica concedes that this could easily place an intolerable strain on many marriages, particularly because Nigel has had to put her interests before his own; however, she feels that the experience has created a more balanced relationship.

Case-study 2.2: Ian and Kate Edwards

Ian and Kate, both in their late thirties, have managed to overcome many of the pressures that running a small business can place on a marriage or close relationship.

Both worked for a large corporation where they had met and formed their relationship. When Ian decided to set up his own financial services consultancy, Kate joined him; she now runs her own word-processing company attached to this, but independently administered. Two important factors in their relationship are, first, the fact that Ian has a partner, Geoff, and, secondly, a seven-year-old son by Ian's first marriage.

Ian highlighted the factors he believes are essential to any relationship coping with the demands of a small business. 'Firstly, there has to be joint acceptance of the sacrifices that will need to be made in the early years, particularly in terms of the household's standard of living. Secondly, there has to be a joint commitment to make the business succeed. This is vital, even if one of the partners is not actually involved in the business. If he or she does not support the other fully, it can prove a very serious handicap. The first few years can be very hard and place great pressures on the relationship. In fact, starting a business is the ultimate test of whether your relationship is a good one. If it is, the pressures and challenges will draw you together. If it isn't it will tear you apart.'

The problems have not always been easy to solve. In particular, the demands made by the business have meant that Ian cannot devote the time he would like to his son, Stephen. That said, Kate finds that the weekends when Stephen comes to visit (Ian's former *wife has custody) are the one time when she can drag him away from the office. 'Ian will work most evenings and weekends as a matter of course. Having Steve there helps him to relax. Even so, he never really switches off. He'll be playing cricket with Steve and, whilst he is doing so, you can see his mind going round all the time.'*

Kate's involvement with the business, through her own company, Letterskills Limited, has given her a greater understanding of the strains Ian is facing. However, her day-to-day presence in the office has meant that she has to be careful in the way she handles her reaction to various issues: 'I have to take care not to get involved or express my own views on business decisions which are outside my role in the office. In addition, I have to act like Caesar's wife in terms of my punctuality and productivity. I wouldn't want or expect any special treatment because I am a partner's wife.'

Kate also feels that, whilst the shared experience of building up Ian's business draws them closer together, it is very important to her to have her own business as well. 'Two-thirds of my time is spent supporting Ian in his business, but that one-third of my time devoted to my own business is very important. It gives me a bit of independence and I think it is healthy to have different things to talk about, rather than being totally involved in the same activities every day.'

Learning points

Although the roles of business owner and supporter are divided differently between the two couples, both Veronica and Nigel and Ian and Kate are remarkably similar in the conclusions they have drawn from their experiences. Both couples stressed that:

- Starting a small business was the ultimate test of a good marriage or personal relationship. If the relationship is well founded, the two partners will be drawn closer together. If the relationship is ill founded, the strain will pull it apart.
- There must be a *joint* acceptance of the sacrifices that will have to be made. This requires that, even if one partner is

not involved on a day-to-day basis, he/she understands the business and feels committed to it.

- The partner who is not the founder should still feel that they are contributing to the relationship on an equal basis. Ideally, they should either be involved in the business itself or be financially contributing to it through work of their own.

Exercise 2.5: Your business skills

Having considered your personal values and your family's feelings, you should now consider whether you have the specific skills needed to market, manage and financially administer your business.

A third questionnaire is provided below. Once again, responses as to your suitability posed by the questions should also be provided by a supporter if appropriate. Because the questions are specifically related to your previous employment, however, the supporter should have had detailed knowledge of your day-to-day work or be a professional business counsellor (see pages 107–12), otherwise you may prefer to conduct this exercise on your own. Remember to summarize your and your supporter's reactions to the exercise on separate sheets of paper for comparison, discussion and further use in Exercise 2.6 on page 45.

1. *Management experience*

- Have you managed part or whole of a business before? YES NO
- If so, for how long?
- How did you get on?
- Did you enjoy it?
- What lessons did you learn?
- If you haven't managed a business before, have you been responsible for running a department or project(s) in your previous employment? YES NO

- If yes, what skills do you feel you acquired:
  - – motivating other people YES NO
  - – negotiating with other people YES NO
  - – counselling and coaching other people YES NO
  - – delegating work to other people YES NO
  - – evaluating your own and other people's performance YES NO
  - – the ability to take decisions YES NO
  - – the ability to identify priorities between courses of action YES NO
  - – the ability to gather information YES NO
  - – other skills (please specify)
- If you haven't held management responsibility, do you feel that you have picked up any or all of the skills listed above in other ways? Please specify how and where.

2. *Selling skills*

- Have you ever received any sales training YES NO
- Have you sold anything before? YES NO
  - – Did you enjoy it? YES NO
  - – What results did you obtain?
- Have you ever had any formal sales training? YES NO
- Have you considered how you would cope with rejection? YES NO
  - – Are you easily put off? YES NO
- Has your pay ever been linked to your performance? YES NO
  - – If not, how do you think you would react?

3. *Your financial skills*

- Have you ever received any financial planning or administration training? YES NO
- Have you ever compiled a business plan? YES NO

- Do you know what should go into one?
YES NO NOT SURE
- Have you been responsible for drawing up and meeting a budget? YES NO
- Are you interested in financial matters, e.g. how businesses tick and make money? YES NO NOT SURE
- Have you had any dealings with arranging finance, preparing accounts, pricing, costing materials, assessing profit, completing a cash-flow forecast, etc.? YES NO
- How do you think that you will handle the financial pressure: the continual awareness required of expenses taking funds away and income bringing funds into the business?
- In your personal life, have you ever had to maintain and service a large loan or overdraft? YES NO
- Could you handle a situation where you might need to maintain either of these external sources of finance for some time? YES NO NOT SURE
- Have you any knowledge of VAT and tax and how they relate to the small business? YES NO

4. *Book-keeping*

- Have you any experience in keeping financial records?
YES NO
- Have you had any training (either formal or 'on-the-job') in book-keeping? YES NO

5. *Managing people*

- Do you foresee the need to employ anyone in your small business? YES NO NOT SURE
- Have you ever hired or fired anyone? YES NO
- Have you had any experience in setting targets for people?
YES NO
- Have you had any experience in helping (coaching or training) people to achieve targets? YES NO
- Have you ever had to discipline anyone? YES NO

- Would that be something you would find very difficult?

  YES NO NOT SURE

- Would you say you were good at motivating people?

  YES NO NOT SURE

- Would you say you were a good judge of character?

  YES NO NOT SURE

Exercise 2.6: Identifying the next steps

Having compiled a substantial amount of information about your values, motivation, family needs and business skills, you now need to summarize how they relate to your plans to start a small business and identify courses of action which will help you to cope with any issues raised or gaps in your skills or experience.

Copy and complete the tables on pages 46–8 to help you consider your next steps in a systematic manner. Return to each set of reactions you have completed and summarize the main issues raised. Then, using the suggested courses of actions and issues listed below as a guide, produce a specific personal strategy tailored to your own circumstances and abilities. As a further guide, a case-study of the completed exercise is supplied on page 49.

Personal values and motivation

Common entrepreneurial characteristics

- A high level of drive and energy
- Enough self-confidence to take carefully calculated moderate risks
- A clear idea of money as a way of keeping score and as a means of generating still more money
- The ability to get other people to work with you and for you productively
- High but realistic, achievable objectives
- A belief that you control your own lifestyle

- A readiness to learn from your own mistakes and failures
- A long-term picture of the future of your business
- An ability to compete with self-imposed standards

Suggested courses of action

- Set up your business immediately
- Postpone your decision until you have gained more:
  - experience
  - contacts
  - research
  - confidence
- Take a part-time job and build up your business gradually (see pages 136–7)
- Take on a business partner to support and encourage your motivation (see pages 148–51)
- Involve your personal partner (for the same reason – see pages 142–6)
- Consult a business guidance counsellor (see page 235)
- Consult an occupational guidance counsellor
- Decide to stay as you are

Notes

Date........................

Issues raised	Initial thoughts on the actions I could take

Considering your family

Questions to consider

- Do they agree with your plans?
- Do they understand the idea?
- Do they accept the risks?
- Are they involved in the planning?
- Do they have any business experience?
- Do they realize the effects if you fail?
- Do they accept that you will have to work long hours?
- Is your home at risk?

Suggested courses of action

- Discuss progress regularly
- Ensure that both partners have balanced lives
- Consider the other partner/relative(s) going out to work to support the business
- Involve the partner/relative(s) actively with the business
- Ensure that you build enough time for family life into your plans

Notes

Date........................

Issues raised	Initial thoughts on the actions I could take

Your business skills

Common business skills

- Selling and marketing
  - identifying markets
  - identifying and researching competition
  - advertising the product
  - obtaining publicity
  - direct selling
  - telephone selling
  - setting the right price
- Financial skills
  - book-keeping
  - credit control (i.e. chasing up creditors)
  - planning cash flow
  - planning capital expenditure
  - budgeting
- Managing people
  - dealing with suppliers
  - dealing with clients
  - recruiting staff
  - organizing and delegating
  - coaching and counselling
  - reviewing and assessing productivity
  - disciplining
- Managing productivity
  - setting and keeping production deadlines
  - arranging delivery or distribution

Suggested courses of action

- Taking on a business partner (who can provide moral support and skills you do not have – see pages 148–51)
- Involving your personal partner (for the same reasons) – see pages 142–6

- Going on a training course for small-business people – see pages 259–62
- Consulting a business guidance counsellor – see page 235
- Consulting:
  – a bank manager (see page 111)
  – an accountant (see page 107)
  – a solicitor (see page 110)
- Joining a small-business club (see page 252)
- Visiting an enterprise agency (see pages 235–49)
- Phoning or visiting your local business advisory service (see page 249)
- Buying books on different aspects of business start-up (see pages 266–72)

Notes

Date.......................

Issues raised	Initial thoughts on the actions I could take

Case-study 2.3: Peter Clarke (a worked example)

Peter Clarke is a solicitor employed by a medium-sized law firm in Reading (Deskins Lentor & Associates). During his six years working for the firm he has specialized in Company Law. The firm has decided to merge with a larger practice and Peter has come to realize that there is no immediate prospect of becoming a partner.

He therefore decides to explore the possibility of setting up his own business, drawing on his specialist knowledge of Company Law. He hopes to base his business on two main services: as a legal consultant, advising individual companies on various aspects of

Company Law; as a specialist writer, contributing to and updating journals, textbooks and directories covering this area of law.

Peter is married and has one child, Nicholas, aged two. He and his family live in a small two-bedroomed semi-detached house close to the firm's offices.

By working his way through the various exercises in this chapter, Peter raises the following issues:

Personal values and motivation

He is strongly motivated by the idea of having a greater degree of control over his lifestyle, and being financially independent. He is also confident of his ability to work methodically and to manage business projects.

He is, however, worried about working on his own. He is used to sharing business decisions and the stimulation that regular contact with business colleagues has brought in the past.

Family considerations

His wife, Helen, is worried about the level of income that he could bring in as an independent consultant. Both of them wish to have a second child and have both children educated privately.

Helen also feels that, due to the age of their son and their desire to have a second child, she would be unable to contribute directly to the business.

Peter therefore feels that he would need to base his consultancy on some form of guaranteed income before setting up on his own.

Business skills

Taking an honest look at his abilities with his 'supporter' (a close colleague at work), Peter feels that he is strong in the following skills:

- *Negotiating with other people*
- *Decision-making*
- *Identifying priorities*

– Financial administration and budgeting.

He feels, however, that he is weak in the following areas:

– Selling and marketing
– Delegating
– Counselling and coaching
– Motivating.

Looking at how these findings relate to his business plans, Peter reaches some conclusions.

He would still like to explore the possibilities of setting up on his own.

But he would need to do so with the help and support of someone else.

He would need to negotiate at least one major contract, which would bring in a regular income, before setting up the consultancy.

He already has a number of important business skills: the ability to make decisions, identify priorities and handle his own financial affairs. He is not unduly worried about his lack of delegating, counselling and motivating skills since he does not anticipate the need to employ more than a secretary in the early stages of the business. He is, however, concerned at his lack of selling and marketing abilities.

Applying these conclusions to Exercise 2.6 and considering the options listed, his three summary tables look like those overleaf:

Personal values and motivation: Notes

Date: 10th February 1987

Issues raised	*Initial thoughts on the actions I could take*
Like the idea of controlling my own lifestyle, and competing for work. *I know where I want to take the business.* *I could work methodically and manage the business.* *Don't like the idea of working alone. I need the motivation of someone else to encourage my work and share business decisions with.*	*Involve Helen? (Difficult because of Nicholas.)* *Stay on at Deskins on a part-time basis until I am more ready? (Not really possible at my level of seniority.)* *Stay as I am? (Not a good idea – my self-confidence will flag rather than increase if I stagnate.)* *Take a business partner? (Sounds a good idea – if I can find the right person.)*

Considering your family: Notes

Date 12th February 1987

Issues raised	*Initial thoughts on the actions I could take*
Helen worried about income (what if we have second child?) *Helen unable to get involved.* *Overheads still very high.*	*Must have the immediate prospect of some regular income – I will use my contacts at Deskins to negotiate a part-time consultancy before leaving.*

Your business skills: Notes

Date: 15th February 1987

Issues raised	*Initial thoughts on the actions I could take*
Feel confident about: *– negotiating deals* *– decision-making* *– identifying priorities* *– finance and budgeting* *Not so happy about:* *– selling and marketing* *– delegating* *– counselling and coaching* *– motivating* *Selling and marketing are skills I will need. The others do not matter so much at this stage.*	*Take a course on selling and marketing (or possibly a small-business course) – good idea regardless.* *Take on a business partner with marketing experience? (Yes – if I can find someone with the right legal background.)*

Summary

As a result of the exercises, Peter comes to a number of decisions:

1. He will go ahead only if he can negotiate at least one large consultancy which will bring a guaranteed regular income. On considering possible organizations to approach, he decides to offer his services to a professional business association whose members require regular advice on Company Law and other legal matters.
2. He will go ahead only if he can find a business partner with marketing experience in the legal profession. This will bring him a number of advantages:
   – It will provide the social and business stimulus that he

will lose by leaving his firm.
- It will bring to the business skills which he cannot provide.
- It will increase the level of personal savings available for investment.

3. In the meantime, he will take a small-business course to provide himself with the skills he currently lacks.

Conclusion

You should now have a much clearer impression of:

- your reasons for wanting to start your own business;
- the skills that you can contribute to the business;
- the feelings of those people in your family who will be most affected by your decision;
- the steps you should now take to respond to the issues you have identified.

As you read through the rest of the book, refer back to your notes and conclusions whenever you need to respond to specific business issues raised in the text. Your written conclusions can also be used whenever you consult outside professional help – for example, from a business counsellor or occupational guidance service.

Above all, bear in mind that, whatever you decide to do about your plans to start a business, the self-assessment process you have just completed has been a useful exercise. Even if you decide to stay where you are, you will have learned something about yourself, your personal needs and the skills you have to offer.

3 *Assessing Your Idea*

Having decided that you have the personal motivation, circumstances and skills to run your own business, you should now consider the idea or concept around which the business will be built. In doing so, you will have to identify:

- what skills, knowledge and experience are required;
- how many of these you currently possess and how many you need to obtain;
- whether the product or service involved will generate sufficient demand.

You may already have a well-defined idea of the product or service on which you will base the business. If you have, you should turn immediately to the sections of this chapter which discuss the skills required (pages 97–106) and the market potential (pages 82–97).

Some people, however, start with the desire to run their own business without any specific idea of the product or service they wish to offer. If this is true in your case, you should read the section below which discusses in general terms ways in which you can identify business concepts appropriate to your own circumstances.

Choosing the right idea

One of the more interesting statistics about self-employed people is that more than half change their occupation when they set up on their own. In addition, something like 60 per cent of self-employed people do not employ anyone else. When considering ideas for a business, it is therefore worth remembering that:

- Ideas for new businesses need not involve extensive

premises, large numbers of employees, expensive and sophisticated equipment or complex financial support. Many can be started by sole practitioners, working from home and using local, easily obtainable support.

- Ideas for businesses may not come only from skills, knowledge and experience picked up from work. They may be based on skills and talents acquired:
  – while bringing up a family;
  – from hobbies and leisure pursuits;
  – from private study or education.

Let's have a look at a few examples.

Ideas from present or previous employment

Ideas from your present job or from a part-time occupation do not have to be based on the specific professional or 'job-specific' skills and knowledge you have acquired through training or on-the-job experience. They can also be based on 'secondary' skills and knowledge which are incidental to your job but which can be used in their own right.

To illustrate this, let us return to the hypothetical study of Peter Clarke (see pages 49–54). Once his consultancy is established, Peter gets his income from three different sources:

– working for a professional institute advising their members on aspects of Company Law;
– writing articles on aspects of Company Law and contributing to/updating an annual directory covering relevant regulations;
– taking part in a local weekly radio programme answering phone-in inquiries on legal problems.

Peter's business is based on a number of talents which he can offer to clients:

- His knowledge of Company Law and legal matters generally. This was acquired as a direct result of his work and his training as a solicitor in a commercial legal firm before he set up on his own.
- His experience of how the law is applied. This is, once again, directly linked to his professional work as a solicitor.
- The underlying skills which he acquired, not from any form of professional training, but from the day-to-day experience of working for the legal firm. These are:
  – the ability to write clearly and effectively;
  – the ability to communicate with people and explain complicated legislation in a way which untrained people will understand.

Looking at his business from another perspective, the actual service he can offer is his knowledge and experience of complicated legislation. But this knowledge and experience could be useless if he lacked the skill to communicate it effectively.

Let us now illustrate this further by looking at a 'real-life' example of how one enterprising employee built a business out of seemingly mundane office skills.

Case-study 3.1: Melanie Frazer

Melanie Frazer started freelancing when she was in her late twenties in order to escape from a nine-to-five office routine.

'Seeing people in the street at eleven o'clock in the morning, I would ask myself, "Why aren't they in an office?" All my life, no one had told me that the world could be a different shape – there had just been an automatic assumption that one would progress up a hierarchy.'

Melanie had rebelled against a humdrum existence before by working abroad as a tourist firm's representative in Spain and later as an English teacher in Egypt. Initially trained as a secretary-linguist, she had also had various office jobs in England – as a PA, translator and manager of a translation agency. It was on her return from teaching in Egypt that she decided she definitely didn't want to 'sink back into the office routine'.

The alternative, as she saw it, was to operate independently, using her language skills. Initially finding work as a translator and interpreter, she later applied her languages to market research and, over a period of years, has gradually worked up to her present position as an independent consultant in the field, carrying out projects both abroad and in England. This was not, however, what she had in mind when she started out. 'I didn't have a plan. I wasn't aware that what I was doing was setting up a business. All I knew was that I needed to find a way of earning my living and not to feel too uncomfortable about what I was doing.'

Melanie initially set about getting work by using any and every contact she had come across in her previous employment. She also visited translating and interpreting agencies, and it was through one of these that she landed her first freelance assignment as a receptionist at an international conference. Then other work came in spasmodically and after about six months Melanie landed a major contract, translating for a consulting engineering company. This went on for some months and it was never very clear when it was going to come to an end. When the work eventually ran out: 'It was almost like starting again. I hadn't realized that what I should have been doing was developing other sources of work – instead, I was back to square one.'

It was from these early experiences that Melanie developed 'a continual fear that there wouldn't be any work next Monday', which dogged her for years to come. 'I was terrified. I understand very much how people feel when they're unemployed. You feel more stress and strain when you're looking for work than when you're actually doing it.'

Nevertheless, she kept going, even though the work was sporadic. Helped by the fact that she was living in low-rent accommodation, she struggled along, without even an overdraft, but it was hand to mouth. She feels that 'I couldn't have done it if I'd had any other liabilities'.

Contacts led to commissions of various kinds, such as translation assignments and interpreting for the Central Office of Information. Then, again, the work ran out; this time, as the result of answering an advertisement in The Times for a student to help with a research project, Melanie found herself spending a few weeks working in Mexico.

When she had finished this assignment, Melanie realized that she was 'good at finding things out' and wondered how she could apply this skill in other ways. A casual conversation with a friend who worked in advertising led to the idea of doing market research as a way of using languages when the translation work ran out. Taking addresses from a copy of the Market Research Handbook, in which the friend had ticked all those companies which he thought might use linguists for overseas research, she did a mailing and immediately received two replies offering research work in French and Spanish.

The first assignments were very straightforward: telephone interviewing, with questionnaires to be completed. This later led to field trips to Spanish- and French-speaking countries.

Contacts gradually led to more and more work. 'The ball started rolling. It was several years before I could really believe that this was happening, and that there'd always be someone else ringing up with an offer of work. I now have to listen very carefully when someone telephones because I have no idea from which angle the approach is going to come. I've built up more and more contacts, each leading to others, so that now when someone rings up and says, "So-and-so gave me your name," I have to concentrate very hard to remember who "So-and-so" is, because it's become a very wide net.'

Over the years, Melanie has built up her expertise, and she now handles complete projects from start to finish. There has been a continual process of learning and developing new skills, both through experience and from formal training. 'In every job I've taken,' Melanie says, 'I've learned whilst doing the work, and I've progressed in a wide range of fields.'

She has sometimes felt, however, that learning from experience is not enough, and that she needs to be taught. This has led her to take a number of courses, both to widen her scope in the market research field, and to help her to use new technology. She has learnt about word processing for business and home computing, and she has attended courses run by the Industrial Marketing Research

Association. Although she hasn't always learnt very much from formal instruction that she hadn't already discovered through experience, she does feel that 'going on a course can lead to contacts and give you confidence, even if the course itself doesn't teach you anything dramatically new'.

Courses, and contacts developed through them, are a means of counteracting one of the major problems of working alone: isolation. It was partly to escape from this that Melanie started working in the market research field, because it offered more opportunities for meeting people than straight translation work. More recently, she has also been coping with the problem of isolation by transferring her operation from home to an office in Barley Mow Workspace, a managed-workshop scheme which provides the companionship of working alongside other small firms and self-employed people, as well as offering other benefits in terms of shared services like reception, photocopying and mailing (see page 166).

It took a long time before Melanie stopped worrying 'whether next week was going to bring anything'. Over the years, though, her confidence has increased, and she now feels that 'you just have to keep your nerve. You have to go on trying. You can't just sit there and hope that something will happen – but, also, you mustn't get despondent because there doesn't seem to be an immediate response. If there isn't any work coming up, you have to busy yourself setting things up.' To remind herself of how she has progressed, Melanie keeps a cartoon on the wall. It shows two large bumble-bees, one of them explaining to the other: 'I used to be a drone, now I'm a pollen consultant.'

Learning points

Melanie Frazer's success is a good example of how basic skills picked up during the course of routine work can be built upon and expanded to provide the basis of a successful business. Points to note include:

- Her language skills arose out of a series of mundane office jobs.

- She spotted the initial market potential of her skills and was able to expand and diversify her activities to much more lucrative fields of work.
- She achieved this partially by getting the right training and investing in a number of relevant courses.
- When not working, she spends her time looking for future market opportunities.

Like many of the examples in this book, Melanie does not come from an exceptional background or possess exceptional skills. It is the way in which she chose to use her skills that set her apart from all the other office workers she worked alongside at the start of her career.

Ideas from hobbies/leisure pursuits

Many people narrow their choice of business ideas to those which relate directly to their work, without considering the wealth of ideas which can be adapted from their hobbies and leisure interests. In many cases, it may also be possible to combine skills and knowledge acquired at work with those acquired in leisure pursuits.

To illustrate this, let us take three common hobbies and examine the businesses which could be based around them.

Writing

Most newspapers and periodicals rely heavily on material from outside contributors, particularly trade journals and hobby/leisure magazines. You would be best equipped to find regular work if you combine a good literary style with a specialist knowledge (aerodynamics, careers advice, model railways, travel, motorcycles, cars, cookery, for example). To develop your writing ability, you may be able to join a local writers' guild or take a relevant course of study.

Outlay. You would need a typewriter or word-processor and a regular supply of stationery. You would also need regular issues of the publications you wish to write for (to check for style, content and layout) and a cassette recorder to aid research. (To be truly competitive, you would be well advised to invest in up-to-date word-processing equipment – this can often cost as little as a sophisticated typewriter.)

Advertising your service. You could generally do this by direct approach, on the telephone or by letter. A full list of those publications which accept freelance contributions can be found in the current *Writers' and Artists' Yearbook*. You could also place an advertisement in the *UK Press Gazette* or *Campaign*, or find work through an agent (details in *Writers' and Artists' Yearbook*).

How to cost. Freelance work is generally paid per number of words published or per number of lines, or by individual negotiation with the editor/agent.

Developing your service. You could team up with a photographer to provide a more complete service. You could also form a writers' co-operative, which covers a wide range of specialisms. You could invest in desk-top publishing software and branch out into more ambitious publishing schemes. If you are relying on freelance writing as your sole form of income, you should always aim to negotiate a 'retainer' or the promise of regular work from at least one – and preferably two or three – publications.

Photography

Depending on your resources, you could offer a freelance service for local newspapers, trade journals and periodicals; coverage of local events on commission (weddings, fêtes, fairs, parties); a freelance service for local auctioneers and estate agents, or an in-house portrait service.

Outlay. You would need a full range of photographic equipment, a room you can convert into a darkroom and, if you want to branch into colour work, access to a local developer. If you offer an outside service, you would need adequate transport for your equipment. If you offer an in-house service, you would need a room you can convert into a studio, with a range of backcloths and suitable lighting facilities.

Advertising your service. This could be done through advertising in your local paper; through notices and professional advertisements in newsagents' windows, registry offices and churches; by direct approach to local auctioneers and estate agents; or through photographic agencies (see *Writers' and Artists' Yearbook*). Video is a new and rapidly growing market, provided you can invest in the right equipment and receive the right training.

How to cost. You could charge according to the hours worked, or ask for a flat fee per print.

Furthering your knowledge. Courses are offered by local colleges and adult education institutes (e.g. towards a City and Guilds certificate).

Developing your service. You could team up with a writer/journalist to provide a complete service to newspapers/periodicals. If you build up enough experience, you can open your own outside studio.

Craftwork

There has always been a demand for high quality craftwork and, if you have developed your amateur interest and can produce highly skilled work, you should be able to find a wide range of retail outlets and, possibly, mail-order custom. You could also sell your craftwork from a market-stall in local fêtes, fairs and festivals. Popular crafts include:

- candle-making (further details from *Simple methods of candle manufacture*, available from Intermediate Technology Publications);
- glass engraving (further details from the Guild of Glass Engravers);
- jewellery (courses are available at many adult education institutes, often leading to a City and Guilds certificate);
- pottery (further information from the Craftsmen Potters Associates);

– soft toys (courses are available at some adult education institutes, usually leading to a City and Guilds certificate).

Courses are available in most crafts at local colleges and adult education institutes, backed up by a selection of residential courses offered by a variety of regional residential colleges. Details of all courses are available from the Crafts Council.

Case-study 3.2: David Hollis

David Hollis, now twenty-five, started making and selling Christmas crackers when he was a schoolboy, to earn extra pocket money. Despite continuing in full-time education up to the age of twenty, he managed to build his hobby over the years into an established business, to the extent that he now employs six full-time staff and around thirty homeworkers, supplying crackers to such well-known stores as Habitat, Heals, Harrods, Paperchase and Rymans.

In the early stages, running the business was very much a case of trial and error and of learning from experiences which, in retrospect, have their humorous side.

As a child, David had always dreamed of running some kind of enterprise; he hit on the cracker-making idea when, aged thirteen, he read in an article in a Sunday newspaper about Christmas crackers that it was possible to buy a kit and make your own.

'I went on nagging and nagging my parents until they sent for this kit, and I made up a few boxes of dreadful crackers. Then gradually I got better, until I thought I could get my family and friends to part with some money in exchange for them.'

By this time, it was the middle of December and David was running out of materials. He hurriedly sent off for replacements but, by the time they arrived, Christmas was over, so there wasn't very much he could do until the following year.

The following Christmas, he was more ambitious. He drew out all his savings – £16 – and spent the money on materials, which he made up into sample boxes of crackers. At the beginning of December, he tried to sell them to local stores, only to be told that they had bought their stocks the previous spring at the gift shows. 'I'd obviously well and truly missed the boat. I was horrified, particularly as it was my own money I'd spent.'

Determined to recoup his £16, the next year David started in September. He phoned the local supermarket, where his mother did her weekly shopping, and actually succeeded in winning his first order – for 150 boxes. 'Looking back, the manager obviously didn't buy them for purely commercial reasons – I think he was fascinated by what I was doing.'

With some financial help from his parents – his father forked out £50 for materials – David made up the order, working in the family living-room after school. His mother helped with the deliveries, taking a small consignment of crackers to the supermarket every time she went shopping.

Unfortunately, the crackers hardly sold at all because they were in a solid box, and the lid had to be removed to see what was inside. Every time David went to the supermarket, they were still there, in a big pile.

Eventually, about a week before Christmas, David decided to do some research to find out why the crackers hadn't sold. He phoned the store, pretending to be a customer, and found out that if the crackers had been packed in a box with a transparent lid, they would probably have been snapped up. The supermarket venture hadn't been a total disaster, however, because David had been paid for his supplies – but the manager refused to speak to him on the phone thereafter.

Learning from his experience, he used better boxes the following year and, undeterred, he went in search of new markets, and managed to get an appointment with the London buyer of the John Lewis Partnership. He messed it up, however, not only by arriving four hours late and with his samples in old carrier bags with torn handles, but also because some little stars which were meant to be glued on to the crackers had fallen off when he took out his first box of crackers. 'I tried to explain, but of course any apologies were useless by then.' At least, however, he learned that 'it's no good taking something in and saying "We're going to do this and that to it," because, of course, they'll ask, "Well, why haven't you?" '

However, in the same year he did manage to win a sizeable order from a local wholesaler for 2,000 giant crackers. They sold extremely well, and the following year the wholesaler upped the order to 10,000.

This time David had bitten off more than he could chew. He worked every night, after school, for months; and he also found several home-workers to help out. Despite this, production simply couldn't keep pace with demand. 'The wholesaler kept saying, "We want more, more – you've got to have two juggernauts outside, full of them." I was doing my best, but I was still only producing five or six hundred a week. Then one day I turned up at his warehouse and found it full of crackers just like mine. He'd found someone else, who'd got a factory, to copy the design and produce the crackers more cheaply.'

By then, David had made the entire 10,000, of which the wholesaler had taken 9,000. With only a verbal agreement, he couldn't force the wholesaler to take the final batch, so any profit he would have made was wiped out.

'After that, I decided to make something that people would appreciate, rather than just pile them high and sell them cheap.' From then on he made high quality, specialized crackers, and was successful in winning an order from Paperchase for 600 boxes. By this time he could drive, and so he hired a van for deliveries. Otherwise he had no overheads, the order being sufficiently small for him to make up the crackers himself.

For the next couple of years David went on making crackers for Paperchase. Then, in his last year in the sixth form, he had almost decided to give up the cracker business and concentrate on his 'A'-levels when an unsolicited repeat order arrived. 'I couldn't turn it down – and that's really why I'm here now.' Perhaps surprisingly in the circumstances, David did manage to pass his exams and, under some pressure from his family, enrolled at the local polytechnic to study law.

After a couple of years, David and the polytechnic parted company prematurely, partly because the cracker business was taking up too much of his time. This was despite the fact that for much of this period David's 'office' consisted of a phone booth in a railway station near the college, and if the door wasn't properly closed the person at the other end could hear the sound of station announcements and passing trains.

Soon after David's abrupt departure from higher education, a real turning point came about. By this time his girlfriend was helping *with the business, and together they took a small stand at the International Spring Fair at the National Exhibition Centre.*

'The fair was an enormous success. That's when we got the business on to a proper commercial footing.' They became a limited company, using the name Robin Reed both to convey the impression of being an established family (David could pretend to be the junior partner, to account for his relative youth) and because the name had associations with Christmas robins.

However, finance became a problem. Previously, everything had been done on a cash basis, but there was now a pressing need to negotiate a bank loan, to bridge the gap between paying suppliers and receiving payment from customers – particularly tricky in a seasonal business.

With some help from his father, David put together a business plan, and started shopping around for a loan. He possessed written orders and samples of the product, but there was nothing he could offer as security, so it wasn't easy to raise the necessary capital. Eventually, however, he negotiated a loan with the local branch of Barclays, who have been extremely helpful and have even exceeded their normal lending limits on occasion.

Since then, the firm has gone from strength to strength. They now occupy a modern factory of 3,500 square feet on an industrial estate, and their plans for expansion include renting the empty premises next door, and employing more full-time staff.

The company's growth certainly justifies these moves – during this period, turnover, now well into five figures, has increased by nearly 50 per cent per annum.

Learning points

What can be learned from David Hollis's successful development?

- His story illustrates how a successful business can be based on a seemingly modest hobby.
- Entrepreneurial spirit does not depend on age or work experience. David started his business at the age of thirteen and built it up while still at school.

This example also illustrates a number of other essential learning points:

- the need for proper market research;
- the importance of not taking on more work than you can cope with;
- the need to get written confirmation of all orders for new business;
- the need to ensure adequate cash-flow.

David's failure to follow these requirements resulted in early failure and disappointment. But, very importantly, his perseverance and his ability to learn from his mistakes enabled him to turn a schoolboy hobby into a profitable and expanding business.

Ideas from looking after a home

The domestic responsibilities of maintaining a home and bringing up a family can also provide skills which could form the basis of a successful enterprise. This can best be illustrated by taking some of the standard chores about the house and working at them in terms of the skills, knowledge and experience acquired.

Shopping. An ability to buy the highest quality goods within a fixed budget. *Skills acquired*: budgeting, quality control, an ability to deal with a wide range of suppliers.

Child care. An ability to educate, and to control the activities of one or more children. *Skills acquired*: an elementary knowledge of child psychology, co-ordination and leadership skills, elementary teaching skills, elementary counselling and care skills, elementary management skills, patience, imagination.

Cooking. An ability to prepare appetizing meals for several people, working to a fixed budget. *Skills acquired*: food preparation, catering skills, presentation skills, manual dexterity, budgeting.

Household maintenance. An ability to run and maintain a clean and well-ordered household. *Skills acquired*: time-allocation skills, laundry and dressmaking skills, furniture care and maintenance skills, self-discipline.

Gardening. An ability to maintain a well-ordered garden and to grow both flowers and vegetables. *Skills acquired*: using a wide variety of tools, manual dexterity, co-ordination, perceptual skills (e.g. spotting and controlling early onset of plant disease); design skills (e.g. designing a vegetable plot and laying it out to achieve maximum crop production); physical strength.

Let us take this process a stage further and look at three potential skills acquired in the course of bringing up a family or maintaining a home, examining how a successful business could be built up around each.

Cooking

You could approach pubs, delicatessens, cafés, wine bars and restaurants in your local area and offer to supply them with jams, chutneys, pâtés, cheesecakes, sweets, pastries, stews, salads and pies. You could also specialize in seasonal fare such as hot-cross buns, Christmas puddings, mince pies, chocolate yule-logs and so on. You could offer a local catering service for individuals and businesses, preparing the food at home and transporting it to the consumers.

Outlay. You would need to have a full range of kitchen utensils and gadgets and a wide assortment of dishes, aluminium foil and plastic film. You would also need to have a large refrigerator/freezer for cold storage and possibly, if you expand your service, a second oven. If you offer an outside catering service, you would also need a van or large car, a full range of cutlery and plates, and additional storage space.

Advertising your service. You could do this by direct approach (see Yellow Pages for a list of potential clients); by notices in the local newsagents' windows; by advertisement in your local paper, or by personal contacts.

How to cost. You could look at commercial brands as a rough guide to cost and add a small extra cost for the fact that it is home made. If you are offering an outside catering service, offer a choice of pre-costed menus which you can prepare easily and efficiently.

Furthering your knowledge. This could be done by part-time courses in advanced cooking at your local college or adult institute; City and Guilds courses at your local technical college; weekend residential course at Denman College in Oxfordshire open only to members of Women's Institutes; Cordon Bleu style courses, etc.

Developing your service. You could team up with another outside caterer to provide a more comprehensive service. If you have an attractive property which is large enough, you could offer teas and/or buffet lunches in the garden/house. If you build up enough experience, you could even open your own restaurant/wine bar/café.

Child care

You could offer a local service looking after under-fives whose parents are at work.

Outlay. You would be expected by the local authority's Social Services Department (with whom you will have to register) to have a safe, warm place for children to play, to have adequate kitchen and toilet facilities and to provide stimulating activities. You would need to buy extra equipment and playthings: cots, small chairs or stools, potties, playpen, building bricks and other robust toys that can be shared by children.

Advertising your service. Once registered with the local authority, the Social Services Department will put you on their vacancy list and you can also advertise yourself direct. You may also consider joining the National Childminding Association (236a High Street, Bromley, Kent BR1 1PQ).

How to cost. There is no scale of charges laid down for child-minding but, in some areas, childminders have grouped together and agreed a uniform rate. The National Childminding Association usually recommends a weekly charge per child, with additional charges for, say, providing extra meals or keeping a child after 6 p.m. or overnight.

Developing your service. If you are a qualified nurse or have similar experience in looking after children, you could consider setting up a private day nursery for pre-school children. Alternatively, you could offer crèche facilities to local employers wishing to recruit part-time female staff who need child-care facilities.

Dressmaking

You could offer an individual made-to-measure service or possibly find a retail outlet in your local area.

Outlay. You would need a high-standard sewing machine with attachments for zips and gatherings, a cutting table, an ironing board, a dressmaker's dummy and adequate hanging/storage space. You would also need a separate room equipped with a long mirror for fittings.

Advertising your service. This could be done through advertisements in your local paper or notices in newsagents' windows.

How to cost. You should generally charge according to the number of hours worked and for the fabric, if you provide it.

Furthering your knowledge. This could be done through City and Guilds courses at your local college.

Developing your service. You could supplement your income by offering an alterations service to local high street outfitters and a repair service to local dry cleaners.

Case-study 3.3: Janet Apperley
Janet Apperley – founder of Greenlay (Hampers and Catering)

Limited, provides haute cuisine for le beau monde . . . and for others. Janet looks as if she was born rich: an inaccuracy she dispels with a certain anger born of the fact that she could get no business start-up grants because she was entering the luxury trade. Fortunately Janet's husband was supportive.

Janet did homework on hampers and found that Fortnums' and Harrods' had to be returned after use. With Henley up the road (they live near Maidenhead in Berkshire), in 1981 Janet went ahead offering appropriate riverside picnics in wicker baskets which clients could keep. 'The first line sold at about £17 – packed with prawn salad, duck and orange terrine, asparagus quiche, cumberland sausages and wine for two.' About £50 was spent on initial menus-cum-leaflets with order forms, which were slipped in specially selected letterboxes in the area.

Local newspaper advertising helped, but costs were kept to a minimum – 'we did all our own designing'. Having taken orders (about twenty-two for that first Henley), preparation went on in their own kitchen. Janet's two sisters and friends helped out and ate the leftovers by way of payment.

'What appealed to me,' says Janet, 'was organizing and presenting high quality food and interesting packaging.' Within a couple of years the business had grown to enable her to take on staff so that she could concentrate on selling, and promote the new 'Light D'light' box, which holds a four-course meal, a quarter-bottle of wine or mineral water and a glass. A major design feature is the way the front unfolds on to the knee to form a handy tray.

Janet gave a local press conference with the hampers on show and then took them to Fleet Street offices for the next day's lunch (having refrigerated the food overnight). Publicity ensued: journalists were impressed by the high standard and imaginative presentation.

Picnics are seasonal, so the company – Greenlay is Janet's maiden name – sought catering orders for occasions like weddings and business gatherings. The result was successful enough to justify a move in August 1985 to larger premises (5,000 square feet) in an industrial area near Heathrow.

Financially the operation could not have reached this point without investment, which came in the form of around £60,000, a considerable proportion raised through friends and associates using the tax-relief Business Expansion scheme (on condition they leave money in for at least five years). That investment has also enabled the purchase of the first refrigerated trailer which can be towed behind the directors' cars. The firm now sounds pretty grand, but in the first month it suffered from bad business and poor accountancy advice; 'only later did we find out we were spending too much on things like graphics'. She changed banks and used a loan to lay the foundations (putting up her house as guarantee).

An old friend, a farmer, showed her how to work out the percentage of profits she should make on sales. That side of the business is now being computerized, along with lists of all clients under various headings, from Christmas hampers and picnics to catering. 'The new mailing list is amazing.'

Janet makes the operation sound smooth, but she has worked all hours for four years. 'I've just started taking off one weekend in four.' This is largely because she has taken on an operations manager who runs timetabling, helps schedule deliveries by a mixture of staff members, datapost and same-day carriers (about £8 per order to central London, for example).

Turnover in the past year was about £200,000 and is expected to expand, but not at the expense of that personal service and imaginative presentation which Greenlay has proved customers will pay for – from buttonholes for each picnicker to a seashell barrow for a company outing. Cakes can be fashioned to look like buildings or logos, and meals can change with fashion: 'Nursery food is back – apricot crumbles, apple charlottes and treacle tarts.'

Janet sets a standard of professionalism which is the key – from walkie-talkies (to keep in contact at large outside events, such as Henley Royal Regatta) to twenty-four-hour ordering, a large library of information on all aspects of food preparation and serving. The solid pattern of growth with the new unit is expected to lead to new and bigger outlets.

Exercise 3.1. Identifying ideas of your own

Having read the section above, it is worth relating the ideas it contains to your own talents and circumstances. The exercise below will help you to do so in a systematic fashion.

1. Make A4 copies of Tables 3.1, 3.2 and 3.3 on separate sheets of paper, using the format shown.
2. Using the information you assembled in Chapter 2 and other sources (your job specification, curriculum vitae, diaries, etc.), list in the left-hand column all the skills you feel you possess.

   The skills you list may relate to ideas and information; to things or products; or to people. They could have been acquired in the course of your work, or from your leisure activities, hobbies, domestic chores, child-rearing responsibilities, holidays or education. If you feel it appropriate, use your marriage partner, a close friend/relative and/or a former work colleague to provide a second opinion.
3. In the right-hand column of Table 3.1, list as many business ideas as you can which could be based on, or supported by, the skills you have listed in the left-hand column. Use the Table of Business Ideas on pages 56-73 if you need inspiration.
4. Using the same process, list all the kinds of knowledge you possess in the left-hand column of Table 3.2. Once again, remember to include everyday knowledge, not only that acquired through work but through hobbies, leisure pursuits, etc., and other personal sources.
5. In the right-hand column of Table 3.2, list as many ideas as you can which could be based on, or supported by, the knowledge you have listed in the left-hand column. Pay particular attention to those which have also appeared in Table 3.1.
6. In Table 3.3, make a shortlist of the three ideas which appeal to you most and for which you feel you are most qualified. (Bear in mind that many of your skills will need to be developed in order to make them commercially viable – see pages 97-106.)

Table 3.1 **My existing skills**

Date:........................

My skills	Business ideas they could support

EXAMPLES OF SKILLS

To do with ideas and information: researching, compiling, presenting, creating, developing, discussing, assessing.

To do with things: making, refining, collecting, assessing, buying, selling, pricing, distributing, transporting, storing.

To do with people: advising, counselling, managing, persuading, serving, taking instructions from, teaching, feeding, transporting.

Table 3.2 **My existing knowledge**

Date:........................

My knowledge	Business ideas it could support

EXAMPLES OF KNOWLEDGE

Art, local services, safety in the home, plant growth, local transport links, legal requirements, business contacts, business suppliers. The principles of: physics, photography, gardening, cookery, freezing foods, chess playing, cookery, hygiene, makes and varieties of cameras, railway engines, vegetables, antiques, trees, wines, malt whiskies and clothes.

Knowledge on how: a committee is run, decisions are made, grants are given, a computer works, a hotel/library/ office is run.

N.B. The essential difference between skills and knowledge is that having a skill implies that you are able to perform or do something. Knowledge may be linked with a skill, or it may lead to the development of a skill. For example, you may already have a good knowledge of French grammar and vocabulary, but will need some years living in France to develop the skill of speaking French properly. An 'adviser' may have a great deal of book *knowledge* but may need to develop the *skill* of advising people how best to use that knowledge.

Table 3.3. **My top three ideas for a business**

Date:

1.

Notes

2.

Notes

3.

Notes

Case-study 3.4: Elizabeth McGovern (a worked example)

Elizabeth McGovern works in the marketing department of a chain of fast-food restaurants. During the course of her life outside her main occupation, she has also been involved in the following activities:

- *She has studied in France and Germany and has a good working knowledge of both languages.*
- *She worked as an assistant and later as an assistant manager in a bookshop.*
- *She is a keen vegetarian and also a very good cook.*
- *She works for a local voluntary work centre, driving elderly people about in her local community.*
- *She organized a local petition to stop the closure of a local maternity clinic.*
- *She helps to run her local CND branch.*

She dislikes the commercialism and products of her current employer and would like to live a more independent life in an occupation more suited to her personal beliefs and interests.

Using the methods outlined in Exercise 3.1, her tables look like those overleaf.

Table 3.4. **My existing skills**

Date: 10th May 1987

My skills	*Business ideas they could support*
Basic marketing skills (from my job). These include: *– market research* *– point of sale* *– advertising on the media* *– press liaison* *– packaging* *Cooking* *Driving* *Relating to older people* *Lobbying and campaigning in local politics (from my maternity clinic petition and CND activities). These include:* *– press liaison* *– making contacts in the local authority* *– writing and arranging the printing of flysheets, posters and press notices* *– organizing local rallies and marches* *How to organize an office from my job and CND activities. These include:* *– choosing and buying office equipment* *– organizing the work of clerical assistants and secretaries*	*A publishing venture (perhaps related to vegetarian food or peace issues?)* *A catering venture (vegetarian fast-food?)* *A local typing or word-processing operation?* *Starting a local bookshop (specializing in 'alternative' publications)* *Starting a marketing consultancy (perhaps for charities or small local organizations)*

– buying stationery – correcting typing and printing errors	
Buying and selling books (from my previous job in the bookshop)	
Buying and assessing health foods	

Table 3.5. **My existing knowledge**

Date: 11th May 1987

My knowledge	*Business ideas it could support*
French and German	*Translation services (after additional training)*
French and German lifestyles and culture	*A tourist or courier service*
The local roads and lanes of my local area (from driving older people to shops)	*A publishing venture*
The local counsellors and Member of Parliament	*A local taxi service*
The basic principles of retailing, and how local government works	*Freelance writing (I wrote press releases and marketing literature, and I could use these skills to write about more important issues)*
The history of vegetarianism and the Peace Movement	*A catering service (maybe linked with delivery?)*
How printing is organized (from my job and CND activities)	
Herbs and spices needed for cooking	
The local and national suppliers of health food	

Table 3.6. **My top three ideas for a business**

Date: 15th May 1987

---

1. A publishing venture

Notes

This would allow me to draw on my marketing skills, the knowledge I have of the printing process and the knowledge I have of how bookshops are run. I could concentrate on publishing books and pamphlets related to health and health foods, political issues and other 'alternative' subjects. I would, however, need training in the printing process, and I would also need to bring in a partner with direct experience of publishing as I am not confident that my own experience is sufficient.

---

2. A catering venture

Notes

There is a growing market for vegetarian and health foods in my local area. There is no reason why I could not apply the same principles and methods used to sell fast junk food to my own cooking. I could open a local restaurant or café for people to eat in, and have a separate counter for take-away food which people could order by telephone. I have seen this work in Covent Garden and I might try to get a part-time job in one of the health-food restaurants there before setting up myself, in order to gain an inside look at how the business works.

---

3. A marketing consultancy for charities and organizations

Notes

Many local community-based organizations desperately need marketing expertise to help them thrive, and the basic principles of marketing I have learned in my job could be used to serve their needs. The problem here is obviously the financial return – few could afford to pay the kind of money a commercial organization has access to. However, my community activities have highlighted the fact that many charitable trusts and local authorities provide grants to help local organizations expand, and this includes money for publicity. To take this idea further, I need to engage in a little market research among my local political contacts to see whether the idea is financially viable.

Conclusion

This case-study is based on a real-life example. The person concerned ultimately chose to start a catering venture – but not the kind outlined in the exercise. Instead, she operated a 'fast health food' delivery service, advertised in the local press and by mailshots. She limited her health-food provision to a small number of popular dishes – the choice selected by conducting a thorough market research exercise – and cooked and froze these in advance. Customers rang to order the food and she then delivered it to their door. This not only allowed her to draw on skills acquired from her previous job and her love of cooking, it was also based on her knowledge of the local community and the local roads picked up through her voluntary work. With the exception of her marketing experience, all the skills and knowledge she needed came from leisure activities or private interests.

Researching your market

Having identified the product(s) or service(s) you wish to use as the basis for your business, you will need to explore the market potential. Any business enterprise has to be based on someone's needs, and there are a number of critical questions you should answer before taking any practical moves to establish yourself.

Exercise 3.2. Assessing your concept and its market

The detailed questionnaire below will help you assess the potential of your product or service in a logical manner. To answer all the questions, you will need to spend time in your chosen marketplace and canvass potential customers or clients to ensure that demand will be sufficient to justify your initial investment of time and money. Remember to keep detailed notes of all your responses. You will need the information when drawing up a detailed business plan (see Chapter 7).

Potential methods you can use and details of possible sources of information can be found between pages 88 and 97. It is important that you conduct the research *before* taking any practical moves to establish yourself. Much of the work can be undertaken in your spare time, while you still have the security of a regular income.

1. *Your product* (if you are supplying a service, turn to 2, below)
   - What product are you planning to make? Describe it in two or three sentences.
   - Have you produced it before in your previous employment?
   - Have you ever sold it yourself before?
   - If YES, what reaction did you receive?
   - If NO, do you have a clear idea of how you wish to sell it?
   - Describe your method in two or three sentences.
   - Have you a clear idea of how you are going to price your product?
   - Do you already have potential customers? How many?

2. *Your service* (if you are supplying a product, turn to 1, above)
   - What service are you planning to offer? Describe it in two or three sentences.

- Now describe it in one sentence or a single word.
- Have you ever provided this service before in your previous employment?
- If YES, what reaction did you receive?
- If NO, do you have a clear idea of how you wish to sell it? Describe your method in two or three sentences.
- Have you a clear idea of how you are going to price your service?
- Do you already have potential customers? How many?

3. *Customers/Clients*

- Who are likely to be the potential buyers of your product/service?
- Are they drawn from:
  - a particular profession or occupation
  - a particular sex, age or ethnic group
  - a particular region or locality
  - a particular class or social group
- Are they likely to be buying your product or service for themselves or on behalf of the organization they work for? (Put another way, are they likely to be using their own money or someone else's?)
- How can you reach this market in the most cost-effective manner?
  For example:
  - by advertising on television, radio, or national, local or specialist publications (see pages 174-9)
  - by direct sale (face-to-face or on the telephone)
  - by mailshots (see pages 178-9)
  - by notices in local post office and/or newsagents' windows (see page 177)
  - by shop-front displays
  - by inserts in specialist directories and/or Yellow Pages (see page 176)
  - by leaflet distribution (see page 177)

- Have you already identified potential clients/customers in your area?
- If YES, have you approached them and asked them questions about:
  - what price they would be prepared to pay
  - how often they would buy your product or service
  - what kind of approach they would best respond to (see list above)
  - what special needs they require which are not currently available at a price they can afford

4. *Your competition*

- Who are your major competitors in your chosen field?
- How much do you know about:
  - the prices they charge
  - the quality of their product/service
  - the resources at their disposal
  - the numbers of staff at their disposal
  - their profitability and current economic state
- How much do you know about customers' or clients' reaction to their product or service?
- Can you list specific reasons why some customers or clients would prefer to use your services or buy your products? For example:

  If you are a manufacturer, are your products:
  - cheaper (while retaining the same quality)
  - finished to a higher standard
  - better designed
  - better packaged
  - presented in a wider range of colours, flavours, shapes, etc.
  - more available locally
  - not available elsewhere

  If you are supplying a service, is it:
  - cheaper (while retaining its effectiveness)
  - more friendly

- quicker
- more specialized
- more well known
- different
- more available locally
- more varied
- not available elsewhere

■ Are you sure that these assets will be sufficient to persuade potential clients or customers to change to you? Is this conclusion based on guesswork or some form of market research exercise?

5. *Nature of demand*

Having identified your potential clients or customers:

■ What regular needs are they likely to have? For example:
- speed
- reliability
- personal service
- attractive premises
- convenience
- advice
- quick service
- access to parking
- good packaging
- wide range of goods
- cleanliness
- friendliness
- after-sales support
- wider choice
- discounts, etc.

■ Which of these needs are you in a position to meet?

■ Which of these needs are you *not* in a position to meet? (How is this likely to affect your profitability?)

■ Is the demand for your product or service based purely on topicality? Is it a fashionable idea that may peter out in a year or is there a potential long-term market?

- Is your market seasonal? Will the demand for your product or service vary according to the time of year/month/week/day?
- Is the demand for your product or service purely local? If it proves successful, can it be adapted or expanded to other areas/fields?
- Is your market in the 'premium' or 'quality' sector (i.e. is the demand dictated by the need for widely available, low-cost products/services or high quality, expensive products/ services)?

6. *Suppliers*

- To meet your demand:
  – what suppliers will you need?
  – how much are they charging for their materials/services?
  – where are they located?
  – how do their materials/services compare, both in quality and cost, with those of their leading competitors?
  – are their charges taken into account in your prices?

7. *Distribution*

- To meet your demand:
  – how are you going to distribute your product/service?
  – is this something you will be able to handle with your own transport or will you need to contract out to an outside firm?
  – what distribution companies exist in your region? How much are they charging for their services? How do their services compare to leading competitors?
  – is the cost of distribution reflected in your prices?

8. *Staff*

- To meet your demand:
  – will you need to employ anyone?
  – if YES, what categories of staff will you require?

- how many hours a week will they be required to work?
- what kind of contractual arrangement is most appropriate (fixed-term? fixed-job? casual? hired through an agency? taken on under a government scheme, e.g. YTS Community Scheme)?
- what legal and statutory obligations will these contracts involve?
- what will be the total cost of meeting your staff requirements?
- what office space will be required to accommodate them?
- is this cost reflected in your prices?

9. *Premises*

- To meet your demand:
  - will you need external premises?
  - have you considered the alternatives (using your own home . . . stalls within other premises . . . community offices or shared facilities)?
  - have you considered the implications, including insurance . . . planning permission . . . legal obligations . . . access to your customers/clients?
  - are they immediately available?
  - is the cost of renting or leasing your premises reflected in your price?

10. *Equipment*

- To meet your demand:
  - what equipment will you require?
  - will it be necessary to: . . . buy it . . . rent it . . . lease it?
  - do you know the necessary suppliers? Have you compared their prices?
  - what maintenance will the equipment require? Who will undertake it? At what price?
  - are there statutory safety requirements?

– is the cost of the equipment and its maintenance reflected in your price?

Conducting the research

The cost of using professional market research agencies will probably prove prohibitive with the financial resources at your disposal. However, there are a number of methods you can use to conduct the research yourself. Most can be undertaken in the leisure time at your disposal before you establish yourself.

Professional or work contacts

If your business idea is related to your current or a previous job, you should take advantage of the opportunity this provides to canvass and consult:

- close colleagues who are suitably qualified or experienced to advise you on the commercial viability of your idea;
- potential clients or customers in the same field who can tell you whether they would buy your services or goods (if you can win their contract in advance, so much the better!);
- suitably qualified contacts whom you may wish to involve directly in the business.

Local community contacts

If your business idea is directly aimed at your local community, you could conduct the same kind of informal survey among likely customers or clients. If your roots in the community are reasonably well established, you can insinuate the vital questions into simple, everyday conversation. At the same time you can start to investigate local suppliers, distributors and sources of equipment.

A more formal survey

Building on the informal information you have gleaned from the two sources above, you could next experiment with a more formal survey of opinion. This could be achieved by:

- A systematic telephone survey of potential customers ('Hello, I represent a new company/consultancy dealing in . . . Would you be prepared to answer a few questions about your current and future needs?').
- A direct-mail survey or sales-response letter asking the same questions (this may well result in a poor response, but could nevertheless yield important information – see details of the Post Office's free mailing offer to local small businesses on page 178).

Bear in mind, however, that this kind of formal approach will yield tangible results only if the list of people you wish to approach is well researched, using the sources of information listed below.

A trial exercise

If the business idea you have developed involves little more than your current home-based skills and equipment, you could experiment still further by taking time off work or your current responsibilities and actively canvass for business on a short-term basis. You could use most of the techniques outlined above in addition to small-ads in the local or trade press, notices in newsagents' or shop windows, and sales letters. If the response is very poor, you should take a closer look at the viability of your idea. Make sure, however, that you have the facilities and the time to cope with a large response. You do not wish to attract a bad reputation even before you set yourself up formally.

Reference material

These practical exercises should be supported by detailed research, drawn from the very comprehensive range of information from reference material readily available throughout the country. Broadly, these can be divided into (a) company and product data, (b) market and industry data.

Company and product data

Information on potential suppliers, customers and competitors, together with the products/services they offer, is available from a number of sources. This should be used to support or qualify the market research you have conducted, rather than replace it. No written source of information can be entirely tailored to the circumstances of your particular business start-up.

Yellow Pages/Thomson Directories. The simplest, and for many small businesses the most effective, source of information on local competitors and suppliers. If your business is serving the local community, these two telephone directories (which you probably already have in your possession) will provide you with a starting point for any informal or formal survey of market opinion and available resources. Yellow Pages and Thomson Directories covering other local areas in your region should be available in the reference section of your local public library or by applying to your local British Telecom office.

Business directories. A number of business directories exist, providing systematic data on companies throughout Great Britain. The principal among these include:

Kelly's Manufacturers and Merchants Directory, which lists over 90,000 UK manufacturers, merchants, wholesalers and firms, under 10,000 trade, product or service headings. The directory is published by IPC Business Press, who also publish *Kelly's Regional Directory of British Industry* (a town-by-town guide to industry), and *Kelly's Post Office London Directory* (which provides business listings street by street).

Key British Enterprises, which provides information on 20,000 UK companies and is very useful for identifying sales prospects, monitoring potential competitors and clients, or finding new suppliers. KBE is published by Dun and Bradstreet in two volumes, alphabetical and geographical. Dun and Bradstreet also publishes a one-volume guide, *Stubbs Directory*, which lists 130,000 UK firms but in slightly less detail; and *Principal International Business*, which gives basic facts about 50,000 businesses in 135 countries.

Kompass. This two-volume directory is published in association with the CBI. Volume One is indexed by product or service, and Volume Two provides basic company information on the 30,000 suppliers identified from Volume One. *Kompass Directories* are also available for Australia, Belgium and Luxembourg, Brazil, Denmark, France, West Germany, Holland, Indonesia, Italy, Morocco, Norway, Singapore, Spain, Sweden and Switzerland.

Sell's Directory. This one-volume directory is published jointly by Sell's Publications Limited and the Institute of Purchasing Management. It lists 65,000 products and services, using a classified cross-reference system. There is also a guide to several thousand trade-names cross-referenced to each company.

These directories, used imaginatively, can help to collate basic data on:

- potential clients
- potential competitors
- potential suppliers and distributors
- those products and services, related to your own, which are already on the market
- useful contacts to approach

The size, scope and detail of the directories vary, and each can be used for different purposes. *Stubbs Directory*, for example, does not have the depth of information of some of the others, but it has one of the widest spreads. It can therefore be used as a starting point to pinpoint which companies you wish to examine in greater depth. *Sell's Directory* is useful if you only know the trade-name of a particular product and wish to find out who makes it, with a view to establishing competitive sources of supply. *Key British Enterprises* is very useful for identifying sales prospects, monitoring competitors or finding new suppliers. *Kelly's Post Office London Directory*, on the other hand, is useful for finding concentrations of a particular type of business or gaps in the provision of a particular type of business.

Most of these directories are available through the major business libraries (see page 95) and some may be available in selected regional public libraries.

Market and industry data

Information on companies and products has been more than matched by publications dealing with specific market-sector data. Much of it is directly relevant to large established companies, but the background information they provide may prove useful in making the final decision as to whether your choice of product is justified. The major publications include:

The A–Z of UK Marketing Data. This basic guide to the size of individual markets covers a very wide range, classified by product area, market size, production imports, exports, together with information on the market share of brand leaders and some attempts at quantified market forecasts. It is published by Euromonitor Publications, 87 Turnmill Street, EC1. Euromonitor Publications also publish *European Marketing Data and Statistics*.

British Business. A weekly journal published by the Department of Trade and Industry which provides basic data on UK markets such as retail sales, hire purchase, industrial production, catering, the motor trade and textiles.

Market Research Sourcebook. Probably the most comprehensive source of market trends. These invaluable journals are published by HMSO and are issued on a monthly, quarterly and annual basis. They are divided into three series (production, service and distribution) and miscellaneous (which covers such areas as shipping, insurance, import/export ratios, cinemas and tourism). They are particularly valuable for gauging market shares and inter-company comparisons.

Key Note Publications. Another series of in-depth analyses, these publications cover 100 market sectors, looking at the market leaders in each, product developments, legislation and products assessed by volume and value. An appendix details further sources of information, including recent press articles and other reports. Further details are available from Key Note Publications, 28 Banner Street, London EC1Y 8QE.

Mintel. A useful way to update existing information. *Mintel* is a monthly publication providing reports on the performance of new products and consumer expenditure. It covers five specific consumer goods markets each month. Further details are available from Mintel, 20 Buckingham Street, The Strand, London WC2N 6EE.

General information

General information on company performance and market trends can be culled from selected reading of the quality national press, local and provincial press, and periodicals.

The quality nationals to read include the financial, economic and management pages of the *Financial Times*, *The Times*, the *Guardian*, the *Daily Telegraph*, the *Sunday Times* and the *Observer*. The general pages of your provincial press may also provide clues to the performance and market needs of local companies.

In addition, there are a wealth of trade and technical publications covering every sector of the market on a monthly or quarterly basis. These are aimed at either the general reader or the trade/industry. A subscription to one or more of the journals concerned is a good investment, not only because they can provide up-to-the-minute trends not covered by the larger directories above (details of future trade shows, seminars, changes in legislation, etc.), but also because they may provide outlets for future advertising or press coverage (see page 169).

The best directory listing all existing trade publications is undoubtedly Brad (British Rate and Data). This 'ad-man's Bible' lists all newspapers and periodicals in the UK and Eire, giving details of their frequency and circulation, price, key executives, advertising rates and readership. Updated copies are not easy to come by (at £100 a subscription, most libraries will not stock it) but slightly out-of-date copies are available from the publishers, MacLean-Hunter Limited, 76 Oxford Street, London W1N 0HH.

Easier to obtain are a variety of other press directories producing a similarly broad listing of existing periodicals but with varying degrees of detail. The best of these include *Willing's Press Guide*, *Benn's Press Directory* and *Pim's Media Directory*.

Where to find this information

The reference sections of selected libraries up and down the country should stock, or may be able to obtain, some or all of the publications listed above. Three types of reference libraries are worth approaching:

Specialist/technical libraries. Of these, the most important are:

Business Statistics Office Library, Cardiff Road, Newport, Gwent NPT 1XG (Tel. 0633-56111, ext. 2973). Open 09.00–17.00 Monday to Friday. Stocks British statistics office data as well as a broad range of related non-official material. The library is open to the general public, and offers an information service by telephone or letter.

Service Reference Library (Department of British Library), 25 Southampton Buildings, Chancery Lane, London WC2A 1AN (Tel. 01-405 8721, ext. 3344). Open 09.30–21.00 Monday to Friday; 10.00–13.00 Saturday. Perhaps the best library of its kind, it has 25,000 journals, 85,000 books and pamphlets and the details of 20,250,000 patents. It accepts telephone inquiries, and visits without prior arrangement, and even offers a linguist service for those wishing to inspect overseas literature in a foreign language.

Attached to the Service Reference Library is a Business Information Service (Tel. 01-404 0406), designed primarily to support the activities of other businesses and industrial libraries, but also available to individual users.

Statistics and Marketing Intelligence Library of the Overseas Trade Board, 1 Victoria Street, London SW1 (Tel. 01-215 5444/5). Open 09.30–17.30 Monday to Friday. In addition to a comprehensive collection of statistics on overseas countries, this library also has a wide range of UK statistics and directories.

Professional associations. A number of professional associations have libraries which can provide information and statistical data on the fields and occupational interests they represent. Three examples are the excellent libraries offered to their members by the Institute of Chartered Accountants in England and Wales, the Institute of Personnel Management and the British Institute of Management. These and other specialist business libraries (including those not listed above) are listed in the *ASLIB Economic and Business Information Group Membership Directory*, available from the London Business School Library, Sussex Place, Regent's Park, London NW1 4SA (Tel. 01-262 5050).

Local reference libraries. While the libraries above will be able to handle particular or specialist inquiries, you may find for more general inquiries that the business information section of your local reference library is enough. Particularly good provincial libraries include:

Aberdeen
Central Library, Rosemount Viaduct, Aberdeen AB9 1GU (Tel. 0224-634622).

Birmingham
Central Libraries, Chamberlain Square, Birmingham B3 3HQ (Tel. 021-235 4511).

Bristol
Central Library, College Green, Bristol BS1 5TL (Tel. 0272-276121).

Cambridge
Central Library, 7 Lion Yard, Cambridge CB2 3QD (Tel. 0223-65252).

Chatham
Chatham Library, Riverside, Chatham MA4 5SN (Tel. 0634-43589).

Exeter
Central Library, Castle Street, Exeter EX4 3PQ (Tel. 0392-77977).

Glasgow
Commercial Library, Royal Exchange Square, Glasgow (Tel. 041-221 7030).

Ipswich
Central Library, Northgate Street, Ipswich IP1 3DE (Tel. 0473-214370).

Leeds
Central Library, Calverley Street, Leeds LS1 3AB (Tel. 0532-462067).

Liverpool
Commercial Library, William Brown Street, Liverpool, Merseyside L3 8EW (Tel. 051-207 2147 and 207 0036).

London
City Business Library, Gillett House, 55 Basinghall Street, London EC2B 5BX (Tel. 01-638 8215).
Deptford Reference Library, 140 Lewisham Way, Deptford, London SE14 6PF (Tel. 01-692 1162).
Holborn Library, 32/38 Theobalds Road, London WC1X 8PA (Tel. 01-405 2706).
Westminster Reference Library, St Martin's Street, London WC2H 7HP (Tel. 01-930 3274).

Luton
Reference Library, Bridge Street, Luton LU1 2NG (Tel. 0582-30161).

Manchester
Central Library, St Peter's Square, Manchester M2 5PD (Tel. 061-236 9422).

Newcastle upon Tyne
Central Library, Princess Square, Newcastle upon Tyne, Tyne and Wear NE99 1HC (Tel. 091 2610 691).

Nottingham
Central Library, Angel Row, Nottingham NG1 6HP (Tel. 0602-43591).

Oxford
Central Library, Westgate, Oxford OX1 1DJ (Tel. 0865-815509).

Petersfield
Central Library, 27 The Square, Petersfield GU32 3HH (Tel. 0732-3451).

Southampton
Central Library, Civic Centre, Southampton SO9 4XP (Tel. 0703-832664).

Developing your skills

You may find the skills you have identified while providing the basis for a successful enterprise need further development. Formal training may be required:

– to enable you to offer a professional service to future clients;
– to broaden the scope or range of your product or service.

Case-study 3.5: Melanie Frazer and Paul Chester
The case-study of Melanie Frazer made earlier in this chapter is a good illustration (see page 57). As we saw, Melanie started self-employment as a translator and interpreter, and later broadened her business to become an international consultant in market research. During the course of establishing and building her business, she took a number of courses to improve and broaden the skills she had acquired from her previous employment. These included:

- a Spanish course at Madrid University to build on her existing knowledge of the language;
- a course for translators at the Polytechnic of Central London;
- a word-processing course at a local college – to improve her administrative skills;
- a 'flexi-time' course in home computing at the South Bank Polytechnic;
- a course on 'The Basics of Market Research' at the Industrial Market Research Association;
- an advanced course on market research offered by the same association.

At the time of writing, she was also considering an MBA course to improve her management skills.

Melanie found that starting a business involved a continual process of learning and developing new skills. As she explained, 'Even when the course itself doesn't teach you anything dramatically new, it can lead to new contacts and give you confidence.'

Her experience is shared by Paul Chester. Along with his wife, Helen, he runs a retail jewellery business in Oxfordshire, selling all types of jewellery from silver and 18-carat gold rings to clocks and general giftware.

Paul left school with only one 'O'-level. 'I knew that I would not be able to climb up in a job to a very high standard and I started my business because I had always wanted to achieve something on my own.'

Paul's basic knowledge of the trade came from working in various jewellery shops for three years after he left school. During the course of his on-the-job experience he learned how to engrave and to undertake small jewellery repairs. He broadened his experience by going to college for one night a week to study gem stones and gain more advanced knowledge of the jewellery trade.

The benefits of the training have enabled him to set up his own business. He was able to move into larger premises after two and a half years. He has vastly increased his stock level and increased his annual turnover from £20,000 to £100,000 in three years.

Where to train or study

In seeking to improve your skills, you can turn to a wide range of educational institutes and training bodies.

Small-business courses. Courses aimed specifically at developing the skills of small-business people are now offered by Government Training Centres, the Open University and the Open College (see below), management training courses and Institutes of Further or Higher Education. Details of these appear in the Appendix on page 259.

Colleges of further education. These are available in most localities and offer a wide range of general education and specific training. The courses generally last from September to June and are available on a full-time or part-time basis. The major qualifications catered for by the courses are:

- City and Guilds qualifications
- RSA secretarial and business qualifications
- B/TEC courses
- Specific professional qualifications such as: Royal Institute of Chartered Surveyors, Institute of Housing, Institute of Personnel Management

Colleges of further education cater for people of all ages, and the increased number of adults using them has led to many colleges offering specific courses for mature students. These include 'return to study' courses, 'GCSE courses for mature students', and refresher or basic courses in typing, secretarial work, gardening, cookery and crafts. There are often playgroup or nursery facilities available to course members and the times offered are varied (e.g. 09.30–11.15, 17.30–20.00).

Universities and polytechnics. Some universities and many polytechnics offer part-time courses in specific vocational skills. These can vary from flexible or modular degree courses through to courses in office technology. Information on the courses offered is available by applying to the institute concerned.

The Open University. The Open University runs a highly successful continuing education programme which offers short, distance learning courses lasting from a week to ten months and costing anything from £150 to £500. They also offer study packs for people to use at home which cost between £5 and £30. The courses on offer are divided into three main areas:

- Courses drawn from the full degree programme, covering a wide range of topics in humanities, social science, mathematics, science, technology and education.
- Courses forming part of the OU's scientific and technical updating programme, covering computer systems, robotics, manufacturing systems and quality systems.
- Courses forming part of OU's highly successful open business school, including 'The Effective Manager', 'Accounting and Finance for Managers', 'Personnel Selection and Interviewing', 'Managing People', 'Introduction to Marketing' and, in particular, 'Starting your own Business'.

Further information about Open University courses, and how to apply, can be obtained from the Information Office, Open University, Walton Hall, Milton Keynes MK7 6AA (Tel. 0908-74066).

The Open College. Very similar to the OU's courses are those offered by the Open College, launched in 1987. The Open College's courses are exclusively vocational. They cover many areas which may be relevant to small-business start-ups, including communication skills, computers in business, time management, marketing – and of course self-employment. The method of instruction draws heavily on the techniques pioneered by the OU. Students are provided with such aids as a workbook, an audiotape, a videotape and practical kits. These are backed up by programmes broadcast on Channel Four and one-to-one tuition from a network of local learning centres. Further information on OC courses is available by writing to: Open College, Freepost, PO Box 35, Abingdon, Oxon OX14 3BR (Tel. 0235-555444).

Henley, The Management College. Distance learning courses similar to those offered by the OU's Open Business School are available from Henley, The Management College. These cover 'The Effective Manager'. 'Accounting for Managers', 'Marketing for Managers' and 'Information Management'. Further information and details of the courses are available from: Henley Distance Learning Centre, Greenlands, Henley-on-Thames, Oxon RG9 3AU (Tel. 04912-571552).

National Extension College (NEC). Many further education qualifications can be obtained by using the correspondence courses offered by the National Extension College in conjunction with your local college of further education (see section on colleges of further education, above).

The NEC also offers a 'How to Study Effectively' course, an Open University preparatory course and a series of home student packages linked to national and regional radio and television series (e.g. 'Mind Your Own Business', 'Women in Society'). Further details can be obtained from the National Extension College, 18 Brooklands Avenue, Cambridge CB2 2HN (Tel. 0223-316644).

Institute of Marketing. The IM, together with Lloyds Bank, the Manpower Services Commission and the Department of Employment, have put together a 120-minute workshop for small businesses, entitled 'Marketing Your Business'. Each workshop concentrates on the essentials of a simple but effective marketing programme. It raises many of the key questions that many small businesses fail to ask themselves, and goes on to explain the simple techniques which can be used to grasp and exploit opportunities. Everyone attending the workshop receives an information pack containing a checklist and action points to help create a marketing programme, a practical video programme and a reference guide. Information is available from the Institute of Marketing, Moor Hall, Cookham, Berkshire SL6 9QH (Tel. 062 85-24922).

Private correspondence college. There is a wide range of these, and they offer courses leading to general education qualifications (University of London external degrees, OU preparatory courses) and professional qualifications (law, accountancy, banking, etc.). The larger ones offer careers advice, occasional seminars, and a detailed prospectus of relevant qualifications. All offer a course tutor, who marks your papers and can be consulted if you are having problems. Some colleges also offer guarantees of your money back or a year's free tuition if you fail the examination.

You should remember to be a little wary: standards and course fees vary enormously. You should try to find out as much as you can about the course and the college before you commit yourself. You should check whether the course materials relate directly to the course you want to take, that the notes are updated regularly and, most importantly, that the course has already been written (can you see a sample?). You should also check to see whether the college has been accredited by the Council for the Accreditation of Correspondence Colleges (CACC, 27 Marylebone Road, London NW1 5JS (Tel. 01-935 5391)).

Other independent colleges and schools. Independent or private colleges provide a huge array of educational possibilities. For example:

- architecture (e.g. The Architectural Association School of Architecture)
- adventure (e.g. the Outward Bound Trust)
- beauty therapy (e.g. London Institute of Beauty Culture)
- computing (e.g. Control Data Institute)
- cooking (e.g. Cordon Bleu)
- craftwork (clock repair, china repair, etc.)
- drama and music (e.g. Rose Bruford College)
- driving (e.g. British School of Motoring)
- floristry (e.g. Constance Spry School of Floristry)
- foreign languages (e.g. Berlitz)
- hairdressing (e.g. Vidal Sassoon)
- secretarial and office skills (e.g. Pitman)

– teaching English as a foreign language (e.g. International House, London)

and many, many others.

Many colleges offer courses leading to nationally and/or professionally recognized qualifications.

You should always be careful to check the admissions policy of the college: is it concerned that only those who can benefit or succeed on the course should be admitted? Also check whether the college is approved by the Department of Education and Science, the opinions of past students and whether the course has the content and leads to the qualification you want.

Informal study

LEA day/evening classes. Thousands of classes exist which meet in local colleges, evening institutes, community centres, schools and adult education institutes. They cover a wide range of subjects that include typing, car maintenance, cooking, yoga and general education subjects such as languages up to 'O'-level standard. The courses usually rely on local demand.

Enrolment is usually in September at a fixed time and is on a first-come, first-served basis. The courses are relatively inexpensive and fees may be waived or substantially reduced for people out of paid work. A detailed prospectus of the subjects offered locally is available from your local college or local public library. Classes are also advertised in local papers and, occasionally, on public transport. For courses in London, *Floodlight* is an invaluable publication (available from most bookshops). Similar courses are offered by local clubs, Women's Institutes, and the Workers' Education Association.

University extramural departments. A number of universities have extramural departments which offer evening classes, part-time day classes, short courses and public lectures in a variety of subjects which include art, transport, photography, literature and languages and which also offer preparatory courses for full-time higher education. Longer diploma and certificate courses are also offered by the University of London extramural department.

The courses are open to anyone and give you the chance to sample aspects of higher education without committing yourself to a full-time course. Detailed information on the subjects offered and when to apply is available from the relevant university.

Short residential courses. Extramural departments of universities, colleges of higher education, schools, charitable trusts and private colleges offer short-term, summer residential courses. The subjects offered include: furniture restoration, landscape painting, weaving, advanced languages, lacemaking and pottery. A full prospectus of the courses, and where they are offered, is published annually by the National Institute of Adult Education, 19b De Montfort Street, Leicester LE1 7GE (Tel. 0533-551451).

Further information and advice. An increasing number of educational guidance services for adults are being established around the country. All provide impartial help on the full range of educational opportunities in the region, although a few are intended as information services only and do not give advice.

The full list of current services is published in a guide produced jointly by the National Association of Education Guidance Services and the Educational Counselling and Credit Transfer Information Service (ECCTIS) and is available from ECCTIS, PO Box 88, Walton Hall, Milton Keynes MK7 6DB (Tel. 0908-368921).

Exercise 3.3. Filling the gaps

This final exercise draws on information you have gathered in the past two chapters and will help you to:

- identify the skills and knowledge you still need to acquire in order to start your business;
- identify the best ways to achieve this.

1. Make a copy of Table 3.7, using the model on page opposite.
2. Collect and compile the information you have gathered in the course of working your way through the last two chapters.

3. In the first column of Table 3.7, below, list the skills and experience needed to start and maintain your business.
4. In the second column, list those skills and items of information which you do *not* currently possess.
5. In the third column, list the courses of action you propose to take in order to obtain these skills and knowledge. Use the suggested action listed in Table 3.8 below as a guide.

Table 3.7. **Filling the gaps**

Skills and knowledge required by the business	Skills and knowledge I do not currently possess	Action I plan to take

Table 3.8. **Suggested actions**

- Take a small-business course.
- Take a course at an institute of further or higher education.
- Take a distance learning or correspondence course.
- Involve your personal partner or a relative (if they possess the necessary skills or knowledge).
- Take a business partner (one or more) who has the necessary skills and knowledge.
- Take on employees who have the necessary skills and knowledge (on a full-time, part-time or temporary basis).
- Employ a consultant.

- Contract out the side of the operation you are not skilled in.

Conclusion

By working your way through the last two chapters you should have a clear idea of:

- The reasons why you wish to set up your own business and the implications for you and your family.
- The product or service around which you are going to base the business.
- The skills, knowledge and experience required to set it up and where you will obtain these.
- The market you are about to enter and its present and future needs.
- The resources you will need and where you will obtain these.

You can now turn to the practical measures needed to set up your business. This is the subject covered by Part Two of the book.

2 Setting up

4 *Seeking the Right Advice*

This section covers the practical aspects of setting up your business. It concludes with an exercise on producing a business plan, which will enable you to pull together in one document the various strands of your business strategy. The finished plan can then be used to help raise the finance needed to start the enterprise.

Throughout this section you will have to confront complex legal, financial and practical considerations. This book can do no more than raise the issues you will face; it cannot provide detailed advice tailored to your own individual needs and circumstances. As a point of principle, you should identify and consult the most appropriate sources of advice *before* you take any major decision which is likely to affect your business. Many businesses fail because their owners choose to seek the right advice only when faced with a crisis – by which time it is far more difficult to provide substantial outside help. The key advisers usually consulted by business people are listed below.

Accountants

The large majority of small-business people choose to seek advice from a professional accountant. An accountant can advise you on most financial issues affecting your business, but you should make particularly sure that you consult his or her opinion when you are:

- considering which business structure to use (sole trader, partnership, limited company);
- considering which source of finance is most suitable;
- choosing the best way to cost your work;
- registering your company;
- designing your business stationery (businesses are required to disclose certain information on their letterheads);
- setting up book-keeping and financial administration systems;
- calculating your income and expenditure for the first 1–5 years;
- drawing up a business plan.

Recent relaxations to the code of professional conduct mean that accountants can now 'announce' (rather than advertise) their services in selected media outlets. Details of the professional firms or sole practitioners available in your region can be obtained from any or all of the following sources:

- Local District Societies of the Institute of Chartered Accountants. Details of these can be obtained from the Institute of Chartered Accountants in England and Wales, Chartered Accountants Hall, Moorgate Place, London EC2R 6EQ (Tel. 01-628 7060).

- Local editions of Yellow Pages or Thomson directories.

- Local newspapers.

- Through local branches of the Small Firms Service (see page 249), Rural Development Commission (see page 249) or Enterprise Agencies (see page 235).

- By recommendation from *reliable* friends, business colleagues or personal contacts.

When choosing an accountant, make sure that you consider all the following questions:

- Will a local accountant be more suited to your needs than one from a regional or national centre? Will his or her superior knowledge of local people and affairs be outweighed by any specialist knowledge or greater experience the latter might have?

- Do the nature of your business or the particular needs of your market mean that you require an accountant who specializes; or will a less expensive professional offering a general service be adequate?

- How much will you be charged? Will you be charged for telephone advice? (Remember, you will get what you pay for – cheap advice is not always the best.)

- Will the work of your financial affairs be carried out by a partner of the firm (who will charge a higher hourly rate) or by an articled clerk or trainee accountant? In what circumstances will either be employed?

- If you have found an accountant by recommendation, does the recommendation come from someone with similar needs to you and your business? Has he or she used the services of the particular accountant you have been recommended to, rather than just the firm?

- How much experience has the particular accountant had of the issues likely to arise with your kind of business, your locality and your size of firm?

- Has the firm or individual had previous experience in advising small businesses generally?

The last two questions apply equally when you come to choose other business advisers, including a solicitor, bank manager and specialist consultants.

Solicitors

The statutory requirements governing small businesses are sufficiently vast and complex to make a solicitor with specialized knowledge of business law another necessity. Once again, you should consult your lawyer whenever you need to, but particularly in matters relating to:

- terms of trade
- partnership agreements (always enter into a contractual agreement with a business partner)
- trading regulations relating to:
  - the office of fair trading
  - health and safety at work
  - the hygienic preparation, handling and storing of food and drugs
  - fire precautions
- the preparation of contractual agreements with:
  - clients and customers
  - suppliers and distributors
  - consultants and employees
- the preparation of purchase and tenancy agreements
- the choice of suitable business premises.
- Planning permission and other statutory regulations relating to the purchase of premises to be used for business purposes.

You may already have a solicitor who has represented you in your personal affairs (for example, in the purchase of your current home). You should check, however, whether his or her knowledge of business law is sufficient for your professional needs. If this is not the case, or if you do not currently have access to regular legal advice, details of firms in your local area can be obtained from:

- Local editions of Yellow Pages or Thomson directories.
- Local newspapers.

- Through local branches of the Small Firms Service, Rural Development Commission, Enterprise Agencies, relevant professional institutions or small business clubs.
- By writing to the Law Society.
- Through *reliable* business contacts in the same field.

Bank Manager

Most small businesses of the type highlighted in this book do not require complicated financing and rely on an overdraft facility or loan provided by the local bank. Full details of the services offered to small businesses by the clearing banks can be found on page 130. However, it is also worth remembering that bank managers can prove a valuable source of business advice. In particular, they can advise you on:

– the best form of finance (although it is a good idea to ask your accountant for a second opinion);
– the most effective way of using your business accounts;
– the various financial and advisory services offered by the bank;
– general guidance on the running of your business.

On the whole, it is usually best to stick with the bank manager you have been dealing with in the past – he or she will know you and have an intimate knowledge of your financial history. At the same time, however, it is worth shopping around to see whether better facilities for small businesses are offered by other banks in your area. Most clearing banks now offer special services for small businesses, but the quality and depth of their support does vary.

Insurance brokers

Insurance cover plays an even greater role in the day-to-day life of business administration than it does in your personal life.

You are legally required to take out comprehensive cover for any vehicles you are planning to use for business purposes. You will also be required to pay employer's liability and National Insurance contributions if you employ anyone (although the amount will vary according to the type and size of your business).

Over and above these recommendations, you may also be well advised to consider policies covering: sick pay, life assurance, personal pension plan insurance, fire and special peril, theft, bad debt, and business interruption. The services of a reputable insurance broker are therefore a real asset. Advice on who to approach can be obtained from any or all of the advisers listed above.

General business advice

There is now a growing network of advisory services which will be able to advise you on any or all of the issues highlighted above, as well as providing guidance on strategic and day-to-day business policy. Among others, business advice is available from:

- Small Business Advice Centres;
- Enterprise Agencies;
- URBED (Urban and Economic Development Limited);
- ARC (The Action and Resource Centre);
- local authorities and agencies.

Details of small business advice centres and enterprise agencies can be found in the Appendix (see page 235). Details of URBED and ARC can be found on page 135.

5 *Assessing Your Financial Needs*

Changing social trends and an increased political commitment to the establishment of small business now means that the aspiring entrepreneur can turn to a much wider range of sources of financial support. Many businesses, particularly those which are home-based and require few human or material resources, can be established quickly and effectively without heavy commitments to financial institutions.

That said, proper financial support and administration are crucial to any small enterprise, be it a home-based consultancy or a limited company operating from business premises with major overheads. A sizeable majority of businesses fail, not because there is an inadequate market for their product or service, but because they are unable to calculate, plan for and meet their financial needs.

The best statistical proof showing how bad financial planning can undermine an otherwise good business service was a research paper, *Causes of Bankruptcy in England*, which was presented at the Durham University Business School Conference on Small Businesses in 1978*. Professor Donleavy, a senior lecturer in accountancy at the Thames Polytechnic, London, surveyed 217 firms out of a total of 10,000 High Court London bankruptcies from the 1960s. Based on these, he plotted five principal routes to insolvency:

- Sales failure (income below expenses)
- Expenses failure (expenses accelerate beyond income)
- Capital failure (expenditure exceeds net revenue cash-flow
- Overdrawing (net cash-flow exceeded by 'proprietorial' drawings)

* Source: DTI

- Tax failure (taxation ignored, leading to failure to meet Inland Revenue demands)

Particularly interesting was Donleavy's description of 'the bankrupt personality', drawn from the factors behind the failures in trading. An extract reads:

> The potential bankrupt believes in himself, fiercely resents working for institutions, sets great store on flair and luck but very little on paperwork of any sort. He (or she) is a worrier and of indifferent health. He distrusts professional advisers but often relies on the judgement of friends or family. He is an optimist but indecisive and defers the facing of problems until they can be delayed no longer (especially tax problems). He usually knows his product and offers a good service but does not sell himself or organize himself . . .

Although the research on which the report was based is now nearly twenty years old, there is no reason to suggest that the findings of a similar study today would be any different. Nor do the basic rules of financial planning vary according to the size of the business. They apply as much to the sole trader as to a large multinational.

Case-study 5.1: Marion Carter

Having spent the last three years trying to establish herself as a freelance textile and knitwear designer, Marion Carter, a graduate of the Central School of Art and Design, has decided to call it a day and return, for the time being, to the security of a full-time job and a regular salary. She is still working on designs in her spare time and hopes at some future point to go back to full-time freelancing. However, her experiences of trying to establish herself, to live independently in London, and to pay her way through part-time work show just how difficult self-employment can be for someone lacking savings or financial help from her family.

Marion started thinking about freelancing towards the end of her last year at art college, mainly because at the time there seemed little alternative in fields related to her degree (in textile design). Her aspirations were encouraged by the interest her work aroused at Fabrex, a trade fair at which the Central School's textile design students were encouraged to exhibit, and by a successful degree show at which she made contact with an agent who was setting up a business selling British print designs to clothing companies in the USA. At the same time, two of her college contemporaries were planning to rent a cheap studio in the East End of London, and it seemed opportune to share space with them, to try to market work through the agent, and 'see how it took off'.

Marion did need an initial financial stake to pay the studio rent and buy materials. Knowing that designing probably wouldn't generate much income for a while, she looked around for some means of paying her way; as well as the studio space, she had to keep a shared flat going and have something left to live on. Claiming social security was one option; but part-time work seemed more viable, particularly since she had already been working as a waitress for a couple of nights a week while she was at college, and she was able to extend this into a 25-hour-a-week job. On the strength of her part-time work, and the fact that by now the agent had agreed to take her on, the bank manager granted an overdraft facility of £500, which Marion thought would be just enough to tide her over until the designs started to pay off.

However, her initial collection didn't go as well as she had hoped: out of a dozen designs the agent had selected, only a couple were sold. After that, the agent began to lose interest and, after submitting further designs with no success, Marion decided to switch to another outlet. The opportunity arose to sell through her two friends in the shared studio. By now they had begun to make sales trips to Europe and America, acting as agents as well as selling their own designs. Marion asked them to represent her, and through them was able to sell more of her work. There were also one-off knitting commissions that came in from time to time – but it still wasn't the breakthrough she had hoped for.

Marion could have done more to promote herself by taking her portfolio to London buyers. But here she ran up against lack of time; the waitressing job left only one completely free weekday. On the other four days she worked in the restaurant from eleven to four; she had thought this would give her the possibility of arranging appointments beforehand and then working from the late afternoon onwards, into the evening, on her work. Perhaps not surprisingly, it proved almost impossible to arrange a morning appointment and still arrive at the restaurant at eleven, and although she often worked in the studio until the early hours, the situation was hardly conducive to producing her best work.

Things appeared to be looking up when she was offered another part-time job, this time as a general assistant with a small graphics company. This, besides being more relevant to her design skills, promised the eventual opportunity of her being able to take work away, and so to be based full-time at the studio. In practice, it didn't work out. Not only did Marion find herself spending more and more hours at the company's premises on this 'part-time' job but, because she was working on a freelance basis, sometimes she didn't get paid for weeks. Eventually there was a confrontation and she left, taking a much-needed break and temporarily claiming social security while she sorted out what to do next. Somehow or other she managed to keep the studio going during this period.

Since she was unemployed and wanted to move into a rather different type of self-employment, Marion found that after 13 weeks on the dole she became eligible for the Enterprise Allowance Scheme. Through the bank, she managed to raise a loan for the £1,000 necessary for acceptance (there was little risk from the bank's point of view since Marion agreed to repay the money, by standing order, during the year she was on the scheme).

With part of the loan Marion bought materials and equipment, and she started designing and making up sweaters. Some of them she sold at the annual Chelsea Crafts Fair, and others through a market stall which she ran for a few months at weekends. Both these activities were valuable exercises in learning how to sell and getting direct feedback from the market; in commercial terms, however, even though they certainly didn't lose money, they didn't make much either. Just making up the garments was very time-consuming, and there was strong competition from longer-established firms, trading at the same street market, that were able to produce similar sweaters more cost-effectively.

Marion also did some sub-contract work, knitting garments for designers who were exhibiting at Olympia. Through them she made contact with yet another agent – this time in the knitwear field. However, although the agent expressed a lot of interest in her work, by this time Marion was more cautious and aware that it would take a long *time for sales to build up. So when, soon after the Enterprise Allowance came to an end, she was offered a full-time job managing a specialist wool and knitwear shop, Marion jumped at the chance. The new job offered security and greater involvement in the knitwear field, albeit from a different aspect. At home, in her free time, she is still working on a collection of designs for her new agent and has plans to sell sweaters through a friend's shop, building up sales gradually in the hope of eventually having 'a strong financial footing on which to succeed in making knitwear design into a full-time occupation'.*

Although Marion hasn't been able to establish a business, she hasn't lost anything – having repaid the overdraft and the loan – and she has gained equipment, as well as valuable experience. 'I've learnt a great deal in the past three years. I've learnt you haven't got time to do everything: I'll be looking for outworkers to produce my designs another time. I've also learnt that I should turn down offers of work if, when I sit down and look into them, I realize they're not going to give me the sort of financial return that I need. I'm able to be tougher and less polite.'

She is now also aware that, 'You do need money to start off – you need money to produce money. I was worrying all the time about paying my bills and not devoting enough energy to the business.

'I've benefited from my mistakes – if only I had known at the beginning what I know now!'

Learning points

Marion's failure to establish herself in business is not untypical. She made a number of mistakes. The most crucial of these were:

- She failed to plan her growth, allowing herself too little time to establish her reputation in a highly competitive market.
- She negotiated an overdraft facility which was far too small for her business needs and underestimated the amount of income she would receive in the early months of the business.
- By relying on part-time work to secure her finances, she

did not allow herself the time to promote her portfolio and products.

- She did not cost her time properly and failed to provide herself with outworkers to produce her designs.
- She accepted all offers of work without calculating whether they would generate enough profit.

It is worth noting, however, that Marion did not feel the efforts she had made to establish her business were wasted and that she will have learned from her mistakes when trying self-employment in the future.

Basic principles

A number of basic principles need to be attached to the establishment of any small enterprise.

- Before and during the period of establishment of your enterprise, you need to *seek the right advice* and ensure that you secure the services of a competent financial adviser (see pages 107–12).
- In planning your business start-up, you should ensure that you *assess accurately your financial needs* for at least two years. In your calculations you should include:
  - the cost of any equipment
  - the cost of any additional training
  - the cost of any business premises
  - the cost of any staff and/or professional services
  - the cost of any tax liability
  - the cost of launching or promoting your product or service
  - the cost of meeting your personal or family needs: mortgage, rent, insurance, school fees, basic necessities, etc.
  - the early sales potential of your product/service.
- Having assessed your financial needs, you should *consider all the possible sources of finance* available to you and select the one(s) most appropriate to your business

needs. These include:
- financial support from banks
- support from other financial institutions
- financial support from enterprise agencies
- financial support from local authorities
- personal savings and/or redundancy payments
- dual incomes, part-time and temporary work
- government schemes.

Assessing your financial needs

Accurately identifying your financial needs is the practical starting point of any business plan. The answers that emerge from your calculations will affect both the degree and nature of the external finance you look for, and may have a considerable influence on the structure and direction your business takes.

Your calculations should cover two major areas: (a) your personal financial needs, and (b) your business financial needs. The following exercises will help you to calculate these in a systematic manner.

Assessing your personal financial needs

Before you assess your business needs, it is vital to appreciate your personal financial position and how it will affect your income requirements in the early years of your enterprise.

The assessment is divided into four parts:

- Exercise 5.1. My immediate cash position
- Exercise 5.2. My current income and expenditure
- Exercise 5.3. Obtaining additional income
- Exercise 5.4. What actions to take

Make copies of the charts using the format shown.

Table 5.1. **My immediate cash position – worksheet**

Status as at / /19

	Self £	Partner £	Comments
1) Available cash:			
■ Bank account current account			
■ Post office savings account			
■ Building society share account			
2) Obtainable cash:			
■ Bank deposit (fixed time) account			
■ Building society term share account			
■ Stocks and shares			
■ Others			
3) Obtainable cash – with penalty:			
■ Endowment policy			
■ Other			

Exercise 5.1. My immediate cash position

Complete the worksheet provided, summarizing your current cash position. The headings are not meant to be totally comprehensive. You may wish to add further examples, if relevant to your particular circumstances. Before starting, briefly refer to Table 5.1 and list below some of the reference items that you may need. For example:

1. building society book(s)
2. bank statement (deposit and current)
3. investment policies
4.
5.
6.

Exercise 5.2. My current income and expenditure plan

Using the analysis sheets provided (Tables 5.2–5.4), systematically assess your current financial position in terms of your own best estimations of income and expenditure. Make sure that you include an assessment for expected inflation into your calculations. Before starting, briefly read through the tables and list below some of the reference items you will require to have close at hand. This will save you time and also help you to focus your concentration on the job at hand. (Some reference items already suggested.) Refer to your data at hand and try to make this exercise as accurate as possible. Remember that the quarterly dates for many bills are January/April/July/ October.

Reference items that I need:

1. Bank statement/standing order listing
2. Cheque-book stubs
3. Credit card statements
4. Mortgage statement
5. Salary slips
6. Tax returns
7. Housekeeping estimates
8.
9.
10.

Table 5.2. **Current expenditure – analysis sheet**

Period: twelve months commencing / /19

	Estimated Annual £	Current month 1 £	Future month 2 £	Future month 3 £	Future quarter 2 £	Future quarter 3 £	Future quarter 4 £
Mortgage/Rent							
General rates							
Water rates							
Telephone							
Electricity							
Gas							
Fuel (oil, gas, etc.)							
School fees							
Life insurance							
House & contents insurance							
Car: insurance/licence							
Transport: maintenance/fuel							
TV: rent/licence							
Holidays							
Annual subscriptions							
Clothing							
Christmas expense							
Food							
Other housekeeping							
Medical							
Entertainment							
Capital goods (furniture, etc.)							
Hire purchase							
Repairs							
Others							
Total expenditure							

Table 5.3. **Current income – analysis sheet**

Major assumptions:

- ■
- ■
- ■
- ■
- ■

Period: twelve months commencing / /19

	Estimated Annual £	Current month 1 £	Future month 2 £	Future month 3 £	Future quarter 2 £	Future quarter 3 £	Future quarter 4 £
Salary (net)							
Investments							
Unemployment benefit							
Child benefit							
Pension							
Others							
■							
■							
■							
■							
Total income							

Table 5.4. Current income and expenditure – summary

Period: twelve months commencing / /19

	Estimated Annual £	Current month 1 £	Future month 2 £	Future month 3 £	Future quarter 2 £	Future quarter 3 £	Future quarter 4 £
Income total (Table 5.3)							
Expenditure total (Table 5.2)							
Income and expenditure							
Balance: Surplus/(Shortfall)							

Comments

- **Risk** (Expenditure is greater than income):

- **Opportunities** (Income is greater than expenditure):

NOTES: 1. At this stage it pays to be well prepared in terms of the accuracy of your budget forecasts.

2. Table 5.2 could also be used as financial tracking sheets by splitting each column into two under the headings 'Estimate' and 'Actual'. At the end of each month/quarter you could then review matters and adjust plans accordingly.

Exercise 5.3. What opportunities are there to obtain additional income?

Exercise 5.3 asks you to consider whether there are any opportunities for you and your family to obtain additional income.

Using the estimates of monthly expenditure calculated in Table 5.5 consider the following:

1. *Personal partner's income*
   - Is my partner willing or able to work?
   - What kind of work is he/she qualified or skilled to undertake?
   - What annual income will it provide?
2. *Part-time work*
   - Can I or my personal partner find part-time work locally?
   - What type of work would be involved?
   - What organizations or personal contacts could help us?
   - Will it interfere with my business plans? (See pages 136–7)
3. *Child benefit*
   - Are we entitled?
   - When can we expect this?
   - How is it paid?
4. *Pension*
   - Have I accurate information on my pension options?
   - Do I need further information?
   - Will it be affected by my business income?
   - Where can I obtain further information and advice?
5. *Lodgers*
   - Could we take in lodgers (students, business employees, etc.)?

– What are the legal implications?
– Would it interfere with my business plans (for example, if the business is run from home)?

Table 5.5. **What opportunities are there to obtain additional income?**

	Estimates		
	Year 1	Year 2	Year 3
1) Partner's income			
2) Part-time work			
3) Child benefit			
4) Pension			
5) Lodgers			
6) Other			
....			
....			
....			

Exercise 5.4. What actions should I take?

Table 5.6 allows you to summarize the information gathered in Table 5.5. It also enables you to summarize ways in which you can reduce your expenditure. When completing Table 5.6, refer to the section opposite which suggests ways in which you can achieve this.

Table 5.6. **What actions should I take?**

Actions to reduce expenditure (what, and how it can be achieved)	Timing (when)
Actions to increase income	Timing

Survival on a reduced income

Even if you succeed in tapping some or all of the sources of income mentioned previously, the difficult early years of establishing a business will probably impose strains on your standard of living. You may have to consider ways in which you can live more cheaply, if only in the short term. Ways you might like to consider include:

- Cheaper food – bargains galore can be picked up from food and non-food markets, with cheap vegetables and fruit available towards closing time.
- Cheaper transport – bicycles, bought or rented, provide a cheaper and healthier form of local transport than the motor car. Now that you do not have to travel during peak hours, you can benefit from off-peak public transport, which can often prove up to 30 per cent cheaper.
- Cheaper entertainment – West End cinemas in London now offer cheaper matinee seats, as do many provincial theatres and cinemas. Many exhibitions and places of entertainment also give reduced rates at certain times of the day. In addition, it is worth remembering that there are many free forms of entertainment – art galleries, country walks, etc.
- Cheaper literature – a wide range of reading matter as well as (in some areas) audio cassettes and records are available from local or specialized lending or reference libraries.
- Cheaper repair services or gardening – if you are an experienced leisure-time gardener, or a keen do-it-yourself enthusiast, you can now use these skills to avoid unnecessary household maintenance costs or to supply the family with home-grown vegetables, fruit and flowers.
- Cheaper household items – radio programmes often run 'swap-shops', and local auction rooms offer the possibility of buying expensive items at a bargain price.

- Cheaper hairdressing – some hairdressing salons give free or reduced cuts and styling if you are willing to act as a model for their trainees.

Assessing your business financial needs

Exercise 5.5. Having reviewed your personal situation, it can now be useful to review in draft form your initial assessments of the financial requirements of the venture you have in mind.

Table 5.7. **Your business financial needs – a draft assessment**

	£
1. *Initial outlay*	
■ Do you need to purchase equipment, e.g. tools, machinery, etc?	
■ Do you require premises (rent/rates, etc.)?	
■ Do you need to refurbish the premises: decoration/furniture?	
■ How much are you going to spend on marketing and promoting your business, e.g. advertisments, business cards, paper and supplies, etc.?	
■ How much do you plan to spend on professional advice: solicitors/accountants/others?	
■ Do you need to purchase raw materials to start you off?	
■ Are you buying into a venture in any way?	
2. *On-going costs*	
■ What operating costs do you anticipate: – telephones – rent/rates – electricity/other fuels – production costs (raw materials, etc.) – labour costs – on-going sales costs (commission and advertising) – distribution costs (couriers, etc.) – equipment/furniture; renewal and repairs – professional charges – bank charges	

You might like to consider here other types of costs pertinent to your particular business venture.

Draft assessment / /19

- Setting-up costs =
- On-going costs =

NOTES:

Sources of finance

Having assessed your financial requirements accurately, you should now search around for the most appropriate source of initial capital.

Anyone wishing to start up on their own can nowadays turn to a wide variety of organizations and schemes offering financial support. In addition, the growth in part-time and temporary work, together with an increase in redundancy settlements and dual-income families means that less conventional but equally effective ways of funding the early stages of a small enterprise now exist. The various sources of financial support highlighted below can be divided into three sources:

- financial institutions
- special schemes
- personal resources

These sources are suitable for small-scale business start-ups and not for more ambitious enterprises involving large initial overheads.

Financial institutions

Banks

In recent years, largely as a result of the Bolton Committee's report in 1971, clearing banks have begun to realize that small firms represent a large source of potential business. Although frequently criticized for their lack of response to ideas for new businesses, in fact clearing banks provide more money to small businesses than any other source. Your local bank will probably be your first and may be your only essential point of contact with an external financial institution.

Traditionally, banks have provided support in one of the following ways:

Overdrafts. Few people need an introduction to overdrafts. They are relatively easy to obtain (given the qualifications listed below). They are, however, subject to fluctuating interest rates and immediate recall. They are therefore best used for working capital needs and to overcome cash-flow problems.

Fixed-term loans. These are usually classified as short (up to three years), medium (three to ten years) and long (ten to twenty years). The banks will usually want to secure the loan against one or more fixed assets or demand a personal guarantee from the director(s), if the business is a limited company. In return, the loan is usually granted at a fixed rate of interest or is pegged to a basic base rate.

Special loan schemes. To cater for a growing number of client entrepreneurs, many banks now offer the kind of tailor-made packages they previously provided only to larger, better-established enterprises. This includes loans on special terms, information and advice, and often some form of counselling. The exact nature and quality of these packages varies from bank to bank, so it is worth shopping around to find the one best suited to your individual business's needs.

Industrial and Commercial Finance Corporation (3i)

Most of the ideas for small businesses covered in this book do not require extensive capital, and people starting them could easily raise sums of up to £5,000 (or more) from a combination of bank loans, the special schemes covered below and/or personal resources (see page 138). However, if you are seeking a loan of more than £5,000, and you do not wish to provide the onerous guarantees required by many financial institutions dealing in venture capital, a useful organization to turn to is the Industrial and Commercial Finance Corporation, commonly known by its popular title of '3i'. Owned by the major clearing banks, the 3i provides tailored financial support for any sound proposition that needs funds of between £5,000 and £2 million. Crucially, from the small-scale entrepreneur's point of view, over half of 3i's clients still receive amounts under £50,000.

Each application is treated on its own merits, with finance designed to meet individual requirements. Application should be made to one of eighteen area offices.

Special schemes

As an alternative to conventional support from financial institutions, or as a means of supplementing their support, small-scale entrepreneurs can turn to a wide variety of special schemes sponsored by national and local government, and local industry. The main ones include:

Finance

The Enterprise Allowance Scheme. The Enterprise Allowance Scheme provides a regular income if you have previously been unemployed and want to start your own business. For up to 52 weeks, you can receive an allowance of £80 every fortnight to supplement the receipts of the business.

To be eligible for the scheme, you must:

- be receiving unemployment or supplementary benefit yourself or through a member of your family at the time of application;
- have been unemployed and actively seeking work for at least eight weeks (time spent under formal notice of redundancy and on certain MSC schemes – such as the Community Programme – can count towards this qualifying period);
- show that you have at least £1,000 available which you are prepared to invest in the business in the first 12 months (this can be in the form of a loan or overdraft);
- be over 18 and below state pension age;
- agree to work full-time in the business;
- not have received the Enterprise Allowance previously for a different business (you are allowed to join the scheme only once).

Also, your proposed business should be approved by the Manpower Services Commission. It must be a new, independent business and be suitable for public support (there are certain excluded categories such as nightclubs and gambling establishments).

If you think you are eligible for the scheme, you should ask at your local Jobcentre to be included in an Enterprise Allowance information session (this is the first stage in applying to join the scheme).

Competitions

A number of important competitions for small businesses are run by enterprise trusts, local authorities, professional associations and private companies. These offer cash prizes, business advice packages and trophies to the winners. Good examples include the 'Award for Business Enterprise Competition', sponsored by Scottish Business in The Community; 'Women Mean Business Award', sponsored by *Options* Magazine; the Arthur Young/NatWest 'Business Award for Young Designers'; the 'Flying Start' competition run in the north-west by Granada TV and the 'Small Business Air Exporter of the

Year'. Details of these and other business competitions or awards appear in the Appendix (see page 254).

The Small Firms Loan Guarantee Scheme

In addition to their own schemes, the clearing banks also take part in a government-sponsored loan guarantee scheme, originally introduced to help small firms with little capital start-up to raise essential funding. This rather controversial scheme was designed to provide support for financial proposals which have been reviewed and considered viable by approved banks but which would not normally be approved. In these circumstances, the government agrees to guarantee 70 per cent of the loan up to £75,000. The loan is repayable over two to seven years and is charged at 5 per cent over basic bank rate.

The history of the scheme has been very chequered. By June 1984, 15,253 businesses had benefited from the scheme, of which 8,187 were new enterprises. However, a report published in Spring 1984 revealed that as many as one in three of the businesses funded by the scheme had folded during the first three years.

Since then, the government guarantee has been reduced from 80 to 70 per cent and the interest charged raised from 3 to 5 per cent over base rate. The success rate has improved and the scheme has now helped a total of 18,000 small firms with guarantees on loans worth over £590 million. For the moment its immediate future seems secure. A leaflet describing the scheme is available from the Loan Guarantee Unit, Department of Employment, Steel House, 11 Tothill Street, London SW1H 9NF (Tel. 01-213 4293).

Local authority loan guarantee schemes

A more successful example of a loan guarantee scheme is the partnership between local authorities and the Co-operative Bank. The Co-op's scheme aims to support business development in economically hard-hit areas of the country where finance would not otherwise have been available. Loans under the scheme have a maximum limit of £50,000 and carry an interest of 3 per cent above basic rate. The local authority guarantees a portion of the loan in the event of failure, and individual packages under the scheme may also include local authority grants or the provision of low-cost premises. Further details appear in the Appendix (see page 265).

Enterprise agencies

The encouragement of small business start-ups has been given the biggest boost by the enterprise agency movement. First started in 1978, there are now over 162 agencies spread over the country, with more on the way. The agencies are non-profit-making companies, usually run by a small staff who can call on the wealth of expertise within the organizations that provide sponsorship and support.

Amongst the growing range of activities and initiatives undertaken by these locally based bodies is the setting up and management of small-business workshops; the promotion and management of small-business clubs or networks; the provision or sponsorship of education and training for business people; and the building of links with voluntary organizations, educational authorities, community programmes and environmental projects.

Almost every sector of the financial, industrial and commercial world, as well as local government and the voluntary sector, is involved in some way with the enterprise agency movement. Sponsors have included local government, chambers of commerce, universities, polytechnics and colleges, industrial and commercial companies, banks and merchant banks, accountancy firms, the media, insurance companies and building societies. Prominent organizations include the Port of London Authority, the General and Municipal, Boilermakers and Allied Trades Workers' Union, British Telecom, Deloitte Haskins and Sells, the CBI and Unilever. A comprehensive directory of all the agencies currently in existence, together with details of the activities they sponsor/organize, appears in the Appendix (see pages 235–49).

Other agencies

In addition, business people looking for financial and counselling support should be aware of three other organizations closely linked to the enterprise agency network:

ARC (the Action Resource Centre). Set up in 1978, ARC concentrates on creating employment opportunities by providing local businesses with financial support and expert advice, using people and resources seconded from industry and business. ARC has regional managers based in Cheshire, Clydeside, Edinburgh, Greater London, Leicester, Liverpool, Nottingham, South Wales, South Yorkshire, West Midlands and West Yorkshire. Details and further information from ARC Greater London, Henrietta House, 9 Henrietta Place, London W1M 9AG (Tel. 01-629 3826).

BSC (Industry) Ltd. The British Steel Corporation set up this subsidiary to encourage industrial regeneration in areas badly hit by steel plant closures. It now offers financial help, either from its own fund or from other UK grants and assistance, and can provide considerable help in putting together financial packages and proposals for approval by banks and other lending financial institutions. It has also set up a wide network of small industrial workshops and offices for use by small businesses. Details and further information from John Northcott at British Steel (Industry) Ltd, NLA Tower, 12 Addiscombe Road, Croydon CR9 3JH (Tel. 01-686 0366).

URBED (Urban and Economic Development) Ltd. Set up in 1976, URBED fulfils the same role for the urban areas that the Rural Development Commission fulfils for rural regions. It has established workshops, working communities, small enterprise centres, industrial associations and local enterprise trusts. It also provides consultancy services, and organizes an eight-week course on creating business ideas, a weekend course on assessing your prospects, and a three-month course on getting a business going. Details and further information from URBED, 359 The Strand, London WC2 0HS (Tel. 01-378 7525).

Personal resources

Businesses with low overheads and those which require little or no initial capital can often be funded from personal resources. In addition, although banks can and sometimes do lend without security if the proposition is sufficiently attractive, this is not common. Most will require some form of personal collateral (like your house), or will want to be convinced that the proposer can offer sufficient security or guarantees to match the risk the bank takes. Even if it is not required, or if the proposer can benefit from the loan guarantee schemes mentioned above, he/she will still have to take into account personal overheads (family, school fees, housekeeping, clothes, mortage, etc.) when planning the initial budget. Most small entrepreneurs may therefore have to draw on their own financial resources at some point in the business start-up. The four main sources involved are:

- part-time or temporary work
- personal savings
- a partner's income
- redundancy payments

Part-time or temporary work

Hand in hand with the growth of opportunities for the self-employed has been a steady increase in part-time work. Some 2.3 million full-time jobs were lost between 1972 and 1984, while 1.3 million new part-time jobs were created. A very wide range of part-time jobs are advertised in local newspapers, Jobcentres and/or local newsagents or post office windows. In addition, there has been a steady increase in temporary positions in the early 1980s, and a similarly broad variety of this kind of work is also offered by Jobcentres and local employment agencies.

From the small entrepreneur's point of view, this means that there are increased opportunities to obtain some kind of regular income in the difficult first months or years of the business's development.

Case-study 5.2: Jackie Holland

Jackie Holland was able to use a part-time job as a very vital source of income while she built up her small business.

Originally a Production Manager in a company publishing children's books, she returned from an extended trip overseas to find the publishing industry in recession and few jobs available. After surviving on temporary work for a few months, she decided to set up her own business providing commercial companies with creative marketing support. She attended a three-month government-sponsored course but, lacking sufficient business capital, she combined her self-employed activities with the earnings of part-time work to cover her immediate expenses.

After working in one job for two days every week, she found a position as a senior secretary every weekday afternoon for a local helicopter marketing company. The arrangement suited her business needs perfectly but she occasionally found that the duties of her job and the demands of her small business came into conflict. 'If I did a mailing, say to a hundred potential clients, I usually found that I got a lot of people ringing up to make an appointment with me there and then. I was therefore having to deal flat out with inquiries, putting marketing plans together and arranging meetings. Whilst doing all that, I was also having to spend my time in a completely different role. As well as the energy it uses up, there is also a culture shock. One minute I was working for myself and wearing all the hats; the next, I was working for someone else and only wearing one.'

The company employing her, however, was very understanding and prepared to be flexible about the hours she worked – provided she fulfilled her duties. 'It was a fairly small company and I worked for the Managing Director and the Sales Director, both of whom knew what I was doing. If, therefore, I had an appointment which was likely to make me late for work, I could change the hours, as I had a fairly fixed amount of work every day. In addition, if I was not particularly busy during office hours, I could do work related to my own business and write my own letters.'

Learning points

With her essential overheads covered by her part-time earnings, Jackie managed to overcome many of the financial insecurities of setting up a small business. However, her business interests often clashed with her part-time duties, and she was able to reconcile the two only because she was employed by managers who were prepared to be sympathetic to her needs.

In the earlier case-study of Marion Carter (see page 114), one of the reasons why she was unable to promote her work as a freelance textile designer was because her waitressing job left her only one completely free weekday. On the other four days, she worked in the restaurant from 11 a.m. to 4 p.m., which cut right across time for appointments in working hours.

In practice, therefore, if you are planning to use part-time or temporary work to subsidize your earnings in the early stages of your business start-up, you need to ensure that:

- you leave enough time to make any necessary business appointments during the day;
- you leave enough time to perform whatever work is required to back up your contracts;
- the work involved in the part-time position is not so physically or mentally demanding that it prevents you from channelling enough energy into your business.

Personal savings

It is likely that you will have to commit some of your own money to the business. Most banks work on the basis that the business risk is shared, and many start-up schemes for small businesses require a similar commitment.

Case-study 5.3: Gloria Claremount

At twenty-two Gloria Claremount runs her own party and promotional planning agency, 'Skylarks', which specializes in staff parties, promotional events, balls and social extravaganzas.

Gloria took her degree in geography at St Edmund's Hall, Oxford, and soon became its social secretary, running both the college and inter-collegiate balls. Before university, she had gained considerable promotional skills as head of her school's functions, and her success at St Edmund's Hall soon led her to become involved with the Oxford Union, which was then desperate for funds. She became the Union's social organizer, with responsibility for the first Oxford Union Society ball, which was a great success and made a handsome £4,000 profit. Allocated a budget from the Union, she redecor-

ated its cellars and transformed them into a cocktail/jazz bar called 'The Bluenote', which she managed herself, and which is now a highly successful enterprise.

All these activities gave her the marketing and financial skills she needed to set up her own agency. She felt, however, that she required additional business training and sources of financial support. She gained the training by applying, and being accepted, for a place on the Graduate Enterprise Programme. This provides a programme of support which lasts eighteen months and includes training, counselling, aftercare and cash grants. The cornerstone of the programme is a period either with the Cranfield School of Management or at Durham or at Warwick University. Residential tuition at these business schools is interspersed with periods of market research in the area where the business will be located.

Gloria also obtained financial support from the Enterprise Allowance Scheme, which provides unemployed people wishing to start up their own business with an allowance of £40 a week for up to a year (see page 253). It is a condition of the scheme that applicants show that they have £1,000 available to invest in the business over the same period. Although many people under the scheme negotiate a loan or overdraft facilities, Gloria was able to raise the money from her personal savings. She had done this by a very wide variety of part-time, temporary and vacation jobs which she took on during her studies. These included temporary secretarial work at the Stock Exchange, strawberry and apple picking, sales assistant duties in a department store, working as a barmaid in a local pub, and working as a waitress in a restaurant.

The most important aspect Gloria took into account when choosing her business was that it required little or no capital investment. 'I paid particular attention to ensuring that I had an even cash flow,' she explained. 'There are few overheads and most functions are paid for in advance.'

Learning points

The most important aspects about Gloria's moves to start her own business are:

- She picked a business idea that required little or no capital investment.
- She raised a substantial proportion of her initial investment herself, by taking on a wide variety of part-time and temporary work. (See also Jackie Holland's Case-study on page 136.)
- Most of the skills she needed to run the business were acquired, not through work experience or as a result of her studies, but through extra-curricular and leisure activities at school or at college.
- She took care to build on these skills by taking part in a small-business course.

Further details of the Graduate Enterprise Programme are available from the Programme Administrator, GEP, Cranfield School of Management, Cranfield, Bedford MK43 0AL (Tel. 0234-751122).

Redundancy settlements

Another very common source of business capital has been redundancy settlements. A small but significant proportion of the self-employed were previously unemployed or had lost their jobs, and the government has encouraged the numbers of unemployed people considering self-employment by the creation of the Enterprise Allowance Scheme (see page 253).

Case-study 5.4: Barry Baines (52) – management consultant
'The company offered me a voluntary redundancy package – it seemed too good to miss out as I had been with them for twenty years. (I also thought that voluntary redundancy might become compulsory, and I would rather make the decision than let someone else make it for me.)

'Naturally I wanted to get another job initially, but over a period of time it became obvious that it was going to be tough to get the right thing. To be honest, things looked pretty bad for a while and anything would have been acceptable. Gradually it dawned on me

that it might be better to consider part-time or even consultancy assignments.

'Instead of sending out c.v.s, I designed a "c.v. brochure" and sent it around to a number of companies, small-business clubs, consultancies, institutes and friends. I had to write my brochure carefully – not too broad, as this could turn people off ("He can do anything!") but also not too narrow, or I would miss out on opportunities. By carefully working this out, I got into some interesting interviews.

'I now work for several companies as a consultant. I am not making a fortune but I'm doing all right, and occasionally I have picked up work for other friends with whom I have an introductory arrangement of 15 per cent. This helps to top up the income.

'I have also teamed up with an old friend on a couple of assignments and we have discussed setting up a formal partnership. A big step, but it would have a lot of potential for us – he is a very good marketing specialist and negotiator and has a lot of contacts. I have a good generalist background plus the ability to produce creative ideas and write well. My only concern is that I am not too sure whether I want to grow at the same pace that he has suggested. Having just got things off the ground, I am a bit cautious. In fact I am usually a more cautious person anyway.'

Learning points

Knowing your strengths and weaknesses is a vital step when composing your business plan, especially when the business is consultancy based.

Businesses do not necessarily grow out of a blinding flash of inspiration; they can simply emerge out of several personal factors all coming together. In Barry's case, it was the merging of:

- a degree of financial independence offered by the redundancy settlement;
- the realization that a job was potentially going to be difficult to acquire;
- the appreciation that the consultancy market was ripe for certain skills.

When choosing a partner, you must have sorted out what you want to get out of the partnership and what you have to put into it.

A personal partner's income

As we saw earlier, one of the most important features of the past thirty years has been the number of women who have gone out to work and developed their own careers. Women now form over a third of the workforce – over 10 million out of a total working population of 27 million. The UK leads the way in the number of women who choose to work, and only one home in twenty has a husband who goes out to work and a wife who stays at home.

The obvious advantage of having 'dual-earner' families is that one partner can rely on the other's income during times of need. In the Case-study of Diana Breeden in Chapter 1 (see page 14), her husband was able to rely on her full-time salary whilst he studied for his Ph.D. In turn, she was able to rely on his income to supplement her profits in the early stages of her business. In the case of *The Grist* (see below), a vital part of Elisabeth's income in the first year of her business was her partner's full-time salary, and they were obliged to make major economies when he left his job to join her.

If you are planning to rely on your partner's salary to subsidize your business, it is therefore important that:

- your partner supports what you are doing and is fully committed to the enterprise;
- there is no immediate prospect of the full-time salary coming to an end;
- if there are real problems with the business's development, your partner's income will cover your essential outgoings.

Case-study 5.5: *The Grist*

Elisabeth Baker and Tony Williamson publish The Grist, *a magazine dealing with the small brewers' trade. They founded it in 1984 and in 1986 it won the* Publishing Entrepreneur *of the* Year *award – recognition of its success and the intelligent way in which it serves its market. Yet* The Grist *is run by two people, from their own home.*

It is based on the principles of a small business with all the associated problems of managing finances and establishing a market.

Both Elisabeth and Tony were editorial staff in major publishing organizations before they started their own magazine. Elisabeth worked on a trade journal for the brewing industry and Tony on a magazine in the food trade. It was Elisabeth who first saw the need to give small brewers a trade news outlet, through her work at the journal for large brewers. She established that the Small Independent Brewers' Association would support a specialist magazine devoted to their world, and she felt that to continue working for large companies would limit her personal aims. With the support of the Small Independent Brewers' Association, she had effectively done market research for the magazine; by being an 'insider', she had captured her market from the outset.

Elisabeth's saved redundancy money was enough to start the magazine and fund it for the first year, which was spent working alone, from home. Tony was still working for a large publishing house and bringing home enough money for their combined living expenses. For the first few months, all money from freelance work, a stall at Camden Lock and every penny of redundancy money was channelled into The Grist.

Financial survival in the first two years was achieved in several ways. First, both Tony and Elisabeth refused to borrow. They reasoned that the interest payments on loans, and the added stress of having to meet those payments, could easily drive the magazine to the wall. Instead they made sure that all bills were paid before they went on to the next stage. They did this by budgeting for all suppliers' bills in advance. If they decided to take on an extra expense, they would make sure that they could cover the cost by, for example, selling advertising space in the magazine in advance of paying the bill.

The major outlay for The Grist *is paying suppliers' bills. Certainly their initial lack of skill in dealing with printers and typesetters was a hurdle. As their knowledge of processes and methods of cost-cutting in producing the magazine increased, they were able to squeeze the last penny out of every supplier in negotiations in order to keep the bills under control.*

Their other ploy in controlling these costs was to ensure that all their suppliers were within walking distance of their home. Careful planning of production costs has been an important contribution to the survival of The Grist. *The decision to work from home cut out another potential financial headache. Working at home with one telephone in the front room reduced overheads to virtually nil in comparison with other magazines – Tony had worked out that the £2,000, which he 'signed away' every month at his employer's organization just for rent and services, would finance the whole of* The Grist *and its production for eight weeks. It also meant that it took two seconds to get to 'the office'. Working hours for small businesses are notoriously long, and working at home gave Elisabeth and Tony even more time for the magazine. A short day for them constitutes ten hours, a long day eighteen. The advantages of being able to fall into bed at the end of a long day are obvious, quite apart from the psychological benefits which being at home under such pressure can bring.*

Early in the magazine's development, Elisabeth and Tony decided that they would not employ staff. They see employees as a luxury and a heavy financial responsibility which, on a par with bank loans, they were not prepared to take on. This decision, while it relieved them of financial burdens, meant that they had to tackle every single aspect of producing the magazine themselves – right down to licking the stamps and putting letters into the post-box. Certainly help was available from friends and family during the heaviest working periods, but they did not take on permanent staff.

After a year Tony left his job and began work on The Grist *full time. It became even more important that the magazine should succeed as both their livelihoods were now at risk. Their expenditure policy is based on being consciously mean. When Tony became full time, this was imperative. There was no longer a salary to rely on if money ran out mid-week. Elisabeth will spend money made by* The Grist *only if there is an extremely good reason to do so. For example, she agreed to buy a telephone answering machine because it would allow them, first, to tape interviews over the telephone and, secondly, to leave the house together during the day if they needed to. The expense of that piece of machinery was justified by the advantages which it gave the magazine. Spending money on clothes, entertainment or any personal luxury is taboo. Yet if somebody in a faraway part of the world requests a copy of* The Grist *Elisabeth never refuses. Her rationale: the more they build up the magazine, the better their future prospects.*

Redundancy money from Tony's former employer was channelled into the magazine, and it was eked out for the first few months of the second year in order to make it last as long as possible. The influx of energy, manpower and ideas brought in by Tony, combined with Elisabeth's sound groundwork and staying power in the first year, meant that by the time Tony's redundancy money ran out, the magazine was beginning to pay for itself and making just enough money to pay for their living costs.

Making The Grist *make money was a gradual process. The first edition was only four pages long. Subsequent editions remained small, unless the advertising pages earned enough revenue to pay for more editorial pages. In simple terms, expansion was achieved by keeping the product to a financially balanced size. Four years on,* The Grist *has reached 52 pages; each page is paid for by the advertising which the magazine holds. Their luck in having two redundancy payments was seen as a means to tide them over, rather than as a way to produce an expensive product.*

While neither Tony nor Elisabeth had great commercial experience, their personal need to succeed and to survive from the fruits of their work has given them the edge which is needed to press customers into spending money with their enterprise. This hard-nosed approach has resulted in increasing respect from the community which The Grist *serves, and this has meant that their publication is taken seriously. Their lack of commercial experience has hindered them only in further expansion, as several of* The Grist's *competitors have come up for sale, and Elisabeth could not envisage taking them over – although she knew that she was considered by the vendors as a serious potential buyer.*

A kind of jigsaw of skills has held the magazine together in the early times. Elisabeth's knowledge of the trade and administrative skills have had obvious benefits, and Tony's design abilities and ideas have kept the magazine rolling forward. Yet they have ensured that they keep good contacts in the trade, to whom they turn for advice and opinions when they need an objective sounding-board. With a few valuable advisers, they can maintain the magazine's path through the maze of requirements which the brewing trade presents.

Learning points

The prospect of starting a magazine was made less daunting for Elisabeth and Tony because they had experience in their field and they were sure that they had a sound market for their product. Without redundancy payments to start the magazine, they would not have been able to stave off the need for a loan, as their capital was vital to keep them afloat in the first two years. In order to increase the size of their product, they paid for expansion in advance. All bills were budgeted for and all payments were made to suppliers before their next purchase. Attention to detail, in terms of counting every penny, has helped to control expenditure. Planning of expenditure has helped to increase profits. *The Grist* has succeeded through common-sense budgeting and personal dedication.

6 *Practical Considerations*

The financial requirements and early strategy of your business plan will depend on decisions you make in confronting a number of key considerations which affect business start-ups:

- choosing the right business structure (see below);
- choosing the right business premises (see page 156);
- developing an appropriate marketing plan (see page 167);
- deciding on whether you should employ additional staff (see page 179).

Choosing a business structure

A very important factor, which will affect your business's development and your tax liability, is your choice of business structure. For most small-scale businesses there are three main options: sole practitioner (or trader); partnership; or limited company.

Sole trader

In this case you would trade under your own name. You need do little more than change your status with the DHSS and inform your local tax inspector that you have started trading (preferably through your financial adviser). You will, however, be personally liable for any debts which your business activities entail. This form of structure is simple, involves few complications and is best suited to business activities in which you are trading largely on your own individual skills. However, it puts you at a much greater personal financial risk should your business fail.

Partnership

A partnership is similar in status to that of a sole trader in terms of tax liability. Taking a partner, however, has three main advantages:

- It can provide you with a vital source of motivation and support during the hard early days of the business when you are likely to feel isolated or become discouraged.
- It can provide you with an additional source of business capital (which the partner can contribute).
- A partner may well broaden the scope of your business or improve its efficiency and profitability by contributing different but complementary skills to your own; for example, it is common for someone with good specialist or technical skills (which will form the basis of the product or service) to team up with someone else who has financial, administrative or marketing experience.

Taking a partner or partners is a critical step, however. There should be a formal legally binding agreement between you; you will need to divide the profits as well as the initial outlay; and you should always bear in mind that partnerships are difficult and messy to dissolve.

It is therefore important that the person you choose should be someone with whom you can work closely on a day-to-day basis in terms of temperament. Above all, they should be someone you can *trust*. Trust is enormously important in competitive commercial markets. It is important also because *you* will be bound by any agreement your partner makes with anyone else.

The key factor to be aware of is that partners will be 'jointly and severally' liable for each other's actions. You need to be quite happy to be bound by the actions of another person.

Case-study 6.1: Ian and Geoff

Let's return to the case-study of Ian Edwards (see page 40). As the earlier account stated, Ian operates a financial services consultancy in partnership with Geoff Parker. Their main consultancy role is supported by a publishing unit (which produces tailored training materials) and a word-processing company, run by Ian's wife, Kate. In order to examine Ian's decision to enter a partnership with Geoff and the way in which they have handled the close relationship which has resulted, two additional facts about the business are relevant: both Ian and Geoff had worked for the same multinational corporation before setting up on their own; whereas Geoff initially had run his own business, Ian had been in a previous partnership which broke up after two years of trading. It was only after this failure that they had decided to form their present enterprise.

Both Ian and Geoff were keen to stress the benefits of taking on a partner.

'Working on your own is very lonely,' Ian explained. 'If you have been used to working in an environment where you have the stimulus of colleagues all around you, you quickly realize how much you took this for granted.'

Geoff agreed. 'I felt a little isolated as a one-man band. I found that I enjoyed the role much more when working with Ian. We both had a mentor in each other and were able to bounce ideas off each other. You had someone to talk to and to share the excitement of winning contracts with. In addition it gave you more flexibility. It meant that, when two clients rang up on the same day, you could service them both. It also meant we were able to take holidays – an unheard-of luxury for a sole practitioner!'

Ian's relationship with Geoff has always benefited from the lessons he learned from his previous partnership. He set out the reasons for its failure.

'I learned faster than my first partner,' he explained. 'Although he had good ideas, he lacked commercial sense. Because he was an older man and I did not want to hurt his ego, I failed to take steps to rectify the balance before it was too late. I learned that partnerships are not just about business strategy. Their success depends as much on personal feelings. Where your commercial skills are unbalanced, your personal relationship will also prove unbalanced.' Ian went on to compare this experience with his successful partnership. 'Unlike my previous partner, I had already known Geoff in a business situation, when we had worked together in the multinational. I knew that his skills and mine would be compatible, and that what we wanted out of the business was very much the

same. In addition, because we had worked independently of each other after we left the corporation, I had been given the opportunity to see him in operation outside big business. In contrast to my first business relationship, therefore, this was not something we slipped into. It was much more carefully planned.'

Geoff stressed that the secret of a successful partnership was an open and honest attitude. 'Ian and I talked an awful lot, particularly in the early stages when I was still based at my original premises in the North of England. If we weren't in direct contact, we would spend hours on the phone, late into the night, to ensure that we each understood what we had been doing during the day. We shared potential problems and we shared potential marketing opportunities. We had no secrets and, above all, we never pursued our own interests to the detriment of the business.'

Geoff went on to explain how this kind of good communication acted as a safety valve in the event of disagreement or problems caused by differences in style. 'No two people can be the same, and there are bound to be occasional differences. Both Ian and I have strong personalities. We work very hard and need to let off steam. In addition, Ian has a body clock very different from my own. He tends to work very late into the evening and wake up slightly later than I do. I am at my best in the morning and tail off towards the end of the day. So I react less well when I get a phone call from him at one in the morning and, conversely, I do not find him at his best when I turn up on his doorstep at eight the following morning to discover that he is sleeping off an all-night session. We have often had disagreements over business decisions and the style of approach in a particular contract. In all these cases, we overcame the problems by sharing our feelings. If, for any reason, Ian gets up my nose I tell him so – and vice versa. We never go off and sulk.'

As the consultancy has grown, it has proved necessary to take on additional staff. This has also caused problems in their differing styles of approach.

Geoff explained that the main difficulty has been the question of delegation. 'When we were simply a two-man band, it wasn't an issue. We both did everything. As time has gone by, however, we have had to seek constructive ways of dividing our energy. Ian has a capability for work which is incredible and takes an awful lot directly upon himself. I like to step back and let other staff do more under their own steam. So the delegation of responsibility has sometimes proved confusing. We found a certain difficulty in solving key issues: who is responsible for certain members of the team? Who ought to be giving them instructions on a day-to-day basis? Who ought to be reviewing and assessing their work? This is something that is, perhaps, inevitable. It's something that we are obviously going to have to come to terms with as we get bigger.'

Conclusion

No operational difficulties have threatened the very strong bonds that exist between Ian and Geoff – the result of careful planning combined with honesty and openness on both sides.

In summing up, Ian identified a number of key questions which aspiring partners should ask themselves:

- Why are you both going into business in the first place? What do you expect to get out of the venture? Are your separate aims and ambitions compatible?
- If either or both of you is married, what do your spouses feel? Do they know the other's partner and feel comfortable about the relationship?
- Do you both trust each other in financial matters?
- Do you both have compatible skills and a clear idea of how they should be used to support the business?
- Do you both share the same vision?

'Both Geoff and I have paid a price,' Ian concluded. 'We both, after all, could have been proprietors of our own businesses and have sacrificed a measure of absolute control. But, having been able to identify the components of that "price" after three years in business, I can still say that I would do it all again if given the chance. That should be the conclusive test that a partnership has worked for anyone in the same position.'

Limited company

Limited companies are generally considered safer than any other formal business structure, principally because you are liable only for the amount of money you put into the business if it goes into liquidation. In a limited company, money can be raised through the issuing of shares (it is often easier and less complicated to find people who are willing to buy shares than take on all the responsibilities of becoming a partner). The legal obligations of a limited company are, however, much greater than those of a sole trader arrangement or a partnership, and a far stricter control is exercised over its financial affairs, with annual accounts requiring a legal audit by a qualified chartered or certified accountant.

There are two common ways of obtaining a limited company: either by forming one yourself or by purchasing a ready-made 'shelf' company. Shelf companies are those formed by agents to speed up the time involved in starting a business. They have the advantage of being already in existence (and therefore requiring no initial deposit), but financial transactions will have to take place under the existing name rather than under one of your own choice.

Advantages and disadvantages

Care should be taken when making your choice of business structure. Many small entrepreneurs rush into forming a limited company when a sole tradership or partnership can prove far more advantageous. Many points should be considered before deciding upon the constitution of your business. The overriding piece of advice is to talk this through with an accountant.

The points set out below compare the advantages and disadvantages of sole trader/partnership structures with those of a limited company. This list is by no means meant to be exhaustive, but it does constitute a useful checklist.

SOLE TRADERSHIP/PARTNERSHIP

Advantages:

- not governed by the Companies Act 1985;

- greater control over your own capital within the business, i.e. it can be withdrawn with relative ease;
- taxed under Schedule D, where tax is paid in arrears based upon the profit shown in your accounts;
- tax is usually paid in two equal instalments on 1 January and 1 July each year;
- certain advantageous tax elections can be made in opening years;
- tax is charged on the proceeding year basis. For example, income falling into the 1988/9 tax year will form the basis of assessment for 1989/90. Schedule D income tax and Class 4 National Insurance contributions are paid in two equal instalments on 1 January and 1 July 1990. In other words, you have 20–26 months' delay between earning profits and paying tax. This can be particularly important in the first year of trading when your resources will probably be very limited;
- sole traders and partners can draw money out of the business without deducting tax, as they are taxed on the profits of the business, not on what they draw;
- confidentiality is maintained as your accounts do not have to be filed with the Registrar of Companies and made available for public inspection;
- the opportunity exists to transfer the business to a limited company at a later stage;
- a tax loss made by the business can be set off against the sole trader or partners' other income, obtaining tax relief at an early date;
- expenses incurred 'wholly necessarily and exclusively' for the purposes of the trade are deductible for income-tax purposes;
- losses incurred during the initial four years of trading can be carried back three years against income;
- there is no audit requirement unless stated in the partnership agreement.

Disadvantages:

- sole traders are personally accountable for all the liabilities of the business. With partnerships, the partners are liable on a joint and several basis;

- the introduction or removal of a partner creates a cessation of trade for tax purposes, unless all the partners both before and after elect for a 'continuance' (confirmation of trading);
- if the business folds, there are closing-year rules to consider for tax purposes which may prove very expensive;
- sole traders and partners are liable to pay Class 2 National Insurance contributions, which entitle you to fewer benefits than those for an employed person. In particular, you will be unable to claim unemployment benefit if your business folds.
- taxation on the business profits can hit the top rate of 60 per cent for income tax;
- if income is not drawn on the business, it will not affect the taxation position;
- pension contributions are limited to 17.5 per cent of earnings;
- a partnership is not considered a separate legal entity in England, although it is in Scotland;
- the maximum number of partners allowed in a partnership under the law is twenty, except for solicitors, accountants and stockbrokers.

LIMITED COMPANY STATUS

Advantages:

- a company is considered to be a separate legal entity;
- it benefits from limited liability, i.e. the members' or shareholders' liability is limited to the paid-up value of their shares. This means that the debts of the company are the responsibility of the company – not of you personally;
- Corporation Tax is levied on the profits of a company; the rate is restricted to 27 per cent for small companies and 35 per cent for larger companies;
- self-administered pension schemes are available and there is no limit to the company's contributions, although the maximum Inland Revenue-approved benefits must

not be exceeded. Such contributions are allowable deductions for Corporation Tax purposes;
- a loan-back of up to 50 per cent of a self-administered pension fund is possible;
- finance can be raised under the Business Expansion Scheme if required (see page 25);
- greater commercial credibility;
- a change in shareholders does not affect the continuity of the business;
- management and ownership can be separated.

Disadvantages:

- any money drawn from the company is subject to income tax and National Insurance contributions;
- the company pays National Insurance contributions in the form of Employer's NIC on money drawn by owner/directors, whereas (with a sole trader or partnership) Employer's NIC is levied only on the salaries of employees;
- all accounts have to be audited by an approved accountant (see page 107) at least once a year;
- accounts have to be filed with the Registrar of Companies and are available for public inspection;
- the withdrawal of capital is restricted by company legislation;
- there must be at least one director and one company secretary, who cannot be the same person unless there are two directors;
- loans to directors are prohibited. A deposit is usually required until the loan is repaid;
- limited liability can be lost when lenders seek personal guarantees;
- a company is subject to the requirements of the Companies Acts;
- there may be 'double charge' to Capital Gains Tax arising when an asset is sold and when the shares in the company are sold or the company is liquidated;
- Corporation Tax is payable on an actual basis, nine months after the company's year-end;

- a corporate tax-loss cannot be set off against the proprietor's other income for tax purposes;
- it is difficult and expensive in tax terms to disincorporate a company;
- directors are taxed upon benefits-in-kind, e.g. company cars, etc.;
- a change of ownership of more than 50 per cent of the shares can result in losses not being carried forward.

Premises

One critical consideration during the initial stage of starting your enterprise will be your choice of where to conduct your business. Factors you will have to take into account when deciding on premises include:

- Will they allow you the space to work effectively and to accommodate:
  - any equipment you need?
  - any transport you need?
  - any employees you need?
  - sufficient storage space for products and/or essential materials?
- Will they give you adequate access to your clients/customers? Should regular visits from clients/suppliers be essential or desirable, are they within easy access of:
  - an efficient train or bus service?
  - good main road or motorway connections?
- Do they give easy access to your essential suppliers and to a range of amenities such as:
  - photocopying/printing services;
  - stationers;
  - postal services;
  - minicab services;
  - restaurants (for entertaining)?
- Will they enable you to meet all the legal obligations

attached to your particular business activity, particularly in respect of:
- the health and safety of your employees, clients and casual visitors?
- hygiene and sanitary obligations?

■ Have you considered all the financial overheads attached to the occupation and use of the premises, particularly in respect of:
- rent;
- rates;
- electricity and gas;
- water rates;
- ground rent;
- porterage and/or security;
- insurance?

Are all these factors taken into account when you draw up your business plan?

The choices open to you

The various choices open to you, particularly if you are a relatively small-scale operation, may be much wider than you think. The most obvious option is to rent or lease your own workspace or office premises; this may prove essential if you are, for example, planning a retail outlet or employing regular staff. Should you choose this option, you should run through the checklist above very carefully. However, the cost of renting or leasing premises can prove very onerous for a small-scale business and, if your needs are fairly modest, a number of other options exist. These include:

- your own home (see below);
- your own home with an extension (see page 161);
- someone else's home or office space (see page 163);
- shared workspaces or community offices (see page 165).

Your own home

A substantial number of small enterprises can be run, without any inconvenience, from present domestic flats or houses. They include businesses such as typing/word-processing services, teaching and private tuition, freelance journalism/writing, dressmaking, craft-work, telephone selling, data preparation, picture-framing, cushion-making and upholstery, childminding, counselling and (with some alterations) cooking and catering, photography, repair services, boarding animals, furniture maintenance, etc.

There are certainly a number of distinct advantages to working from home, most notably:

- your immediate overheads will be reduced;
- you have more choice as to the hours you work;
- you do not have to commute;
- you will find it easier to combine your work with your family life, possibly (depending on its nature) involving them in the enterprise.

At the same time, working from home can prove extremely demanding. If you rely on self-employment to provide a substantial percentage of your income, you may have to work long hours, often into the evening and sometimes over the weekend. In familiar surroundings close to your family, it is easy to be distracted. The work in front of you will always be competing with household chores that need to be finished, gardening which is long overdue and the television programme your family is watching next door. So you will need to have a far greater degree of self-discipline than when you worked on separate business premises, isolated from the sights and sounds of your home life. You will have to fix yourself a set number of hours to work each day and be able to stick to your target.

In addition, the seemingly simple step of using your home to work, as well as to live, from can have major financial, legal, contractual and social implications. Some of these are listed below. You should consider them all before making your decision.

Insurance

Most normal householder's insurance policies specifically exclude damage, loss or destruction caused by any business activity. Before you 'set up shop', you should approach your insurance company and ask them to review your policy in the light of your work. In many cases, the company may be willing to continue covering the premises as a private dwelling (if, say, you are merely giving music lessons or providing a typing service). But for some business activities, it will be necessary to take out additional cover, For example:

Fire: In the case of craftwork which involves the storage of inflammable materials such as plastic foam and large quantities of adhesives.

Burglary. If you are buying and selling on a regular basis and have a large number of visitors or clients entering your premises.

Public liability. To cover you in the case of illness or damage to your clients or their property because of the sale of defective goods or produce. A good illustration would be if someone suffered from food-poisoning as a result of eating insufficiently warmed up pre-cooked food which you may have provided as an outside caterer.

Use of your car. If you need to use your car for business purposes, you may have to take out extra cover, for example a 'goods in transit' policy.

It is very important to check your insurance policy, even though your business activities may not affect the cover. *If you lose your home, you will also lose your livelihood.*

Breach of covenant

There may be a covenant in force on your house or flat, whether you rent it or own it, which may prevent you from operating business activities there. You may, for example, have said that the property was for residential purposes only when you applied for a mortgage. Before you become committed, you should:

– check with your building society, if you have a mortgage;
– check your lease, if you are a tenant;
– check your deeds, if you are an owner-occupier (you can obtain these by completing form A44 available from Her Majesty's Stationery Office and sending it to the Land Registry).

Neighbours

If your work is likely to affect your neighbours (for example, if it involves additional building, a steady stream of visitors who may have to park in front of the house, or machinery which they are likely to hear), consult them first and try to be considerate to them when you are working. Unless it is absolutely necessary, do not work late at night or early in the morning if it is likely to keep them awake. Ask any visitors to park tidily.

Investigations into home-based businesses are often prompted by complaints from the neighbours. On the other hand, neighbours can often be a great source of support, and your contact with them is likely to be much closer if you are spending most of your working day at home.

Laws that will affect you

There are myriad laws that might affect any service you provide or goods you produce. For example:

- The Food Hygiene (General) Regulations 1970, lays down strict guidelines about the preparation and sale of food for public consumption, particularly relating to the cleanliness of the premises and equipment, the handling of the material and the disposal of any rubbish or waste. This will obviously have a great effect on you if you are considering selling food from home or outside catering.
- The Toys (Safety) Regulations 1974 give the Local Authority the right to prosecute anyone producing unsafe or dangerous toys, as defined in the regulations.

Damage or injury caused by the sale or supply of defective goods are grounds for court action. So, always check the regulations governing the manufacture or supply of anything you are proposing to market, and consult your legal adviser before setting up the business.

Your own home (with extension)

From the start, or as you outgrow the space you have available, you may need to extend or make alterations to your home to meet your business requirements. This might involve, for example, extending or adapting your garage, or building an annexe to your house.

Case-study 6.2: Bill and Alison Cooper – Computer consultants
'The business started very humbly from the lounge and second bedroom. Everything always seemed cramped but it's amazing how we managed for so long – around nine to ten months. At the outset we thought we would remain working from home for about twelve to eighteen months but, after six months, we realized that we were growing too quickly – one of the prices of success!

'We needed somewhere to place about four microcomputers on display so that, first, they could be used for programme development projects, and secondly we could train clients in their use. We also required space to accommodate an administration assistant and three computer trainers who would need to call in every so often for briefings and the opportunity to work on the machines.

'We researched local premises – rent, leasehold and even a few freehold properties. However, when we put the figures on to paper we became less excited. Given our fast start, we had not built up a regular core of "bread and butter" clients. To commit ourselves to this kind of financial outlay involved enormous risks unless we could achieve the sales required. On balance, we decided to look at other means of solving our problem. The main choices were: a portakabin at the bottom of the garden; looking for a spare room in part of an existing operation; or extending the house by building on an annexe. In the end we chose the annexe. It could offer us a way to keep costs down and keep the business in our local area, and it would provide the space we needed. It also had the added advantage of a return on investment. The annexe could be turned into a fourth

bedroom or combined with the lounge to make a very large reception room when we came to sell.

'This happened a year ago. Already the question of space has cropped up again – we are expanding very quickly!'

Learning points

- Before you commit yourself financially, think through your precise requirements.
- Many businesses fail in the early stages because they create overheads they cannot guarantee to meet. There are many other options besides renting, leasing and buying specific properties – an imaginative use of lateral thinking can reap great dividends.

If you are choosing this option, however, you should once again check that:

- your extension will be covered under existing insurance agreements;
- you are not in breach of any covenant;
- your extension is not likely to cause problems with your neighbours;
- your extension is built to a standard that will conform to the legal regulations governing your business activities.

Planning permission

This leads to the important subject of planning permission. Regardless of whether you are physically extending your property, you should always check with the local authority to find out whether you need planning permission to carry on any business activities in your home. Permission will certainly be needed if you are intending to make any material changes to your home (for example, adding an extra room to work from or receive clients in, or converting a garage into a storeroom). Permission may not be needed in the case of private research or what the council may regard as a 'profitable hobby' (the distinction between a business and a profitable hobby is often very fine).

You will probably not need permission if you type, write articles, give private music or language classes, sell over the telephone or engage in data preparation. However, check up, whatever you intend to do. You may be commiting an offence if you carry on without permission. Once again, it is also advisable to consult your legal adviser before taking any practical steps.

Someone else's home or office

For various reasons, it may be inappropriate to work from your own home, but you may still lack the financial resources to rent or lease your own workspace. Two alternatives are either to use someone else's home, or to have the use of someone else's workspace in exchange for the free or reduced-rate use of your professional services, or for a percentage of your earnings. Perhaps you have a close friend, relative or parents who can offer you the use of part of their home to work from. This could well prove a useful temporary solution, but it is worth bearing in mind that:

- Whoever owns or rents the premises will incur the same legal and financial obligations outlined above. At the same time they will enjoy none of the tax advantages gained from using a home for business purposes. It is therefore important that:
  - they understand fully all the obligations they are likely to incur from having their premises used for business purposes;
  - they have ensured that they are legally and contractually permitted to do so.
- You will need to have easy access to the premises and may have to have clients/suppliers visiting. You may also need to bring in office equipment. Have your temporary 'landlords' considered the social implications and the disruption to their daily lives or privacy?

In practice, this option could disrupt or damage what previously were positive and fulfilling relationships, unless the implications are carefully considered and the implementation carefully planned. It is really suitable only for freelance activities such as writing, craftwork, typing, etc.

A far more positive alternative is to come to an arrangement with someone who can offer you an office or workspace within their own premises. Clearly, the most secure and binding arrangement would be to rent the necessary space officially. However, if you are not in a financial position to offer a regular rent, you might like to consider two other options. The first is offering a royalty or percentage of your earnings.

Case-study 6.3: James Mitchell – Fishing tackle dealer

'I couldn't afford a shop-front myself, this would have meant an enormous outlay. I calculated what would be needed to break even each month – and it was a large sum. I did see a local need, however. There was only one major supplier of fishing tackle and they were very big. They tended to be a bit impersonal and many people were disillusioned with their attitude.

'I didn't want to compete with them on an equal scale – my initial costs would have been too great. I was, however, in a position to offer a more personal service: to make flies and rods to order; to sell a select range of rods, reels and equipment; and to offer a bait delivery service to local fishing clubs (nobody else was doing this).

'The most important requirement was not to get saddled with the necessity of making a big investment in premises. The solution came out of a conversation with one of my wife's friends who commented, "Why doesn't James have a booth or a stand in an existing sports shop?"

'After negotiations with four possible retail outlets, we eventually struck a business deal with MacGregor's, the sports shop. The arrangement is very simple, I have a counter area plus a store room; 15 per cent of all sales goes to MacGregor's. The advantages are mutual. I have a high-quality shop-front with a name behind me. MacGregor has more customers as well as a financial return on space that was not being utilized properly anyway.

'Needless to say, before I went ahead I did consult with my solici-

tor and accountant, and MacGregor and I do have a legal agreement between us.

'The arrangement has worked well to date, and I am currently discussing ideas with MacGregor's on the joint marketing of our services under the general banner of leisure goods and services.'

The second alternative to paying a regular rent is exchanging your services for the use of the workspace. This kind of 'mutual aid' scheme is a new idea for many people (although it should not be forgotten that the barter system of exchanging goods, services and time preceded the use of money in most countries). Under this arrangement, you could offer your professional services (or produce) at a reduced or free rate in return for the use of workspace or office facilities. To protect yourself, however, it is important that you formalize the agreement under a written contract and that your obligations to your new 'landlord' leave you sufficient time to build up your business. There are also tax implications connected to this form of barter, so it is important to discuss the agreement with your financial adviser before committing yourself.

Shared workspaces or community offices

Perhaps the most imaginative response to the needs of small-scale entrepreneurs who lack the resources or do not need to rent premises of their own has been the emergence of local community workspaces, by which a variety of small businesses share office facilities and common business services. These offer two distinct advantages:

- Because facilities are shared, the cost to individual business people of running their enterprise is far lower than if they were operating on their own.
- Because many people operate better in a social atmosphere, and do not like the isolation starting a business may involve, shared workspaces offer a place where you can literally (in the words of the sales brochure) 'work on your own where you are not alone'.

The address of the National Managed Workspace Group can be found in the Appendix (see page 258). An example of one is provided below.

Case-study 6.4: Barley Mow Workspace

One of the earliest and best examples of a successful community office in action is the Barley Mow Workspace, established in 1976. Around 150 small companies, including individuals and partnerships, operate from this converted Victorian factory (originally belonging to the Sanderson Wallpaper Company) in Chiswick, west London. The premises are on four floors, and provide office, studio and workshop space divided by sound-absorbent screens into units from 100^2 feet up. A few workshops are enclosed, where noise and security make this advisable.

Member firms pay a licence fee (workshops less than offices) and a service charge which covers common services and facilities. These include: cleaning, heating, lighting, maintenance, rates and water rates, and all other statutory charges. They also include the use of conference rooms and (very importantly) a communal receptionist and telephone answering service. Individual business people furnish and equip their own space and pay telephone and telex charges, which are metered. Everything else is covered by the monthly Barley Mow bill.

When it was originally founded, the workspaces were used mostly by graphic designers and architects. Nowadays an astonishing range of businesses operate from the premises, covering such activities as advertising, surveying, accountancy and auditing, charity administration, film and video animation, industrial purchasing, music, sculpture, electronic aids for the blind, car hire, table making and photographic developing and printing. This wide variety of services has helped to make the premises almost self-sufficient. As the organizers put it: 'you could almost run your own business without leaving the building'. Examples of recent services on offer include: Barley Mow secretaries; a dark-room and dyelining services; and a courier service offering both motorbike and car delivery.

As one tenant put it: 'It's full of different abilities. Say I want an exhibition stand designed, or a brochure, a trophy or an audio-visual presentation, some label designs or sales incentive prizes, all

I have to do is walk a few steps and then say so. The work will be done as well and priced as competitively as anywhere in London.'

Finally, a key business in the premises is a restaurant, Lesley Faddy's, which acts both as a useful place to entertain clients for lunch and, perhaps more importantly, as a focal point for the social life of the workspace. For it is contact with other business people sharing the same problems (and many of the solutions) which makes Barley Mow so special. 'It's never static,' said one founder tenant. 'There's always a trickle of people coming or going, new faces and new things happening. Sometimes people come to grief, but usually they outgrow Barley Mow and find it suits them to take on a set of offices or something on their own. The result is that this place is constantly being refreshed, it's always alive.'

Marketing

The effective marketing of your product or service is likely to prove an essential factor of your commercial success. Yet, ironically, marketing is an area to which small-business people devote far too little attention. This is frequently for either of two reasons:

- They mistakenly perceive the cost of effective marketing as being far higher than it actually proves.
- They do not build enough time into their daily or weekly schedule to create a practical marketing plan.

In this section we shall show that, for many small-scale enterprises, the creative use of easily accessible services will make the cost of effective marketing a small burden, easily compensated for by the increased business it will generate.

The options available

The options open to small businesses are, in fact, broader than you might think. The main alternatives include:

- effective use of letterheads and business 'logos' (see below);
- brochures and publicity material (see below);
- media coverage (see page 169);
- advertising in the press and on radio and television (see page 175);
- cheaper ways of advertising (see page 177).

Company letterheads and logos

Your best marketing tools are also your simplest: the design which appears on all your written communications and publicity material. Standard design or logo, using matching typefaces, colours and format, should appear on all your headed paper, calling cards, invoice or account statements, compliment slips and brochures. You may wish to invest some money on buying in a designer who can produce a variety of approaches to choose from. If this is beyond your resources (even a local designer will probably charge you at least £200), many of the growing network of high-street copying services (see below) are increasingly specializing in stationery design.

A set of complementary letterheads, calling cards, compliment slips and invoice sheets may initially set you back by as much as £500, particularly if you are using more than one colour in the design. This is one business resource you should not stint on, however. A written letter, calling card or compliment slip may be the first tangible contact many potential clients will have with your business. The quality, imagination and creativity they reflect will create a favourable impression and improve your professional image.

Brochures and publicity material

Another important marketing tool is some form of publicity material which sets out:

- the business's main products or services;
- the qualifications and background of the main personnel;
- the rates charged or price list (if appropriate);

– the business's major clients (if appropriate);
– the business's location and other details.

This can be sent out, not only on request, but with all routine correspondence to create as wide a market awareness as possible. Unless your enterprise is reasonably substantial, or you have access to considerable initial capital, a glossy colour affair will not be necessary. Depending on the nature of your business, the information may need to be reproduced on just a single A4 sheet, provided it:

- is printed professionally, using good-quality stock;
- is well designed, employing maximum use of colour;
- is clear, concise and well laid out;
- makes effective use of your company logo or design (see above).

The availability and cost of well-designed, well-printed stationery and publicity material have been greatly improved by the recent growth of high-street copying services. Most can design and/or print stationery, including letterheads, calling cards, compliment slips, etc.; they can also produce reports, discussion documents, presentation material, mail order slips (see below), menu cards, price lists, etc.; most are also able to offer substantial discounts for bulk copying.

The copying services available in your immediate area can be contacted through your local Yellow Pages or Thomson directory. Alternatively, it may well be worth buying in the necessary equipment to create your own publicity material. A word processor (or even a good electric typewriter) used in combination with a reasonably flexible photocopier (which can copy on most paper formats, collate, enlarge and reduce) should cope with all but the most sophisticated needs.

Media coverage

In addition to using the media as an outlet for advertisements and inserts (see below), you should also consider ways in which you can get yourself some form of editorial coverage, particularly when you choose to launch your business. This is preferable to placing advertising, for two fairly self-evident reasons: it is cheaper and it carries more weight. Getting and maintaining press attention, however, requires a little skill and an awareness of how journalists evaluate the material they receive.

Written material

Any journalist worth approaching is on the receiving end of huge amounts of written material, all designed to induce him or her to write about, or devote 'airtime' to, that particular organization/individual/product. Most are obliged to adopt fast and brutal ways of reducing the pile of paper on their desks to manageable proportions. Generally, the decision to 'chuck or keep' is made by the beginning of the second paragraph (sometimes even on the response to the opening headline). For this reason, material sent to the press should be:

- 'targeted' directly at the newspaper, magazine, journal or broadcasting station concerned;
- sent to the right journalist;
- sent at the right time;
- clearly written, with the main points brought out in the headline and first paragraph.

Choosing the correct angle

Different journalists look at the same piece of news through different eyes, depending on the particular publication unit they work for or the particular area they specialize in. Any publicity material sent to them should recognize this fact. Looking at your business, particularly at the time of its launch, you may be able to pinpoint a number of possibilities. For example:

- **Professional**: Your product or service may be sufficiently original or creative to attract attention on its own merits. The trade or business press could therefore prove possible outlets for media coverage.

- **Local**: A new company in the district, particularly with an interesting or original product/service, could attract an interest in the local press which it might fail to do in national or trade outlets.
- **Human interest**: Alternatively, the interest might focus on you personally. A good example might be if you were disabled or if you found a sufficiently original way of raising the capital. Local newspapers in particular are always on the look-out for human-interest stories, and small businesses remain a good source.

Writing the material

The main vehicle for any written information sent to journalists should be a 'press release'. As we saw earlier, the release should be clear, concise and tailored to the particular publication concerned.

There are a number of ground rules:

- The paper release should be typed on one, or at the most two, sheets of A4 paper. It should be double-spaced and use broad margins.
- It should incorporate the company letterheads, the words 'PRESS RELEASE' and the date of release.
- There should be a heading which clearly indicates what the gist of the story is. This should be tailored to the type of publication involved (local, trade, national, etc.).
- The information you wish to publicize should appear in the first three paragraphs, with the essential details appearing in the first. Always remember that:
  - the vocabulary used should be appropriate and comprehensible to the readership of the publication(s). Save professional jargon or technical terms for the trade press.
  - sub-editors usually cut from the bottom upwards. No essential information should therefore appear near the end of the release.
- The essential information should include:
  - a direct quotation from the named manager/founder of

the business of (if appropriate) a local celebrity connected with the business.
- a contact who can provide further information and whose telephone number is featured.
- a photograph illustrating the business in operation or the people behind it is always a great help, provided it is: lively and imaginative; professional and well printed. (If you are providing a photograph, always remember to caption it on a separate sheet of paper or using a self-adhesive label.)

- Always bear in mind the deadline for the publication. Remember that:
  - local weekly newspapers which appear on a Friday are often printed as early as Tuesday or Wednesday.
  - monthly publications require information up to six weeks in advance.

Case-Study 6.5: *The Grist*

To illustrate how a press release is written, let's return to the case study of Elisabeth and Tony (see page 142). As we saw, they were two trade journalists living in North London who decided to start their own journal for small brewers. The key points to note are:

- *The journal was aimed specifically at small brewers.*
- *The business was home-based, with all the tasks performed by the two founders.*
- *The business was based in Islington.*

PRESS RELEASE

'Cottage publishers launch magazine for small independent breweries worldwide.'

A cottage publishing house in Highbury, North London, has launched a technical magazine for the small independent brewer worldwide on 1 February 1985.

Elisabeth Baker, formerly Deputy Editor of Brewers' Guardian, recently sold by International Thomson Publishing and Tony Willi-

amson, recent past Editor of Meat Industry, *a current Thomson publication, have just joined forces to produce* 'The Grist International', *aimed at the growing number of tiny craft breweries which have become a worldwide phenomenon.*

The Grist International, *a 20-page quarterly, carries technical, financial and marketing advice as well as classified and display advertising. Produced entirely by Mr Williamson and Ms Baker, the magazine is typeset and printed locally, and the pair see themselves very much as part of the grassroots economy being fervently encouraged by current Government policies.*

The tiny Highbury publishers hope to go bi-monthly with their magazine at the end of the year. They are also planning to run a PR service for brewers and continue freelancing.

A carefully thought-out distribution of this press release resulted in the new business being mentioned in the London Standard, *the local weekly newspaper, the* Business Opportunities Digest, *twelve trade magazines and newspapers including:* Brewers Guardian, Brewing and Distilling, Home Brewer *and* What's Brewing *(the newspaper published by the Campaign for Real Ale). The publicity they received from the* Business Opportunities Digest *proved particularly valuable, with a number of key subscribers originating from this source of publicity.*

Using a press conference

Some small entrepreneurs feel sufficiently confident about the originality of their product or service to launch their business using a press conference. Since press launches are expensive (booking the hall, catering, printing invitations, etc.), time-consuming and attract an unpredictable response, it is important to ensure that the likelihood of resulting publicity is sufficient to justify the effort. Questions to consider include:

- How many journalists is the conference likely to attract? Are they from the right magazines, radio stations or newspapers?

- Would you attract an equally large response (in terms of the column-inches devoted to your business) by the distribution of a well-written press release (see above)?
- Is the conference conveniently located and at the right time? (11 a.m. is a particular favourite with journalists – it gives them enough time to get to the venue and the prospect of an early finish before lunch.)
- Will journalists be given enough warning (at least two weeks) and will they be given clear instructions on how to get to the venue?

In reality, there are few occasions in a small business's development to justify press conferences. Unless the launch of the business is really newsworthy, the product is particularly innovative or you have won an exceptional award, you will probably find the response disappointing and not cost-effective.

Advertising

When considering advertising as a means of reaching potential clients or customers, it is worth bearing in mind a number of points.

- Advertising is expensive and often ineffective if incorrectly used.
- It is therefore sensible to use it only after:
  - finding out (preferably with the expert help of a counsellor or advisory service) what the total cost is likely to be;
  - exploring all the other, less costly, ways of reaching the potential market (press releases, stickers, notices in post office windows, etc.) as an end in itself or a means of testing the ground before attempting more systematic advertising);
  - making sure that the cost of any advertising is reflected in the price of the service or product;
  - making sure that you have chosen the right medium (again, preferably with the help of expert advice);

– making sure that the message is correct and uses language which the customer or client will understand.

Selecting the media

When deciding where to advertise, you should ask yourself a number of questions:

- How much will it cost to reach each prospective customer? Is it worth the price? Can you afford it?
- How often do you want the message to reach each customer? Is it better to place one large advertisement or several smaller ones?
- Do you want to restrict your message specifically to the prospective customer or client who represents the best sales prospect? Or is there a case for more general advertising to get your name known in the particular market in order to attract less immediate sales?
- Always bearing in mind that you are limited by your financial resources, have you explored all the less expensive methods of reaching your customers?
- Having decided to advertise, have you made sure that the advertisement:
  – is easily recognizable, reflecting the style and personality of your business (use a logo if possible);
  – is written in a style with which your audience will identify;
  – uses a simple, easy-to-assimilate design and layout;
  – stresses the main benefits of your product or service;
  – provides all the information needed to contact you (address, telephone number, etc.)
  – is appropriate to the medium of your choice?

Sources of advertising

Newspapers

If you are a retail or service industry, local newspapers should prove the most effective outlet for paid advertising.

Points to consider

- Be selective. Look at all newspapers in your area rather than the one you happen to read. Make sure that their readership are likely customers of your product or service.
- Compare each paper's charges. Ask for the paper's 'Rate Card' which sets out the price of display, classified and special feature ads. Check to see whether they offer special rates for a series of inserts (most do).
- Be systematic rather than sporadic. Remember that:
  - a series of consecutive ads in the same favourable position may prove more effective (and cheaper) than sporadic advertising over an extended period;
  - a carefully written classified ad may prove as effective as (and considerably cheaper than) a display advertisement requiring costly artwork and proofing.

Local commercial radio

A much overlooked medium. There are now nearly 50 local commercial radio stations spread around the country.

Points to consider

- Radio advertising is quick to arrange and brings an immediate response.
- Although expensive (a 15-second 'slot' can cost up to £500) it reaches a much wider audience who may not subscribe to local newspapers.
- For both these reasons, local-radio advertising should be used on specific occasions – for example, when launching your business, a new product or service, or when circumstances demand a rapid increase in sales.

Yellow Pages/local directories

Both Yellow Pages and its commercial competitor, Thomson Directories, offer considerable potential to reach a wide audience.

Points to consider

- Advertising in local directories allows you the potential to reach every household or company with a telephone.
- Sales people at the directory company will help you in drawing up a suitable insertion.
- Response is spread over a longer period than radio and newspaper advertising.
- There are, however, a number of disadvantages, not least of all:
  - most of your commercial competitors are also listed;
  - it is expensive (up to £50 for a classified insertion and up to £200 for a display ad);
  - there is a long lead-time, since most directories are only published every one or two years.

Cheaper ways of advertising

As already mentioned, there are many less expensive means of advertising your product or service which could prove as effective as the costly methods specified above. Some of these include:

Notices in local stores. Most newsagents and some local stores provide display boards for postcard-size advertisements for a very small weekly charge. This is the cheapest and simplest way of advertising. Yet for a small-scale business serving the immediate community, it can often prove as effective as a newspaper ad costing ten times as much.

Leaflets. Another effective method for a small-scale business. They are cheap to produce (£6–8 per thousand) but, to be really effective, they should be distributed by a reputable firm (find one in Yellow Pages) rather than by friends or personal volunteers. Careful attention should be paid to layout and a response mechanism should be devised to check that the leaflets are actually reaching their destination.

Stickers/posters/vans signs. Although the cost of posters on buildings or hoardings would be outside the scope of most small businesses, stickers and small point-of-sale posters should be within the scope of all but the most modest businesses. If you are using a van or car, remember its potential to advertise your product or service through a bright and easy-to-read sign on its bodywork.

Direct mail. A possible alternative to the use of directly targeted sales letters. Provided you have done your market research properly, this has the advantage of reaching the specific audience you wish it to; it also makes it easier to compile customer records, once the business has become established. In conducting direct-mail exercises, you can also take advantage of a very welcome free mail service recently introduced by the Post Office for new businesses. You provide the leaflets or letters together with a reply-paid card or addressed envelope, and the Post Office will send them to up to 1,000 potential customers.

All of these less expensive options can be used as an end in themselves for small businesses which lack the budgets for conventional paid advertising. However, they can also be used as a means of testing the market before any systematic advertising is undertaken; for example, a good way of testing the market for a new business is to print a leaflet advertising the product or service and place it through the door of 500 houses in a defined geographical area. By gauging the response (in terms of the number of replies and the number of sales made) you can calculate what it might cost if you were to advertise in a more systematic manner.

Case-study 6.6: Veronica Jones Associates

The word-processing and printing service started by Veronica Jones (see pages 39-40) is a good example of a small enterprise that has marketed itself effectively but at a reasonable cost.

'My most successful marketing was initially achieved through cards placed in local shop windows,' she explained. 'This method brought me my first client; it also brought some of my biggest clients. I was amazed at the response received through this method – which must be one of the cheapest forms of advertising!'

Confident of her success in attracting business, Veronica then experimented with a direct-mail sales letter sent to 120 local businesses. The results were disappointing. 'It wasn't undertaken with enough care,' she commented. 'Although I was targeting a certain type of business, I had not spent sufficient time researching the "hit list", with the result that many of the recipients were not certain clients. In addition, I didn't consider following up the sales letter with any telephone contact.

'On the second mail-shot I did; I offered incentives within the letter, and followed up with a telephone call a few days later. This produced a more rewarding result and, in any case, the follow-up calls provided some very interesting information, and the marketing exercise was therefore worthwhile.'

Veronica has learned from the experience. 'We have now started to specialize, and this will make direct-mail exercises far easier to conduct. We are also advertising in carefully selected trade magazines – which have a more positive response and are therefore more cost-effective for our type of business: but in any marketing we do now, we find the hours spent in the local reference library really pay off.'

Employing staff

Either from the very start of your business or in the early stages of its development you may need to consider employing staff to provide back-up support or additional services.

For businesses of the size and nature discussed in this book, taking on employed staff is an important step and not to be considered lightly. In the first years of trading, a business needs to be flexible. Too many overheads could hinder its ability to cope with potential fluctuations in trade, perhaps fatally. On the other hand, inadequate support could also make it difficult for you to exploit new business opportunities, forcing you to cope with trivial administrative tasks when you should be concentrating on more important and creative aspects of the business.

Considerations will obviously vary from company to company, but the basic questions you should be asking yourself include:

- Do you have a clear idea of:
  - exactly what the job will entail?
  - how many hours a week it will require?
- Do you know what the current hourly/daily/weekly rate for the job is likely to be? Will it be necessary or desirable to offer the person concerned some kind of stake in the business (shares or profit sharing, for example)? Can you really afford it?
- Will the job require you to employ someone under a permanent contract of employment or can it be performed:
  - under a temporary contract;
  - by a temporary agency worker;
  - by a regular self-employed consultant;
  - under a casual arrangement;

  (all of which could enable you to bring in employed help only when you need it)?
- Do you have a clear idea of where and how you can recruit the staff?
- Do you have a clear idea of the legal implications and obligations involved?

Statutory legal obligations

Employing someone imposes a number of legal obligations. The main obligations include:

Discrimination:

Sex. Under the Sex Discrimination Act 1975 it is illegal to discriminate against a person on the grounds of their sex (or their marital status) in terms of selection, promotion, training or dismissal.

Race. Under the Race Relations Act 1976, it is illegal to discriminate against a person on the grounds of 'colour, race, nationality or ethnic or national origin', in terms of selection, promotion, training or dismissal.

Equal pay. Under the Equal Pay Act a woman has the right to equal treatment when she is employed either on work of the same or a broadly similar nature to that of men or in jobs which, although different from those of men, are considered to have the same value.

Health and safety

Under the Health and Safety at Work Act 1974, all employers have a responsibility to 'secure the health, safety and welfare at work of their employees'. They also have a duty to protect other people from risks to health and safety caused by people at work. 'People at work' include contractors, part-time, temporary and agency staff and casuals, as well as permanent full-time staff. This legal obligation covers the necessity to explain how potentially dangerous equipment works; taking steps to ensure that staff are aware of their responsibilities under the Act; and ensuring that equipment and policies exist to combat dangerous or hazardous situations.

Employment protection

Employers also owe their staff a number of obligations relating to their job security. These increase according to the length of continuous employment with the employer concerned. The basic obligations, all covered by the Employment Protection (Consolidation) Act 1978, include:

from the beginning of the contract:

- not to be dismissed for trade-union membership/activities, on racial grounds or grounds of sex
- have time off without pay to take part in trade-union activities and public duties
- to payments in the event of the firm going bankrupt
- to receive an itemized pay statement

after four weeks:

- not to be dismissed because of a medical suspension
- to receive notice of dismissal

within 13 weeks:

- to receive a written statement of his/her terms and conditions of employment (if subsequently changed, the new terms must be given within four weeks)

after 2 years:

- not to be unfairly dismissed
- to a redundancy payment in the event of being laid off
- to time off to look for work or arrange retraining in the event of being laid off
- to maternity pay (six weeks) in the event of pregnancy
- to return to work after pregnancy

Conclusion

The list of statutory obligations above is only a brief summary of the legal requirements you might be expected to comply with. The exact circumstances in which they might affect you will vary according to the size, structure and nature of your business. Many statutory obligations, including some of the above, are waived or reduced in the case of small businesses. It is therefore important that you consult closely with your legal adviser, before taking on any member of staff, in order to determine your individual obligations.

Choosing the best contract

As we saw above, your need for staff is likely to be fairly flexible in the early days. Taking on permanent full-time staff is only one option open to you. Other, more open-ended alternatives include:

Contract staff

Under a fixed-term contract: This contract sets a fixed duration to the length of service. If the term is for less than two years, the worker concerned will not have any legal protection against unfair dismissal or redundancy pay under employment protection legislation (although they may be entitled to some or all of the other rights listed above on page 181). If the term is for two years or more, the employer has the right to include a valid binding 'contracting-out' clause, under which the employee effectively gives up any right to protection against unfair dismissal and redundancy pay. This waiver will apply only when the fixed term expires, but it can sometimes be 'fair' under the law to dismiss an employee for refusing to accept its insertion into the contract.

Under a fixed-job contract. As opposed to fixed-term contracts, where the contract expires on the completion of a fixed period of time, a fixed-job contract expires when the specific work the employee has been engaged to do is completed. Here the employee is not entitled to any protection against unfair dismissal under employment protection legislation because he or she is not deemed to have been 'dismissed' when the contract expires.

Temporary agency staff

A very wide range of employment agencies now hire out temporary staff. Many agencies not only cover conventional secretarial, word-processor and administrative staff, but also specialize in professional staff – accountancy, personnel, computer staff (programmers and analysts) and drivers. These can usually be hired out on a daily, weekly or monthly basis.

There is a very ambiguous three-party relationship between the workers, the agency who hires them out, and the client who hires them. The agency has a statutory obligation to deduct the worker's tax and NI contributions, but agencies have frequently been held not to be the employers of the workers they hire out on the basis that, as agencies, they have insufficient control over them. In addition, it is worth noting that, whatever the relationship you have with the agency workers you hire, you will be obliged to take such steps as are reasonably practical to look after their health and safety whilst they are working on your premises. The provisions of the Health and Safety at Work Act 1974 extend to those whom you do not employ but who are 'affected by your undertaking', and this has been held to include agency workers performing services for the agency's clients on the clients' premises.

Casual staff

Finally, if you are simply looking for an occasional helper to work odd hours (for example, clearing out a room, decorating, packing or unpacking boxes, etc.) you can bring someone in as a casual worker.

Legally, 'casual' employment is usually defined as an arrangement where the worker concerned can choose whether or not to work at a particular time. In other words you, as his prospective employer, may phone and say, 'There is some work I need doing today, are you available?' and the worker decides for himself whether or not he wishes to accept the offer.

It is commonly assumed that, in cases of this kind, the worker concerned is not an 'employee' under the law, and therefore enjoys none of the rights of an employee. However, this is not always the case. A worker's status as an employee does not necessarily depend on whether he or she was under an obligation to accept regular work. It has been held in the courts to depend on whether he or she worked regularly in practice.

Permanent part-time staff

From your business's point of view, 'part-time' can mean anything between eight and 48 hours a week. Common part-time shifts include:

- 10 a.m.–3 p.m. (a favourite with mothers because they can drop off and pick up their school-age children)
- 9 a.m.–1 p.m.
- 1 p.m.–5 p.m. (good for job-sharers)
- Evenings
- Saturdays only (good for students)
- Saturdays and Mondays

- 2/3 days a week

Where to look

Most of the support staff you need can be found through one or more of the following outlets:

- recruitment consultants
- classified pages of local newspapers
- relevant trade journals
- general or specialist employment agencies
- Jobcentres
- notices in local post offices and newsagents' windows
- notices in your own premises' windows

For relatively unskilled work which pays a low salary, a small ad in local newspapers or notice in the windows of your premises or on the notice-board of a local post office or newsagents will often prove a quite adequate outlet (as well as being relatively inexpensive). For more skilled staff, a specialist employment agency or recruitment consultancy may be the better choice than directly placed advertising (provided you can afford the fee). Remember also to tap your own network of former colleagues and personal contacts if they are qualified or skilled in the right areas.

7 *Writing a Business Plan*

For the past six chapters you have been gathering information and making decisions in respect of a number of key areas:

- your reasons for starting the business;
- the market potential of your business idea;
- the financial support you will need;
- the resources you will need;
- the way in which you will market the business.

This chapter will demonstrate how all this data can be brought together in a comprehensive business plan. Putting together a business plan will help you in the following two ways:

Internally. It will crystallize and put into focus your ideas. Nothing sharpens the mind better than seeing the business facts and projections in black and white. Lots of people have good ideas. Whether you can make money out of them is a very different matter! The business plan will therefore answer the critical question, 'Do I have a viable proposition?'

- It will help you to set objectives so that your subsequent performance can be monitored against them.
- It will also help you to test out your assumptions and intuitive assessments. For example:
  - 'Will it give me the income of £x that I projected and need?'
  - 'I assume that I can get my first order in one month.'
  - 'Will it allow me to set aside £x for my pension?'
  - 'I assume that a percentage of my customers will want . . .'

– 'Can I do it on my own, as I forecast, or do I need to hire someone?'
– 'I assume that I will start producing on *y* date and that it will take me three weeks to finish the processes.'
– 'I believe that in Year 2 I will be able to afford premises. Is this realistic?'
– 'I assume that there will be no rise in raw materials until October.'

Externally. A coherent, well-thought-out business plan is essential if you are to gain the confidence and support of key potential supporters. In particular, it will gain you the support of:

- bank managers and financial decision-makers to whom you will turn for overdrafts, loans, business capital and other forms of financial support;
- key partners or staff whom you wish to involve;
- solicitors, accountants and other business advisers who will be responsible for advising you on a regular basis.

A business plan will help you to respond with confidence to questions like: 'What is the maximum overdraft facility you will need?', 'When do you expect your business to break even?' and 'How sensitive is the business to changes in your sales forecast?' That confidence will be transmitted to whoever you are turning to for financial support, making your case that much more convincing.

Given all of the above needs, a business plan typically addresses three questions:

- Where is the business now?
- Where is the business going in the future?
- How is it going to get there?

Writing a business plan is not a rigid one-off exercise, involving the manager of the business and a few 'back-of-an-envelope' calculations. It is an opportunity to investigate and assess the various directions open to the business and to select the course of action that should lead to the most beneficial results.

Every business can be said to be made up of three vital elements: the people, the idea and the money. It is therefore essential that you, the proprietor, write the narrative to your own business plan. An outsider will find it more difficult to capture your spontaneity and enthusiasm which, in many cases, will be critical to the success of the business plan. However, it is advisable to seek the professional advice of a firm of chartered accountants in pulling together the cash-flow forecasts and projections. Whilst the figures will be your projections, an independent professional adviser will ensure that the figures 'stack up' and link into the narrative of the business plan. The guidelines outlined below cover every possible aspect of business development. Some (for example those relating to the employment of staff) may not be relevant to your own circumstances. The outline should therefore be used selectively according to your own needs.

The format

A well-structured business plan will revolve around a carefully considered format. The plan should be easy to follow and cover all the key areas of the business. It is usually advisable to relegate all the actual forecasts and projections to the appendices, enabling a non-numerate person to read through the plan and get the feel of the purpose.

Any business plan should have a contents sheet at the front of the document, a typical example of which follows.

Case-study 7.1: Example of the contents sheet of a business plan

1. Introduction/overview
2. Corporate profile
   (a) Business objectives
   (b) Permanent information about the business
3. The product and/or service
4. The management
5. Market analysis and marketing
   (a) Industry description and outlook

(b) Target market
(c) Competition
(d) Marketing activities
6. Manufacturing and operational procedures
7. The People Plan
8. Finance requirement
9. Sensitivity analysis

Appendices

A. Cash-flow forecast for the first 12 months/2 years
B. Projected profit and loss account for the first 12 months/2 years
C. Projected balance sheet at the end of the first 12 months/2 years
D. Capital expenditure budget and method of finance
E. Assumptions made in the projections
F. Illustrations of the product and sales literature

1. *Introduction*

The introduction is possibly the most important page of the business plan, as it will explain the business aims and purpose of the plan.

This section can be written on one page and will provide a précis of the information to follow. Areas that are usually covered in the introduction are:

- your personal details;
- the business purpose;
- the geographical location of the premises;
- the product or service;
- the funding required.

2. *The profile of the business*

This section can be split into two sub-sections.

(a) **Business objectives**

The business objectives set out the direction of the business and establish a list of short-, medium- and long-term objectives aimed at achieving the ultimate corporate goal.

The objectives are better presented as a list and examples might be:

- To obtain the premises and develop and refurbish these into the desired business property.
- To purchase the business property ultimately.
- To develop a product superior in every way to its rivals.
- To market the product in a particular geographical location only.
- To build a good reputation for having a reasonably priced and reliable product or service.
- To expand the number of locations.
- To diversify into other products, services or businesses.
- To consolidate the business for the first '*y*' years and widen the number of services offered.
- To expand into export markets.
- To be considered as good employers.
- To share the success of the business with the people involved in making it a success.
- The return required on capital employed, i.e. a specific percentage required.

This list is not meant to be exhaustive; it is meant to act purely as a memory-jogger for the entrepreneur when preparing the business plan. The key point here is that objectives are set and that the plan is drawn up around achieving the objectives.

(b) **Permanent information about the business**

This sub-section illustrates all the permanent information about the business, and can be set out on one or two sheets. The information would usually be:

- The constitution of the business, i.e.
  – sole-tradership

– partnership
– limited company

- Names of owners/shareholders and directors.
- Name of the company secretary.
- Registered office address.
- Trading office address (if different from registered office).
- Company name and number.
- Trading name.
- Details of bankers.
- Details of solicitors.
- Details of accountants/auditors.

It is important that professional advice be sought when deciding upon the constitution of the business, i.e. sole-tradership, partnership or limited company, as each has different legal, accounting and taxation implications. It is vital for you to understand the differences and decide upon the appropriate constitution before preparing the business plan and commencing to trade.

3. *The product and/or service*

This section should define exactly what is to be developed and marketed. Its length will vary according to the number and complexity of the products and/or services planned, and it should be written in layman's language.

Other areas to be covered in this section will be:

- The specific characteristics of existing products and/or services.
- The features distinguishing your products and/or services from those of your competitors.
- Whether the products are, or should be, patented.
- Plans for the development of existing and new products.
- Superior product technology.

- Ease of use and versatility, or the ability to adapt quickly to customer needs.
- Low production costs, etc.
- Product life and adaptations to meet changing market needs.
- Details of any regulatory constraints, e.g. product approval procedures.
- Future developments with the possible emergence of competitive technologies.
- Research and development of new products, considering new technologies and scientific approaches that may become practical in the next five years.

With new products and technology, it is important to compare your future products with your competitors' future products rather than your future products with their existing products.

4. *The management*

In the early stages of a business, external investors (e.g. the banks, financial institutions and venture capitalists) are investing in the management of a business rather than the shell of the business. In practice, this means that your skills in managing, developing, executing and adapting appropriate plans to exploit the potential of the business are of great importance.

It is important, therefore, to communicate your managerial and technical skills and competence to the reader of the business plan. The best way to relate this information is by detailing the curriculum vitae (personal details) of everyone involved. Your track record and previous experience are critical to the success of the business and should therefore be identified in the business plan. Detailed c.v.s can either be set out in this section or included in the appendices to the business plan; this is entirely at your discretion. If the c.v. is included in the appendices, then Section (4) should concentrate on your achievements and experience relevant to achieving the business's objectives.

If you are starting the business with others, then details of all the people concerned should be included. Highlight roles and responsibilities as well as specific skills and experiences.

5. *Market analysis and marketing*

This section covers the marketing plan of the business. An effective marketing strategy should be based on:

(a) a review of the current position, both within the industry and within the company;
(b) the corporate objectives of the company;
(c) a consideration of the possible opportunities.

With a new business it is impossible to predict market-share potential from the size of the market, but it is possible to plan and establish the marketing approach of the business.

(a) **Industry description and outlook**
This sub-section is a useful introduction to the marketing plan, establishing the direction of the business from within the industry sector. Therefore definitions of the industry you are operating in, and the size of this industry and whether it is shrinking or expanding, are important when deciding upon the potential for your business.

The objective of an analysis of the industry and outlook for the future is to associate the reader with the nature and potential of the general market areas in which the company is operating. Points to cover will be the major trends in the industry, the key customers and any expected future changes in the above.

(b) **Target market**
Business development or marketing, in a very broad sense, can be defined as 'the management process responsible for identifying, anticipating and satisfying selected customer requirements profitably'. Consequently, a business needs to select with great care the target market that it will attempt to satisfy. You will need to demonstrate an understanding of the market and your particular niche within it. This understanding will require an analysis of the characteristics of the target market, e.g.

- the typical customer and his/her market-segment characteristics;
- the typical customer's requirements;
- typical order sizes;
- the buying habits of customers;
- seasonal or cyclical characteristics;
- benefits for the customer in using the product or service.

(c) **Competition**

An awareness of the competition should be demonstrated in the business plan, identifying who they are, who the market leaders are, and what can be learned from them. An assessment of the potential of the competition and a comparison of products and services should be illustrated showing the following:

- the geographical location of the competition;
- how successful they are;
- product and/or service attributes;
- pricing comparatives;
- delivery-period comparatives;
- the danger of future market entry by new competitors.

The strength of the competition can affect the prospects of any company, and a detailed analysis of the attributes of successful competitors (and the shortcomings of unsuccessful competition) should feature prominently in the business plan.

(d) **Marketing activities**

Sub-sections (a)–(c) above all revolve around the analysis of the current position and objectives of the company. This section forms the marketing strategy and concentrates upon reaching and communicating with the target market.

The main reason for communicating is to obtain publicity for the company and/or its products, hopefully leading to profitable sales. Effective publicity will arouse interest among potential customers, which can then be followed up by good 'selling', to achieve profitable sales as efficiently as possible.

It is important to decide upon your sales objectives before setting the publicity objectives. For example, it may be that a 'hit list' of key customers is drawn up and that the publicity is centred around reaching and communicating with that market segment.

An analysis of the target market, linked to the results of market research and the buying habits of the customers, will give critical clues as to the structuring of the marketing activities, i.e. is the price or the quality more important? Stress safety/reliability, etc.

The business plan should set out the respective media to be used in attempting to communicate with the target market. Examples of some of the most common methods of obtaining publicity are set out below:

- **Advertising:** The advertising policy may be advised by an independent advertising agency; however, if embarking on this marketing activity without agency advice, state in the business plan the respective media to be used, i.e. newspapers, television, radio, magazines/periodicals, technical press, poster campaign, the cinema. If an actual campaign has been planned, then a précis of this should appear in the plan.
- **Direct mail:** This can often produce effective results when combined with advertising or exhibitions.
- **Sales literature:** Well-structured sales brochures and other literature are important. Both this literature and direct mailers can be included in the appendices if applicable.
- **Exhibitions:** Often an expensive way to communicate with the customers, but nevertheless an important medium. The business plan may include notable exhibition dates.
- **Public Relations:** A 'free' press release can often prove to be an effective form of publicity.

A secondary marketing activity can be corporate image. A good image, well communicated, can be as effective as an advertising campaign. This area can cover everything from the helpful telephonist to the after-sales service and product support. In the modern times of high technology, marginal price differences on products can be ignored in favour of product support and back-up.

The business plan will also identify the selling activities of the business within this section, and the methods and approach should be documented, i.e. whether sales representation is necessary and, if so, geographical locations, etc.

The importance of a well-structured market analysis and marketing section within any business plan cannot be over-emphasized. You should therefore devote an appropriate amount of time to its consideration. The marketing plan may well be prepared as a separate document and only parts of it included in the business plan. Whichever way it is provided, it must be covered.

6. *Manufacturing and operational procedures*

Whilst considering the marketing of the products and/or services and the sales projections of the business, it is essential to review the manufacturing side of the business if applicable. For example, can you produce the volume of goods that you intend to sell? For a manufacturing concern, it is useful to establish within the business the following factors:

- Whether a manufacturing or assembling process is to be adopted by the business.
- Whether any of the products will be manufactured or assembled by external sub-contractors.
- The productivity effect and profitability effect of both the above.
- Overtime working plans.
- The production capacity of the business from its current premises.
- Future growth in production capacity through new technology or obtaining larger premises.
- Any production or operating advantages you have over your competitors.
- The product life – which will also determine the useful life of specialist jigs, etc.

- The useful life of the equipment and machinery and whether this was purchased new or secondhand.
- The procedure for scheduling, costing and planning production.
- The system for monitoring production.
- The projected lead-time between receiving and delivering an order.
- The quality control system.
- The purchasing of materials and buying controls.

Again this list is not meant to be exhaustive but to act purely as a memory-jogger when writing the manufacturing section of the plan.

Operationally, the hours of work and projected normal level of production hours should be illustrated, together with the procedures and controls to be followed in manufacturing and stock control, particularly when considering raw materials, work-in-progress and finished goods. Obviously, if the business is to start with the owner-manager performing all duties, then the system of control and costing, etc., needs to be less elaborate. However, it is important to plan and instigate the appropriate systems initially for the business to grow into.

For a non-manufacturing business, this section will cover the purchasing of products and services and operational procedures from customer order through to eventual delivery. The degree of control is just as important in a non-manufacturing operation, and initial constraints will probably centre around the working capital of the business, i.e. a limitation of stocks due to credit periods allowed by suppliers and credit periods offered to customers. Other constraints to be discussed in the plan are:

- storage;
- transport;
- administration.

It may be that external third parties are to be used for storage and transport, but the administration function rests in the hands of the entrepreneur.

A strong administration side to the business will ensure that effective systems are implemented and controls enforced. This business plan should cover the following administration elements:

- the accounting system;
- sales order processing;
- the purchasing controls and documentation;
- the wages and salaries functions;
- the frequency and type of management reports, including management accounting.

Efficient production and operational procedures will be major factors in the success of any business. Many businesses starting 'on a shoestring' will have insufficient funds available to set up a full in-house manufacturing system. The important thing is to start at a simple enough level and to try not to do everything in-house from the first day of operation. Different approaches to producing the same product will result in different labour and material costs, needing differing amounts of working capital and investment in plant, leading to different levels of profit. Whatever methods you select to begin with can be changed and developed as sales increase and profits are generated.

7. The People Plan

As a supplement to the management section, 'the People Plan' will identify the staffing infrastructure of the business. When 'starting a business on a shoestring' the careful selection of key personnel is essential to the success of the business.

This section will cover the numbers of employees required and the function each will perform within the business. If possible, this would be better illustrated by way of an organization chart showing clearly defined levels of responsibility and channels of communication.

As the business grows, there will be a need for further employees, and these should be planned and identified in the plan accordingly.

The hours of work should be set out and rates of pay, etc., detailed. Other considerations for this section are:

- Recruitment methods and descriptions of the people you are looking for.
- Possible training schemes.
- Wages/salary increases and how they will be assessed.
- Other factors affecting skills and skill costs.

8. *Finance requirement*

The completion of this section will come after the cash-flow forecasts and financial data in the appendices have been completed. The bottom line of the cash-flow forecast will show the maximum finance required; it will also illustrate the month that it will be required in. Reference should be made to the cash-flow forecast in the appendices so that the reader can trace back to the build-up of the financial requirement, if necessary.

This section will cover the initial finance requirement, together with any future requirements after the foreseeable (next five) years. It can make reference to how these funds will be used and how the overall debt is to be structured. Projecting beyond a 12-month period is always very difficult and it is useful to emphasize that any projected borrowings beyond 12 months are forecast on a general basis and subject to change.

The finance requirement should show the total cost of starting the business and how this cost is to be met, i.e. what element relates to the capital introduced by the entrepreneur, how much is required from the bank, what level of debt will be required from other financial institutions.

If equity is to be forgone, the amounts should be quantified and the intended external shareholders indicated. This section will state how the borrowings are to be repaid and over what period they are to be borrowed, i.e. whether the entrepreneur is seeking short-term or long-term borrowings.

Should an overdraft be required from the bank, then the size of this facility will be indicated in the cash-flow forecast. Moreover, the cash-flow forecast will show the expected monthly movements in the bank overdraft/balance.

It is useful to extract key financial information from the projections in the appendices to supplement this section, and this can act as an *aide-mémoire* to the reader:

From projected profit and loss account:

- Projected turnover for first 12 months
- Projected gross profit
- Projected gross profit percentage
- Projected overheads
- Projected net profit
- Projected net profit percentage

From projected balance sheet:

- Projected net assets at end of Year 1
- Projected borrowings at end of Year 1

If any of the assets are to be financed on hire-purchase, then this should be stated in this section, as all borrowings have a bearing on the business. Gearing can be loosely described as the relationship of external borrowings of a company to the capital introduced by the entrepreneur.

Should any of the assets be leased, then this should be mentioned because such borrowings constitute what is known as 'off balance sheet' financing, since the assets are treated purely as hired and appear only in the profit and loss account of the business.

9. *Sensitivity analysis*
(how changes can affect the business)

It is important to know how vulnerable the forecasts are so that risks are appreciated and potential problems anticipated. One essential attribute of a good business plan lies in establishing that you are aware of all the potential pitfalls and can react appropriately to minimize their effects, should they occur.

One method often used to demonstrate that risk has been taken into account is sensitivity analysis work. This section therefore provides certain analyses of the projections, showing how changes in them can affect the business; for example, the effect on the business if there were to be a reduction in the projected level of sales or an increase in the level of overheads. It may be useful to consider the effect of such a shortfall in sales (or indeed a capital overspend), and to have contingency plans available should these circumstances arise.

The sensitivity analysis section tends to 'prove' that the figures make sense, and this generates the confidence of any financial backers – especially if it can be shown that the absolute or relative failure of one project or one area within the business will not bring the whole business down with it.

The sensitivity analysis should be presented in brief summary form, leaving the detailed calculations out of the actual business plan. One useful form of sensitivity analysis is break-even analysis, which shows by what margin the key factors can change before the business will break even.

To familiarize the reader of the business plan with the figures, an extract of the projected profit and loss account is shown in this section of the plan. The extract will usually take the following format:

Shoestring Business Limited

Extract of projected profit and loss account for the year ended 31 December 19*yy*

	£	£	
Sales		xxxxxx	(A)
Cost of sales		xxxxxx	(B)
Gross profit		xxxxxx	(C)
Gross profit percentage		xx%	(D)
Wages	xxxxx		(E)
Other overheads	xxxxx		(F)
		xxxxx	(G)
Net profit		£xxxxx	(H)
Net profit percentage		xx%	

From this extract the sensitivity analysis will be carried out as follows:

For the company to break even, the gross profit (C) would equal the wages and other overheads (G). Assuming a fixed gross profit percentage (D), then the gross profit (C) divided by the gross profit percentage (D) will give the sales figure (A). Therefore, to break even, if wages and other overheads (G) are divided by the gross profit percentage (D), then the break-even sales figure will be given.

The sensitivity of this figure can be calculated as a percentage reduction, i.e.

$$\frac{\text{Original sales} - \text{break-even sales} \times 100\%}{\text{Original sales}}$$

This gives the percentage reduction in original projected sales to break even. If this percentage is low (say 5 per cent), then the projected sales are very sensitive to reductions. If the percentage is high (say 50 per cent), then the projected sales are not very sensitive to reductions; indeed the sales can fall by half and the business would still break even.

Other key factors to analyse are as follows:

- increases in cost of sales;
- reductions in gross profit percentage;
- increases in wages;
- increases in other overheads.

This section is fairly complicated and is difficult to demonstrate. If you are in any doubt about your figures, the advice of a chartered accountant should be sought. Such professional advice is recommended in validating the financial data before approaching the relevant financial institutions.

When carrying out sensitivity analysis work, the theoretical side often overcomes the practical side and too many figures are generated. This is something to beware of when compiling the data.

The example above considers the effect of changes on one figure only. It may well be the case that several figures change at once and the interrelationship of those changes should be considered when calculating the sensitivity. For example, it may be that sales could fall by 20 per cent before a business reached break-even. If a reduction of sales was linked to a reduction in gross profit percentage and an increase in overheads, the same sales may need to fall by only as little as 5 per cent before the business reached a break-even position.

It would therefore appear that this type of analysis work would lend itself well to a spreadsheet package on a microcomputer. However, too much sensitivity analysis can be as bad as too little if the assumptions used have little chance of happening in real life. The use of a spreadsheet financial modelling package is advisable also for preparing cash-flow forecasts linked to projected profit and loss accounts and balance sheets. If any of your forecasts are at all complex, this method can save enormous time and effort, while at the same time enabling you to examine more plans and variations than if you had to do it all by hand.

Summary of the narrative section and style

When the sensitivity analysis section has been written, there is no further narrative necessary for the business plan. The remaining part of the plan is contained in the appendices and comprises the financial data.

It is useful at this stage to review the text of the business plan to date in order to consider the style and approach to writing it. If you rigidly follow the foregoing sections then your business plan could end up being too long and indigestible. Therefore only write about the areas that apply to your business and try to address the key issues. The narrative should be well structured and designed and, if brevity aids clarity, then it should be as short as possible. The key phrase to consider when writing the business plan is 'Think of the reader'. To this end, it is often advantageous to get your supporter to read and review the document at regular stages.

Cash-flow forecasts (Appendix A)

The purpose of the cash-flow forecast is to show the cash effect of the sales, purchase and overheads forecasts. It is a statement of cash receipts and payments over a projected time-period. The usual time-period is 12 months, although it can vary from 12 months to five years.

In simple terms, the cash-flow forecast is a projection of the likely movements in the bank account over a given period of time. As the forecast is usually constructed on a monthly basis, then the bank balance can be projected only as at the end of each month.

The construction of the cash-flow forecast involves several stages; the best place to start is by deciding upon the time-period concerned, i.e. when the receipts and payments are to commence and when the 12-month period will end.

Sales projections. The sales projections are the first stage in compiling the forecast. This is relatively easy: simply project from month 1 up to and including month 12 the likely sales (excluding VAT), allowing for seasonal variations. See Table 7.1(A) for a projected sales forecast.

Cost of sales. The next stage is to project the cost of sales. Assuming a fixed gross profit percentage, this figure can be accurately projected on a monthly basis. Table 7.1(B) shows a cost of sales forecast assuming a 30 per cent gross profit, i.e. cost of sales are 70 per cent of the sales figure at Table 7.1(A).

Forecasting gross profit. The third stage is to perform a gross profit forecast by bringing together the sales and cost of sales forecasts (see Table 7.1(C)).

Forecasting overheads. The fourth stage is to produce an overheads forecast. This shows the overheads costs which must be incurred in order to achieve the forecast level of sales.

Having completed the initial four stages of forecasting, the background information will have been collected for the preparation of the cash-flow forecast.

To illustrate how these all fit together, we have constructed a hypothetical set of figures for an entrepreneur who is starting a business with £15,000 of capital. We have assumed that his business will make a 30 per cent gross margin by purchasing and reselling a product. The example is illustrated by following the key steps in preparing a cash-flow forecast and consists of a series of points in narrative form (they follow directly), plus four financial example sheets:

- Table 7.1: A: Sales forecast
  B: Cost of sales forecast
  C: Gross profit forecast
- Table 7.2: Cash-flow forecast
- Table 7.3: Projected profit and loss account
- Table 7.4: Balance sheet

Steps in preparing a cash-flow forecast

1. From the sales forecast (Table 7.1(A)), a customer credit period should be decided. The usual trading credit is 30 days. While 30 days may well be the terms of credit of the business, many customers will take longer than this period to pay, some will take less. As a cash-flow forecast should be drawn up on a pessimistic basis, Table 7.2 assumes the debtors will take 60 days on average to pay for their goods. Therefore the £3,000 for sales in January are not expected to be received until March, etc. At the end of December, the outstanding debtors appearing on the balance sheet (Example 7.4) will represent the sales from November and December.

2. We have just made an assumption of a 60-day debtors' collection-period, so the next step is to record this on a separate list and start a schedule of assumptions to be updated as the cash-flow forecast is prepared.

3. Working down the cash-flow forecast line by line, the only other item of income to the business will be the capital introduced by the entrepreneur, being £15,000 in January. It is essential that the entrepreneur introduces his capital, however small, at the initial stages of the business, because any bank or financier will wish to see a commitment from the entrepreneur.

4. The income from sales is then added to the capital introduced to give a total income row.

5. Moving on to the payments side of the cash flow, the next step is to apply the trade credit period allowed by suppliers to the forecast 'cost of sales' figures at Example 7.1(B). In the cash-flow forecast, a 30-day credit period has been assumed, so January purchases will be paid for in February, etc.

6. 'Purchases for stock' are an area often overlooked by people starting a business. The example shows a £5,000 stock level being purchased, £3,000 in January and £2,000 in February, and paid for in February and March respectively.

7. Wages and NI Contributions. This line shows two persons working within the business. The entrepreneur initially starting on a salary of £6,000 p.a. (i.e. £500 per month plus 10.45 per cent employer's NI Contribution = £552) from January to May. In June an assistant is projected at £3,000 p.a. (i.e. £250 per month plus employer's NI Contribution at 10.45 per cent = £276.)

8. The rent and rates have been estimated on a small office premises, being a £750 per quarter all-inclusive charge for rent and rates by the landlord.

9. The insurance premium of £600 p.a. has been negotiated with the broker to be paid over five monthly instalments of £120 from January to May.

10. An estimate for repairs and maintenance has been made at £50 per month. No credit period has been assumed. All purchases paid for in the month of purchase.

11. Carriage has been assumed to vary directly with sales, and a figure of 5 per cent of sales value has been included in the cash-flow forecast. This again has been pessimistically assumed to be paid in the month of purchase. In practice, a period of credit would be expected.

12. Other overheads such as motor expenses, printing and stationery, advertising, telephone and postage, bank charges and sundries are self-explanatory and assumed to be paid in the month of purchase.

13. Professional fees assumes the preparation of quarterly management accounts by the entrepreneur's accountants to monitor performance.

14. Capital expenditure has assumed a van for £2,000 and £4,000 for fixtures, fittings and equipment in January and £2,000 of equipment in February.

15. The expenditure lines are all totalled to give a total expenditure row.

16. The expenditure row is then deducted from the income row to give a net monthly figure.

17. As all the above figures have been calculated excluding VAT, account has to be taken of this figure as it can have a serious effect on cash flow. The example assumes for simplicity that VAT is accounted for on a cash basis, i.e. upon cash received and paid, rather than on an invoice basis. Output tax is calculated at 15 per cent of the income from sales. Input tax is calculated at 15 per cent on the following items of expenditure:

- purchases for resale
- purchases for stock
- repairs and maintenance
- carriage
- motor expenses
- printing and stationery
- advertising
- telephone
- professional fees
- sundries
- capital expenditure

18. The repayments/(payments) line accounts for the projected monies to be received from or paid to HM Customs and Excise on a quarterly basis (outputs less inputs). The heavy initial expenditure in the first three months on stock, purchases and capital expenditure linked with a low level of income from sales shows a repayment from HM Customs and Excise due in April of £3,407. All following periods are payments and, as at 31 December, the amount owing to HM Customs and Excise as a creditor is the output tax less the input tax for October, November and December.

19. The next step shows how we reach a net flow position on the statement. Add the 'Income-Expenditure' figure to the output tax, deduct the input tax, and either add any repayments or deduct any payments to reach a net flow position.

20. Bank interest should then be calculated on any overdraft outstanding. The example has assumed a rate of 14 per cent, i.e. a base rate of 11 per cent plus 3 per cent. Bank interest has been calculated on a quarterly basis as the average of the opening balance at the beginning of the quarter and the closing balance at the end of the quarter, multiplied by the rate of interest and divided by 4 to represent a quarterly charge. This is an approximate method. In practice, interest accrues on a daily basis on the outstanding balance and is charged every quarter.

In the example, the interest at March is calculated as follows:

			£
Opening balance			Nil
Closing balance	−5023 − 9010	=	−14033.00
			−14033.00
Average =	$\frac{-14033}{2}$	=	−7016.50
Interest for 12 months	$\frac{-7016.5 \times 14}{\%}$	=	982.00
Interest for 3 months	$\frac{982}{4}$	=	246.00

21. The final step is the cumulative monthly bank balance which is calculated as the balance of the previous month added to the net flow of the current month, adjusting for any bank interest charged in the month.

The cumulative bank balance shows the expected balance at the end of the month. In the example, the maximum overdraft required is £14,357 in May. The entrepreneur would therefore approach the bank and request a £15,000 overdraft facility to cover all eventualities.

A useful exercise to review the arithmetic of the cash-flow forecast is to check that the closing balance at the end of December (an overdraft of £644) is the same as the final figure in the total column (−£644). If it isn't, a mistake has been made somewhere through the forecast.

NOTE: If extensive capital expenditure is being incurred in developing and refurbishing premises, then it may be necessary to prepare a separate three- or four-month cash-flow forecast showing the likely effect on cash flow of this expenditure prior to trade commencing.

Projected profit and loss account (Appendix B)

The information for the projected profit and loss account is drawn from the sales, purchases and cash-flow forecasts excluding VAT (see Table 7.3).

The one additional figure added in Table 7.3 is depreciation, which is a provision in the accounts to allow for the wearing-out of the assets. In the table, £1100 depreciation has been calculated as follows:

	£
Fixtures, fittings and equipment £6000 × 10%	600.00
Motor vehicle £2000 × 25%	500.00
	£1100.00

The net profit of £21175 shows a respectable return for the first year's trading.

Projected balance sheet (Appendix C)

Once the cash-flow forecast and profit and loss account have been prepared, it is a fairly simple matter to prepare the projected balance sheet at the end forecast period. The balance sheet is also a self-checking statement, as the balancing of this document proves the foregoing figures. If the balance sheet does not balance, then a mistake has been made.

- Fixed assets are taken from the cash-flow forecast capital expenditure line (£8000) and depreciation is deducted (£8000 – £1100 = £6900).
- Stock is the closing stock at the end of the period, which in the example is £5000 in the profit and loss account.
- Debtors are those sales not yet received. In the example November sales of £20000 plus December sales of £18000 = £38000.
- Creditors are those purchases not yet paid for. In the example, these are December sales of £12600.
- The VAT creditor is the outputs less inputs for October, November and December from the cash-flow forecast.
- The capital introduced is the £15000 from the cash-flow forecast.
- The profit and loss account is the net profit from that statement.

The balance sheet total is otherwise known as the 'net assets' and the bankers and financiers tend to place a certain amount of importance on this projected figure.

A schedule of assumptions made in the projections should be appended, setting out (as previously described) all assumptions made.

Having reviewed the financial sheets and the key points made in the cash-flow example, return to the business plan contents sheet (page 189). Start to make notes on the major headings – don't try to dot all the i's and cross all the t's but simply write down your initial thoughts and ideas.

Table 7.1.

(A) Sales forecast
For year ended 31 December 19*YY*

	Jan	Feb	Mar	Apr	May	Jun	Jul	Aug	Sep	Oct	Nov	Dec	Total
Sales (£) (exc. VAT)	3000	8000	12000	15000	20000	18000	16000	13000	13000	16000	20000	18000	172000

(B) Cost of sales forecast
For year ended 31 December 19*YY*

	Jan	Feb	Mar	Apr	May	Jun	Jul	Aug	Sep	Oct	Nov	Dec	Total
Cost of sales (£) (exc. VAT)	2100	5600	8400	10500	14000	12600	11200	9100	9100	11200	14000	12600	120400

(C) Gross profit forecast
For year ended 31 December 19*YY*

	Jan	Feb	Mar	Apr	May	Jun	Jul	Aug	Sep	Oct	Nov	Dec	Total
Sales (£) (exc. VAT)	3000	10000	13000	17000	20000	18000	14000	13000	13000	16000	20000	18000	175000
Cost of sales (£) (exc. VAT)	2100	7000	9100	11900	14000	12600	9800	9100	9100	11200	14000	12600	122500
Gross profit	900	3000	3900	5100	6000	5400	4200	3900	3900	4800	6000	5400	52500

Table 7.2. Cash flow forecast
For year ended 31 December 19*YY*

	Jan	Feb	Mar	Apr	May	Jun	Jul	Aug	Sep	Oct	Nov	Dec	Total
Income (£)													
From sales			3000	10000	13000	17000	20000	18000	14000	13000	13000	16000	137000
Capital introduced	15000												15000
Total income	15000	0	3000	10000	13000	17000	20000	18000	14000	13000	13000	16000	152000
Expenditure (£)													
Purchases for resale		2100	7000	9100	11900	14000	12600	9800	9100	9100	11200	14000	109900
Purchases for stock		3000	2000										5000
Wages & NI contributions	552	552	552	552	552	828	828	828	828	828	828	828	8556
Rent & rates	750			750			750			750			3000
Insurance	120	120	120	120	120								600
Repairs & maintenance	50	50	50	50	50	50	50	50	50	50	50	50	600
Carriage	150	500	650	850	1000	900	700	650	650	800	1000	900	8750
Motor expenses	250	250	250	250	250	250	250	250	250	250	250	250	3000
Printing & stationery	300				100				100				500
Advertising	400	100	100	100	100	100	100	100	100	100	100	100	1500
Telephone & postage	320	20	20	140	20	20	170	20	20	200	20	20	990
Professional fees				200			200			200			600
Bank charges			150			150			150			150	600
Sundries	50	50	50	50	50	50	50	50	50	50	50	50	600
Capital expenditure	6000	2000											8000
Total expenditure	8942	8742	10942	12162	14142	16348	15698	11748	11298	12328	13498	16348	152196
Income – Expenditure	6058	−8742	−7942	−2162	−1142	652	4302	6252	2702	672	−498	−348	−196
VAT: Output tax			450	1500	1950	2550	3000	2700	2100	1950	1950	2400	20550
Input tax	1128	1211	1518	1611	2021	2306	2118	1638	1548	1613	1901	2306	20916
Repayments/(payments)				3407			−63			−2496			848
Net flow	4930	−9953	−9010	1134	−1213	897	5121	7314	3254	−1487	−449	−254	286
Bank interest 14%			−246			−485			−214			15	−929
Bank balance	4930	−5023	−14278	−13145	−14357	−13946	−8825	−1511	1529	43	−406	−644	−644

Table 7.3. Projected profit and loss account

For year ended 31 December 19*YY*

	£	£
Sales		175000
Purchases	127500	
Less: closing stock	5000	
Cost of sales		122500
Gross profit 30%		52500
Less: Overheads		
Wages and NI contributions	8556	
Rent and rates	3000	
Insurance	600	
Repairs and maintenance	600	
Carriage	8750	
Motor expenses	3000	
Printing and stationery	500	
Advertising	1500	
Telephone and postage	990	
Professional fees	600	
Bank charges	600	
Bank interest	929	
Depreciation	1100	
Sundries	600	
		31325
Net profit		£21175

Table 7.4. Balance sheet

as at 31 December 19*YY*

	£	£
Fixed assets		6900
Current assets		
Stock	5000	
Debtors	38000	
	43000	
Current liabilities		
Creditors	12600	
VAT	482	
Bank overdraft	644	
	13725	
Net current assets		29275
Net assets		36175
Represented by:		
Capital introduced		15000
Profit and loss account		21175
Net assets		36175

From this intuitive start, consider the following before you go on to do any more work.

Some points to consider now

- Have I identified any areas where I just don't have the information? List them.
- Have I started to identify the types of assumptions that I will have to make, e.g. time-scales, judgements about costs, assessments on wages, etc.? List them.
- What information do I have and what questions does it raise? List them.

Action

- Referring to your lists, who can help you collect and refine the information required? Start talking to relevant people: the bank, an accountant, a business adviser (the Small Firms Service, a representative of a business association/chamber of commerce/enterprise agency), relevant contacts and friends.
- Decide on how you are going to go on to the next stage: the preparation of your own detailed business plan. You could use the format provided here or, alternatively, you could:
  - use an approach suggested by an accountant;
  - use a business package provided by your bank. All the major banks have produced business start-up materials, and it is worth reviewing them;
  - simply enrol yourself on a business start-up course, use your basic material and fit it into whatever method is being used.

Approaches may differ but the end results will not vary greatly – any differences will be more to do with emphasis, degree of detail and presentation format.

Whatever you decide upon, do make sure that you take advice before entering into any firm contractual or financial arrangements.

Simplifying the business plan

It is very difficult for us to try and simplify the business plan, as we are writing a book to cover many different readers and many different kinds of business. The key for you to follow is to concentrate on the basic contents sheet and produce a little narrative on each heading, using the text already written as an *aide-mémoire*.

Three symbols are provided below to assist you in deciding what type of action to take:

Action category

+ Thought process
› Action process
* Seek professional advice

A guide to preparing a business plan

Steps:

1. Decide upon the type of business. +
2. Decide upon the geographical location. +
3. Find the appropriate premises/outlet. ›
4. Carry out market research activities, e.g. demand, competition, pricing, etc. ›
5. Ascertain the amount of capital you have available to introduce to the business. + *
6. Decide upon your business objectives. +
7. Consider the legal structure of your business, e.g. sole trader/partnership/limited company. + *
8. Ask yourself why you will do well in this particular business. What is so good about your product/service? +
9. Do you have a market niche? If so, exploit it. +
10. Identify your target market. +
11. Prepare your marketing plan, showing how you are going to reach your target market. › *
12. Plan the manufacturing and operating procedures. + › *

13. Decide upon the number of employees you will need. +
14. Decide upon the fixed assets required and the cost of this capital expenditure. +
15. Start to prepare draft budgets and cash-flow forecasts for the business, noting any assumptions made. › *
16. Write the business plan and set out the finance required to fund the business. › *
17. Inquire about any government or local authority grants before entering into any transactions or agreements to purchase assets, take on premises or employees. › *

Summary

- The preparation of your business plan will help you to answer the critical questions: 'Is this business viable?', 'Can I make the return that I want from it?'
- The way in which you set up your business is important and one in which you will need to take advice. The main forms are:
  - sole trader
  - partnership
  - limited company

  The form of business start-up will affect not only the business plan in terms of the way it should be developed, presented and resourced, but will also have legal and personal business tax implications.
- The business plan is a reflection not just of facts but also of business assumptions and personal views.
- The plan will reflect you, your personality, skills and experiences and your motivation to make the business succeed. An important element is the details concerning you, together with your business objective.
- Business planning advice is available from a variety of experienced sources; do make sure that you use it.

8 *Reviewing Your Business Development*

You may feel that, once the initial business planning for your enterprise is completed and you have raised the necessary finance to enable you to start trading, the whole question of financial review and control can be dropped until you have built up a regular stream of business.

This a common, but classic, mistake. Once you start trading, become fully involved in meeting deadlines and are confronted by day-to-day administrative difficulties, keeping track of your financial targets will often become impossible. As we saw earlier (see page 113), bad financial administration is responsible for more business bankruptcy than any other factor.

The message is therefore quite simple. *Before* you start trading, you should set up some basic but key procedures to help you monitor performance and control of your operation. By this means, you can compare actual progress against the targets set out in your business plan. A failure to meet essential targets can therefore be spotted quickly and corrective action taken to bring your performance in line.

The system you design need not be very complex. It should involve a process which:

- you understand (even if you do not have a financial background);
- fits the needs of your business;
- is simple to operate and does not take up too much of your time.

As your business grows, and you can afford to 'buy in' or employ greater financial expertise, you can add more sophisticated methods of financial control. For the moment, however, you need a system which will simply give you the security of having your immediate financial position at your fingertips.

Designing your financial control systems

Before you set up your system, it is important that you discuss with your financial adviser(s) what elements of information your system should highlight. Common systems used by small businesses include:

- a cash-flow forecast;
- a debtor/creditor list;
- a working capital requirement sheet;
- a profit and loss account.

The following sections cover ways in which you can monitor your business week by week, month by month, or year by year.

Weekly control – an example

Jeff and Mike started a small business called Word Processing Training Services (WPTS). Neither of the partners had any formal financial training – only the budget experience acquired through working in management positions in a large company.

They both identified that they must keep tabs on the business in the early growth stages, having heard many disaster stories due to failure to control costs and getting the cash flow out of phase. They worked out the following weekly control sheet to be produced at the close of business early Friday night.

Week No. .... *Date* ....

		£
(1) Last statement date	No	Amount ....
(2) Cheques/DDs not on statement	....	
(3) (see explanation		....
(4) Deposits banked, not on statement	....	
(5) (see explanation)		....
(6) Purchase invoices outstanding	....	

(7) (see explanation) ....
(8) Total of outstanding sales invoices ....
(9) (see explanation) =======

The Weekly reconciliation sheet explained

(1) Take your last bank statement figure.
(2) Total the cheques and direct debits not cleared through the statement.
(3) Add or subtract (1) and (2), depending upon whether the original balance was positive or negative.
(4) Total the deposits not cleared through the statement.
(5) Add or subtract (3) and (4).
(6) This is the total of all your outstanding *purchase* invoices.
(7) Add or subtract (5) and (6).
(8) This is the total of all your outstanding *sales* invoices.
(9) Add or subtract (7) and (8).

The cumulative total at Step 9 tells you that, if all the purchases were paid and all the sales received, your end figure or business position would = £......... as at the end of that particular week.

The system is illustrated by the following two examples. The first highlights an overdraft account.

Example 8.1. *Overdraft account*

Week y				*Date*..................
				£
(1)			Amount	3750.00 O/D
(2)		2162.00	add	
	(3)		,,	5912.00 O/D
(4)		4750.00	subtract	
	(5)		,,	1162.00 O/D
(6)		1325.00	add	
	(7)		,,	2487.00 O/D
(8)		7965.00	Subtract	
	(9)		,,	£5478.00

The second highlights a normal credit account.

Example 8.2. *Normal credit account*

Week y Date.................

				£
(1)			Amount	4625.00
(2)		3162.00	subtract	
	(3)		,,	1463.00
(4)		3750.00	add	
	(5)		,,	5213.00
(6)		2165.00	subtract	
	(7)		,,	3048.00
(8)		8260.00	add	
	(9)		,,	£11308.00

Monitoring your finances

A monthly review

A weekly summary will give you a 'snapshot' of your immediate cash flow. However it is clearly important to summarize your total business performance in order to obtain a broader picture of the flow between your revenue and your costs. The key data are summarized below.

A monthly financial monitor

Date

	Month		*Year to date*	
(A) Sales (exc. VAT)	£		£	
(B) Cost of sales (exc. VAT)	£		£	
(C) Gross profit	£		£	
(D) Gross profit %age ((C) ÷ (A) × 100)		%		%
(E) Reconciled bank balance/(overdraft)	£		£	
(F) Stock and work-in-progress	£		£	
(G) Debtors	£		£	
(H) Average collection period (debtors at end of period × no. of days in period ÷ Sales for period (inc. VAT)		days		days
(I) Creditors	£		£	
(J) Average payment period (Creditors at end of period × no. of days in period ÷ Purchases for period (inc. VAT)		days		days
(K) Wages and NI contribution	£		£	
(L) Wages and NI contribution as %age of sales ((K) ÷ (A) × 100)		%		%
(M) Bad debts	£		£	
(N) Key overheads	£		£	

The monthly financial monitor should give an overview of the business at the end of each month, although for it to be effective it must be timely and accurate.

Another useful document for controlling the cash of the business is an accurate list of debtors. This list can be set out as follows:

Name of debtor	*Total*	*1 month*	*2 months*	*3 months*	*Over 3 months*
	£	£	£	£	£
ABC Ltd	100.00		100.00		
DEF Ltd	250.00	100.00	50.00	50.00	50.00
GHI Ltd	2000.00	500.00	1500.00		
JKL Ltd	60.00			60.00	
MNO Ltd	400.00	400.00			
PQR Ltd	500.00				500.00
	3310.00	1000.00	1650.00	110.00	550.00

Such a list will help you to concentrate collection efforts on the appropriate debts.

Monitoring your finances

A quarterly review

All of the information you have gathered can be summarized on a quarterly basis, using the two model charts set out below.

When monitoring your financial control sheets, it is always important regularly to ask yourself the following questions:

- In your trading calculations, are you on target with the projections you made in your business plan?
- Does your gross profit margin agree with your projections or is it necessary to make adjustments?
- Does your profit and loss account compare well with the cash-flow forecasts in your business plan? Are adjustments necessary?

Example 8.3. A working capital assessment sheet

Date

	Month 1	*Month 2*	*Month 3*
Current assets			
Reconciled bank balance credit	£	£	£
+ Debtors	£	£	£
+ Stock/work-in-progress	£	£	£
= Total current assets (A)	£	£	£
Current liabilities			
Reconciled bank balance overdraft	£	£	£
+ Creditors	£	£	£
= Total current liabilities (B)	£	£	£
Working capital (A) – (B)	£	£	£

Example 8.4. A profit and loss assessment sheet

Date

Profit

Trading account

Sales		£
Opening stock	£	
+ Purchases	£	
	£	
– Closing stock	£	£
		£
– Direct labour costs		£
= Gross profit		£

Gross profit margin

Gross profit £ × 100%=
Sales £

Profit and loss account

Gross profit		£
Salaries (including your own drawings)	£	
+ Light & heat	£	
+ Insurance	£	
+ Rates	£	
+ Repairs	£	
+ Advertising	£	
+ Bank Int./HP	£	
+ Rent	£	
+ Tel./post	£	
+ Other expenses (e.g. depreciation of fixed assets)	£	£
= Net profit		£

You will also need to decide, from the outset, to what extent you will handle your own book-keeping and to what extent you will rely on outside help. The key questions to consider are:

- Have you the experience to undertake all the work yourself?
- If not, will you rely on a book-keeper to monitor your finances:
  – every week;
  – every month;
  – every quarter?
- How much will this cost?

Assessing your business

A quarterly review

Regular business reviews do not just involve an assessment of your financial performance. They are also necessary to assess:

- where you are now;
- the direction you are travelling in;
- the means you will employ to get there.

Without returning regularly to your basic objectives, it can become very easy to drift, as you are caught up in an uncontrollable sea of business activity.

The following checklist will help you to focus on the key elements of a general business review. You should run through the questions that are relevant to your own business every quarter if possible and certainly every six months.

Reviewing the business: a general checklist

(a) Review business objectives:
- Have any of these been achieved?

- Have any of these changed?

Action – update the business objectives and amend business plan accordingly.

(b) Review the product and/or service:
- Are they up to date?
- What is your policy for developing existing and new products or services?

(c) Review the marketing plan:
- Has your target market changed?
- Are you reaching your target?
- How effective are your marketing activities?
- How are your competitors performing by comparison with yourself?

(d) Review the People Plan (if this is relevant):
- Do you have the right people performing the right jobs?
- Are your employees suitably motivated?
- Are you using your time efficiently and effectively?
- Is there a regular performance review process?

(e) Review the working capital requirement:
- Is the overdraft facility sufficient?
- Is the business under-capitalized?
- Is the business generating sufficient profits?
- Are you carrying too much stock?
- Are debtors too high? Is there a long collection period?
- Are you under pressure from creditors?
- Is the load of work-in-progress too high?

Assessing your business

An annual review

At the end of your first year of trading, apart from congratulating yourself and your family, you should take the opportunity to make a major review of your performance. If you are not in the trading position you had projected in your original business plan, you should take a close look at the reasons why.

The checklists below will help you to do so in a systematic manner. They cover three main areas:

– business description;
– business organization;
– business performance.

The questions draw on many of the issues already covered in this book (so they should be familiar by now). Not all of them will be relevant to your own business and they should be used more as 'thought-provokers' than as a universally applicable interrogation.

A further exercise (page 232) will help you to examine your business in terms of its strengths and weaknesses. The business issues cover four key areas:

– **Strengths**
– **Weaknesses**
– **Opportunities**
– **Threats**

A regular assessment of all four factors (commonly called a '**SWOT**' analysis) is a feature of all well-run businesses, from a multinational corporation to a local corner shop.

(All the checklists which follow are based on those which appear in the MSC Training Kit *Business Success through People* and are reproduced by kind permission of the Manpower Services Commission.)

Checklist 1: Business description

General

- What industry are you in?
- How large is it?
- What are the major trends inside the industry?

Products and/or services

- What products and/or services do you currently sell?
- What are their special characteristics?
- What distinguishes them from those of your competitors?
- Are they, and should they be, patented?

- Are they up to date?
- Do you have a plan for the development of existing and new products/services?
- What is it?
- What is the trend of your sales?
- What is the customer reaction to your products/services?
- What is your current level of returns?
- Is the level of product/service quality satisfactory from your customer's viewpoint?

The markets and competitors

Analysis of your market

- What is your target market?
- How large is this market?
- Does your market have export opportunities?
- Who are your major customers?
- Where are your major customers?
- Are they mainly regular or casual customers?
- Is the market subject to seasonal fluctuations?
- What is your normal delivery period?
- Is your delivery period as good as that of your competitors?

Analysis of your competitors

- Who are your immediate competitors?
- Where are they located?
- What competitor do you most respect and why?
- Are they successful?
- Are you expanding or shrinking in relation to your competitors?
- How does your product/service compare with that of your competitors?

- What are its distinguishing features?

General financial considerations

- Who owns the business?
- How much influence and control does each owner/shareholder/manager have?
- How has the business generally raised the funds needed for expansion in the past:
  - from bank loans;
  - from shareholder/manager loans;
  - from within the business, by restricting share dividends or drawings?
- Have you identified and considered alternative ways of raising capital for investment?
- Have you analysed their advantages and disadvantages?
- How are investment decisions made (for instance, buying an expensive item of equipment)?

Checklist 2: Business organization

Manpower and organization

- Do you have a manpower plan (i.e. a plan which predicts your future need for employees)? What information does it provide you with? Do you have enough information?
- How many people do you have working for you? What hours do you work? Can you relate the hours worked to business activity?
- Do you have job descriptions? Are they up to date?
- Are there clearly defined levels of responsibility?
- Are working policies and procedures clearly communicated to all employees? Are they regularly updated?

Employees: skills and knowledge

- What are your relationships with your staff like?

- Have you established regular methods of telling your staff what is happening and listening to their response? What are these methods?

- What is your sickness and accident record? Is this acceptable?

- How much do you know of your employees' skills, interests, ambitions and potential?

- What are your policies regarding recruitment and dismissal?

- Are there any formal/established staff-training and development programmes? If so, what purpose do they serve? How effective are they?

- Are there staff succession plans (i.e. if someone leaves, do you know who will step into his/her place)? Have you identified your high-fliers (i.e. those who can be expected to fill senior management positions)? Have you also identified your low-achievers?

- How are promotions decided? What are the key jobs in the business? Do you have replacements already identified within the business?

- How do you assess your wage rates?

- Does each person understand his/her job? Have you or your colleagues ever clarified the job specification of each member of staff?

- Is there a regular performance review process? If not, how is individual or team performance measured?

- Have you recently/ever carried out an audit of the skills/knowledge requirements of the business and matched this against what is actually there?

- Is the management team developing by making the best use of their skills and knowledge and using their time effectively?

Checklist 3: Business performance

The people in the business

Have your results been affected by . . .

- . . . low activity or low work quality due to lack of knowledge, lack of skills or problems with staff attitudes? If so, has the problem come from an individual, an activity or function, a department, site or throughout the company?
- . . . not having the right people in the right job at the right time? Should the company change its policies on when to hire staff and how many to recruit, to take this into account?
- . . . overstaffing in certain parts of the business? What are the options – retraining, reorganizing, changes in working hours, reduction in the labour force?
- . . . a lack of management planning, direction or control?
- . . . communication problems between key people and key activities? How can this be improved?
- . . . not enough attention to policies designed to help people cope with changes to the organization or technology? How can this be put right?
- . . . labour turnover? What are the major causes? How can they be overcome?

Turnover (Sales)

How is turnover affected by . . .

- . . . changing demand?
- . . . your market rates or fixed prices?
- . . . the competitive nature of your business?
- . . . the quality of your after-sales service?
- . . . the efficiency of your delivery performance?
- . . . the quality of your products and/or services?
- . . . your ability to manufacture the quantities needed to meet sales requirements?

- . . . the effectiveness of selling?

Gross profit

Is your gross profit affected by . . .

- . . . the prices at which you are selling your products and/or services being too low?
- . . . having to offer more discounts than you would like to in order to get sales?
- . . . the prices at which you are buying your materials/stock being higher than you recover from your selling prices?
- . . . obsolete stocks?
- . . . waste of materials?
- . . . the cost of production labour being too high?
- . . . production labour not being used as efficiently as it could be?
- . . . not being able to get the right quality of materials/stock?
- . . . not being able to get the right quality of labour?
- . . . the cost of production supervision?
- . . . direct factory overheads (e.g. heat, fuel, power)?

Overheads

How effective is your control of overheads?

- Do you employ too many staff (for example, sales people, accounts clerks)?
- Do you employ too few staff?
- Are your sales overheads too high (for example, in terms of advertising and commission)?
- Are your administration costs too high (for example, insurance, stationery, postage, telephone)?
- Is the cost of your premises too high (for example, rent, rates, repairs)?

- Do you have a major burden in repaying the interest on loans?

Working capital

How is working capital affected by . . .

- . . . the level of stocks?
- . . . the level of work in progress?
- . . . the effectiveness of your credit control?
- . . . bad debts? At what levels do you experience these?
- . . . pressure from creditors?
- . . . banking facilities?
- . . . the level of day-to-day cash requirements?
- . . . short-term and long-term borrowings?
- . . . lack of adequate security to guarantee a loan or overdraft?
- . . . not being able to finance growth?
- . . . directors' pay/proprietors' drawings?

Financial planning and control

- How frequently is management information (i.e. sales, revenues, outgoings, etc.) prepared?
- How accurate and timely is this information?
- Are actual results compared with a budgeted target?
- Is this management information used to:
  – put right what has been going wrong?
  – measure the performance of management and staff?
  – provide the basis for planning?

Production capability and facilities

- Do you manufacture/assemble your sales products, or do you sub-contract this function? What is the balance between in-house and sub-contracted work? How does this affect productivity and profitability?
- What levels of overtime working do you need?
- Are your premises adequate for present and future production?

- What production or operating advantages do you have?
- What is the 'useful' life of your equipment and machinery?
- Do you have an established procedure for scheduling, costing and planning production? Does it operate well?
- How do you monitor your production? Is this system accurate and timely?
- Do you have problems meeting delivery dates? If so, for what reason?
- What system of quality control do you use? How do you set standards?
- What is the level of production rejects or customer complaints? Is this rising or falling?
- How do you rate the quality of your product or service compared with that of your competitors?
- How is purchasing of materials controlled?
- How do you check the performance of your suppliers, in terms of price, quality, delivery dates, etc.?
- How do you identify scrap and obsolete stock?

The analysis of strengths and weaknesses – now

Exercise 8.1. List as many factors that apply to your company now as you can under each heading:

S (strengths):
W (weaknesses):
O (opportunities):
T (threats):

What does this tell me about the business?
List the key issues:

An alternative method of looking at strengths and weaknesses

This analysis looks at the following areas for both the present and the future (6–12 months ahead).

S (strengths): the things that we are good at and the things that are moving us forward, e.g. strong design skills, committed workforce.

W (weaknesses): the things that we are not so good at and the things that are holding us back, e.g. high wastage, quality control.

O (opportunities): the potential in front of us, e.g. growing market, new ideas.

T (threats): the risks we are facing, e.g. increasing competitors, rising interest rates.

It will also help you to highlight some key issues facing the business, both current and future.

The analysis of strengths and weaknesses: the future

Exercise 8.2. List as many factors that apply to your company in the future as you can under the appropriate heading.

S (strengths):

W (weaknesses):

O (opportunities):

T (threats):

What does this tell me about the business?
List the key issues:

Summary

- Weekly/monthly/quarterly financial controls are a must, for you to be able to understand what is happening to the business.
  These should be set up *before* you start trading.
- Monitoring procedures need to be tailored to your requirements; advice from your bank/accountant/other sources (business club, advisory service, chamber of commerce, business friends) is worth considering.
  Make sure that your procedures are simple to complete and don't take up too much of your time.
- It is worth considering at the outset of trading how you propose to organize your book-keeping/accounting requirements and how much support you are prepared to pay for.
- A general financial/business review once a quarter would appear to be a sensible balance between time available and the requirement for critical business information to be reviewed.

Appendices

compiled by
Helen Steadman

I *Advice on starting a small business*

During the 1980s there has been an enormous growth of advisory services for small businesses. There are so many different bodies it can be difficult to know which one to contact, but in **most** cases your first port of call should be a local Enterprise Agency. Information on these agencies, and their addresses, is given on pp. 235–49.

If you are still a student in higher education, or have recently graduated, you could start instead by contacting your careers service, which will provide information about small-business initiatives specifically for graduates, particularly the Graduate Enterprise Programme (see p. 260).

Alternatively, if you live in a country area (in England), and plan to do rural crafts, or start a small manufacturing or retail business, then CoSIRA, the Council for Small Industries in Rural Areas, can help. (See p. 249 for addresses and further information.)

There are other sources of information, such as the government's Small Firms Service, and local authorities. And there are professionals – particularly accountants and solicitors: you will need their advice later on, but since you have to pay for it, investigate the free advisory services first.

Enterprise Agencies

Enterprise Agencies (and Enterprise Trusts in Scotland) are local bodies, usually funded by the business community and local authorities.

They provide free, independent and confidential counselling on all aspects of starting up a small business.

The Enterprise Agency movement is relatively new: most of the agencies have started since 1979. They vary considerably in size and scope; Lenta, the London Enterprise Agency, is one of the largest and longest established; its services include training courses, a 'Marriage Bureau' to link private investors with small businesses, managed workshop schemes and various forms of marketing assistance. Some of the other agencies, more recently formed, are much smaller, but they all provide free information, advice and counselling. Many are closely involved in activities such as the provision and management of small business workshops, promotion and management of small business clubs, and education and training. They are strongly recommended as a first point of contact for anyone who is considering setting up a small business, or is in the early stages of developing it.

The 'umbrella' organization for Enterprise Agencies is: Business in the Community, 227A City Road, London EC1V 1LX (Tel. 01-253 3716). Scotland has an independent but associated organization, Scottish Business in the Community, at: Romano House, 43 Station Road, Corstorphine, Edinburgh EH12 7AF (Tel. 031-334 9876).

Enterprise Agencies currently in operation are listed below. The symbols denote activities as follows:

W = has managed workshops/offices
C = runs a small business club
E = has contact or involvement with Enterprise Zone
I = co-operates with or manages ITECHS
T = provides or has access to education and training for people setting up their own businesses

North Region

Alnwick: Alnwick Small Industries Development Group, 1 The Shambles, Alnwick, Northumberland NE66 1HU. Tel. 0665 605075

Cleveland: Cleveland Enterprise Agency, 52/60 Corporation Road, Middlesbrough, Cleveland TS1 2RN. Tel. 0643 222836

Consett: Derwentside Industrial Development Agency, Berry Edge Road, Consett, Co. Durham DH8 5EU. Tel. 0207 509124. **EIT**

Darlington: Darlington & SW Durham Business Venture Ltd, Imperial Centre, Grange Road, Darlington DL1 5NQ. Tel. 0325 480891. **CIT**

Hartlepool: Hartlepool Enterprise Agency Ltd, 5th Floor, Titan House, York Road, Hartlepool. Tel. 0429 221216; also HANDS, Old Municipal Buildings, Upper Church Street, Hartlepool, Cleveland TS24 7ET. Tel. 0429 66522, ext. 374

Newcastle: Newcastle Youth Enterprise Centre, 25 Low Friar Street, Newcastle upon Tyne NE1 5UE. Tel. 091 261 6009. **WCEIT**

North-East: Enterprise North, Durham University Business School, Mill Lane, Durham DH1 3LB. Tel. 0385 41919

Northumberland: Northumberland Business Centre, Southgate, Morpeth NE61 2EH. Tel. 0670 514343. **T**

Project North-East: Marseilles Chambers, 45 Groat Market, Newcastle upon Tyne NE1 1UG. Tel. 091 261 7856. **WIT**

S.E. Northumberland: South-East Northumberland Trust Ltd (SENET), 20 School Road, Bedlington Station, Northumberland NE22 7JB. Tel. 0670 828686

Shildon and Sedgefield: Shildon and Sedgefield District Development Agency, BREL Offices, Byerley Road, Shildon, Co. Durham DL4 1PW. Tel. 0388 777917

Tyne and Wear: Tyne and Wear Enterprise Trust Ltd (Entrust), SWS House, Stoddart Street, Newcastle upon Tyne NE2 1AN. Tel. 091 261 4838. **T**

Tyne and Wear also at 19 Beach Road, South Shields NE33 2QA. Tel. 091 254 3346; 9–11 Princess Square, Newcastle upon Tyne NE1 8EN. Tel. 091 261 9195; 81–83 High Street West, Wallsend NE28 8JD. Tel. 091 234 0895; 1 Walker Terrace, Gateshead NE8 1EB. Tel. 091 277 6675; 62 High Street West, Sunderland SR1 3DP

Tyneside Economic Development Company Ltd: Business Enterprise Centre, Eldon Street, South Shields, Tyne and Wear NE33 5JE. Tel 091 255 4300. **WI**

North-west Region

Barrow: Furness Business Initiative, 111 Duke Street, Barrow-in-Furness, Cumbria. Tel. 0229 22132. **CIT**

Birkenhead/Wirral: In Business Ltd, The Business Centre, Claughton Road, Birkenhead, Wirral, Merseyside L41 6ES. Tel. 051-647 7574. **WCIT**

Blackburn: Blackburn and District Enterprise Trust, c/o Blackburn and District Chamber of Industry and Commerce, 14 Richmond Terrace, Blackburn BB1 7BH. Tel. 0254 664747. **EIT**

Blackpool and Fylde: Blackpool and Fylde Business Agency Ltd, 20 Queen Street, Blackpool, Lancashire FY1 1PD. Tel. 0253 294929. **CIT**

Bolton: Bolton Business Venture, Bolton Centre, Lower Bridgeman Street, Bolton, Lancs. Tel. 0204 391400. **CT**

Bury: Bury Enterprise Centre, 12 Tithebarn Street, Bury, Lancashire BL9 0JR. Tel. 061-797 5864. **WIT**

Carlisle: Business Initiatives Carlisle, Tower Buildings, Scotch Street, Carlisle, Cumbria CA3 8RB. Tel. 0228 34120. **T**

Chester: Chester Enterprise Centre, Off Hoole Bridge, Chester CH2 2NQ. Tel. 0244 311474. **WCIT**

Clitheroe: Ribble Valley Enterprise Agency, c/o Mr P. Bailey, Ribble Valley Borough Council, Council Offices, Church Walk, Clitheroe, Lancs. BB7 2RA. Tel. 0200 25111

Ellesmere Port and Neston: Enterprise Trust Ltd, 72A Whitby Road, Ellesmere Port, South Wirral L65 0AA. Tel. 051-356 3555

Hyndburn: Hyndburn Enterprise Trust, 19 Avenue Parade, Accrington, Lancashire BB5 6PN. Tel. 0254 390000. **EIT**

Knowsley: Knowsley Enterprise Agency, Knowsley House, Charleywood Road, Knowsley Industrial Park, Kirby, Liverpool L33 7SG. Tel. 051-548 3245. **IT**

Lancaster: Business for Lancaster, St Leonards House (Room B32), St Leonards Gate, Lancaster. Tel. 0524 66222. **WCT**

Leyland: South Ribble Business Venture, 176 Towngate, Leyland, Preston, Lancs PR5 1TE. Tel. 0772 422242

Liverpool: Business in Liverpool Ltd, The Innovation Centre, 131 Mount Pleasant, Liverpool L3 5TF. Tel. 051-709 1231

Macclesfield: Macclesfield Business Venture, Venture House, Cross Street, Macclesfield, Cheshire SK11 7RG. Tel. 0625 615113. **WCT**

Manchester: Manchester Business Venture, Tootals Ltd, 56 Oxford Street, Manchester M60 1HJ. Tel. 061-228 1144. **CET**

Manchester: Mr Volney Harris, Manager, Areas Economic Development Unit, 8/12 Parisian Way, Alexandra Centre, Moss Lane East, Manchester M15 5NQ.

Merseyside: Merseyside Education, Training & Enterprise Ltd (METEL), 6 Salisbury Street, Liverpool L3 8DR. Tel. 051-207 2281. **WCEIT**

Oldham: Business in Oldham, Acorn Centre, Barry Street, Oldham OL1 3NE. Tel. 061-665 1225. **WIT**

Pendle: Pendle Enterprise Trust Ltd, 19/23 Leeds Road, Nelson, Lancashire. Tel. 0282 698001. **ET**

Preston: Preston Business Venture, 43 Lune Street, Preston, Lancashire PR1 2NN. Tel. 0772 25723. **CT**

Rochdale: Metropolitan Enterprise Trust Rochdale Area (Business Help), c/o TBA Industrial Products Ltd, PO Box 40, Rochdale OL12 7EQ. Tel. 0706 356250. **WCIT**

Rossendale: Rossendale Enterprise Trust Ltd, 29 Kay Street, Rawtenstall, Rossendale, Lancashire BB4 7LS. Tel. 0706 229838. **WCET**

Salford: Salford Community Enterprise Development Agency Ltd, 9 Broadway, Salford M5 2TS. Tel. 061-872 3838

Southport: Sefton Enterprise Trust, 54 West Street, Southport, Lancashire PR8 1QS. Tel. 0704 44173

St Helens: Community of St Helens Trust, PO Box 36, St Helens, Merseyside. Tel. 0744 696775. **CIT**

South Cheshire: South Cheshire Opportunity for Private Enterprise Ltd (SCOPE), SCOPE House, Weston Road, Crewe CW1 1DD. Tel. 0270 589569. **WIT**

Stockport: Stockport Business Venture Ltd, PO Box 66, Crossley Road, Heaton Chapel, Stockport, Cheshire SK4 5BH. Tel. 061-432 3770

Tameside: Tameside Business Advice Service, Charlestown Industrial Estate, Turner Street, Ashton-under-Lyne. Tel. 061-339 8960. **I**

Trafford: Trafford Business Venture, 8th Floor, Six Acre House, Town Square, Sale, Cheshire M33 1XZ. Tel. 061-905 2950. **E**

Vale Royal: Vale Royal Small Firms Ltd, The Mid-Cheshire Business Centre, Winnington Avenue, Winnington, Northwich, Cheshire CW8 4EE. Tel. 0606 77711. **WCT**

Warrington: Warrington Business Promotion Bureau, Barbauld House, Barbauld Street, Warrington WA1 2QY. Tel. 0925 33309. **CIT**

West Lancashire: The West Lancashire Enterprise Trust Ltd, The Malthouse, 48 Southport Road, Ormskirk, Lancashire L39 1LX. Tel. 0695 78626. **C**

Widnes/Runcorn: Business Link, 62 Church Street, Runcorn, Cheshire WA7 1LD. Tel. 092 85 63037 and 73549. **WIT**

Wigan/Leigh: Wigan New Enterprise Ltd, 45 Bridgeman Terrace, Wigan WN1 1TT. Tel. 0942 496591. **CIT**

Workington: Enterprise West Cumbria, MOBET Trading Estate, Workington, Cumbria CA14 3YB. Tel. 0900 65656. **WIT**

Wyre: Wyre Business Agency Ltd, Colchester House, Burnhall Industrial Estate, Fleetwood Road, Fleetwood, Lancs FY7 8JS. Tel. 0253 864014. **WCT**

Yorkshire and Humberside Region

Barnsley: Barnsley Enterprise Centre, 1 Pontefract Road, Barnsley, South Yorks. Tel. 0226 298091 **WCI**

Bradford: Bradford Enterprise Agency, Commerce House, Cheapside, Bradford, West Yorks BD1 4JZ. Tel. 0274 734359. **I**

Doncaster: Doncaster Business Advice Centre, 50 Christchurch Road, Doncaster, S. Yorks DN1 2QN. Tel. 0302 734665

Grimsby and Cleethorpes: Grimsby & Cleethorpes Area Enterprise Agency, 2nd Floor, Norwich Union Chambers, 27 Osborne Street, Grimsby DN31 1EY. Tel. 0472 52109. **WEIT**

Halifax: Calderdale Small Business Advice Centre, Unit OP53, Dean Clough Industrial Park, Dean Clough, Halifax HX1 1XG. Tel. 0422 69487. **CIT**

Hull: Action Resource Centre, Hull Business Advice Centre, 24 Anlaby Road, Hull HU1 2PA. Tel. 0482 27266. **T**

Leeds: Leeds Business Venture, 4th Floor, Merrion House, The Merrion Centre, Leeds LS2 8LY. Tel. 0532 446474 and 0532 457583. **T**

Rotherham: Rotherham Enterprise Agency Ltd, 2nd Floor, All Saints Buildings, 21 Corporation Street, Rotherham S60 1NX. Tel. 0709 382121, ext. 3463. **WET**

Scarborough: Scarborough Filey & District Business Development Agency, 4th Floor, Skipton Chambers, 32 St Nicholas Street, Scarborough YD11 2H5. Tel. 0723 354454

Sheffield: Sheffield Business Venture, 317 Glossop Road, Sheffield S10 2HP. Tel. 0742 755721. **T**

South Humber: SoHBAC (South Humber Business Advice Centre) Ltd, 7 Market Place, Brigg, South Humberside DN20 8HA. Tel. 0652 57637/8. **ET**

Wakefield and Kirklees: Kirklees and Wakefield Venture Trust, Calder Vale Road, Wakefield WF1 5PF. Tel. 0484 531352. **CET**

York: Vale of York Small Business Association, York Enterprise Centre, 1 Davygate, York YO1 2QE. Tel. 0904 641401. **CT**

Whitby: Whitby & District Business Development Agency, 3 Bagdale, Whitby, North Yorks YO21 1QL. Tel. 0947 600827

West Midlands Region

Birmingham: Birmingham Venture, Chamber of Commerce House, PO Box 360, 75 Harborne Road, Birmingham B15 3DH. Tel. 021-454 6171. **WT**

Burton: Burton Enterprise Agency, Midland Railway Grain Warehouse, Derby Street, Burton-on-Trent DE24 2JJ. Tel. 0283 37151/2. **WCIT**

Coventry: Coventry Business Centre, Christchurch House, Greyfriars Lane, Coventry CV1 2GY. Tel. 0203 22775. **T**

Dudley: Dudley Business Venture, Falcon House, The Minories, Dudley DY2 8PG. Tel. 0384 231283/4/5. **EIT**

Hereford and Worcester: Herefordshire Enterprise Agency Ltd, 15–17 St Owens Street, Hereford. Tel. 0432 276898. **IT**

Lichfield: Lichfield Business Advisory Service, Redcourt House, Tamworth Street, Lichfield, Staffs. Tel. 05432 58683

Sandwell: Sandwell Enterprise Ltd, 22 Lombard Street, West Bromwich, Sandwell, West Midlands B70 8RT. Tel. 021-569 2231. **CT**

Stoke/Staffs: Business Initiative, Gordon Chambers, 36 Cheapside, Hanley, Stoke-on-Trent ST1 1HE. Tel. 0782 279013. **T**

Telford: The Shropshire Enterprise Trust, National Westminster Bank Chambers, Church Street, Wellington, Shropshire. Tel. 0952 56624. **ET**

Tamworth: Tamworth Business Advisory Service, Marmion House, Lichfield Street, Tamworth, Staffs. Tel. 0827 64222.

Walsall: Walsall Small Firms Advice Unit, Jerome Chambers, Bridge Street, Walsall WS1 1EX. Tel. 0922 646614. **WI**

Warwickshire: Warwickshire Enterprise Agency, Northgate South, Northgate Street, Warwick CV34 4JH. Tel. 0926 495685. **CT**

Wolverhampton: Wolverhampton Enterprise Ltd, Lich Chambers, 44 Queen Square, Wolverhampton W1 1TS. Tel. 0902 713737. **T**

Worcestershire: Worcestershire Enterprise Agency, Berross Centre, Hylton Road, Worcester WR2 5JL. Tel. 0905 424191.

East Midlands Region

Chesterfield: Action Resource Centre, Business Advice Centre, 34 Beetwell Street, Chesterfield, Derbyshire S40 1SH. Tel. 0246 208743

Corby: Corby Industrial Development Centre, 37 Queens Square, Corby NN17 1PL. Tel. 0536 362571

Derby: Derby & Derbyshire Business Venture, Saxon House, Heritage Gate, Friary Street, Derby DE1 1NL. Tel. 0332 360345

Grantham/Kesteven: Kesteven & Corby Glen Enterprise Trust, 57/58 London Road, Grantham, Lincolnshire NG31 6ET. Tel. 0476 68970. **C**

Leicester: Leicestershire Business Venture. Business Advice Centre, 30 New Walk, Leicester LE1 6TF. Tel. 0533 554464

Lincoln: Lincoln Enterprise Agency, 10 Park Street, Lincoln LN1 1UF. Tel. 0522 40775

Northamptonshire: Northamptonshire Enterprise Agency Ltd, 67 The Avenue, Cliftonville, Northampton NN1 5BG. Tel. 0604 37401. **E**

Nottingham: Nottingham Business Venture, City House, Maid Marion Way, Nottingham NG1 6BH. Tel. 0602 412334/470914

Eastern Region

Basildon: Basildon & District Local Enterprise Agency Ltd, Keay House, Room 101A, 88 Town Square, Basildon, Essex SS14 1BN. Tel. 0268 286977. **I**

Braintree: Braintree District Enterprise Agency. Enterprise Office, Town Hall Centre, Market Square, Braintree, Essex CM7 6YG. Tel. 0376 43140

Bury St Edmunds: Mid-Anglian Enterprise Agency Ltd, 79 Whiting Street, Bury St Edmunds, Suffolk IP33 1NX. Tel. 0284 60206. **T**

Cambridge: CEA (Cambridge Enterprise Agency Ltd), 71A Lensfield Road, Cambridge CB2 1EN. Tel. 0223 323553. **T**

Chelmsford: Chelmsford Enterprise, Small Business Office, Civic Centre, Chelmsford CM1 1JE. Tel. 0245 261733. **WCT**

Colchester: Colchester Business Enterprise Agency, Gate House, High Street, Colchester, Essex CO1 1UG. Tel. 0206 48833. **T**

Essex: Essex Small Business Advisory Centre, Church Street, Chelmsford, Essex. Tel. 0245 350388. **CT**

Great Yarmouth: Great Yarmouth Business Advisory Service, 165A King Street, Great Yarmouth, Norfolk NR30 2PA. Tel. 0493 856100. **WT**

Harlow: Harrow Enterprise Agency, 19 The Rows, The High, Harlow, Essex CM20 1DD. Tel. 0279 38077. **T**

Huntingdonshire: Huntingdonshire Enterprise Agency, Castle Hill House, High Street, Huntingdon PE18 6TE. Tel. 0480 50028. **T**

Ipswich: Ipswich Enterprise Trust (IPSENTA), 30A Lower Brooke Street, Ipswich, Suffolk. Tel. 0473 59832. **T**

King's Lynn: West Norfolk Enterprise Agency Trust Ltd, 7 King Street, King's Lynn, Norfolk P30 1ET. Tel. 0553 760431

Loughton: Forest Enterprise Agency Trust (FEAT), c/o Manager's Flat, Loughton Swimming Pool, Traps Hill, Loughton, Essex. Tel. 01-508 7435. **T**

Lowestoft: Lowestoft Enterprise Trust, 19 Grove Road, Lowestoft, Suffolk NR32 1EB. Tel. 0502 63286. **WT**

Maldon: Maldon Branch of Colchester BEA, Planning Department, Maldon District Council, Market Hill, Maldon, Essex CM9 7QN. Tel. 0621 54477, ext. 386. **T**

Norwich: NEAT (Norwich Enterprise Agency Trust), 112 Barrack Street, Norwich NR3 1TX. 0603 613023. **CT**

Peterborough: Peterborough Enterprise Programme, Broadway Court, Broadway, Peterborough PE1 1RP. Tel. 0733 310159. **CI**

Southend: Southend Enterprise Agency Ltd, Commerce House, 845 London Road, Westcliff-on-Sea, Essex. Tel. 0702 78380

Sudbury: Sudbury Enterprise Agency, Guthrie House, 67 Cornard Road, Sudbury, Suffolk CO10 6XB. Tel. 0787 73927. **WT**

Tendring: Enterprise Tendring Limited, 27A Pier Avenue, Clacton-on-Sea, Essex CO15 1QE. Tel. 0255 421225. **T**

Thurrock: Thurrock Local Enterprise Agency Ltd, 79A High Street, Grays, Essex RM17 6NX. Tel. 0375 374362

Wisbech: Fens Business Enterprise Trust, 2 York Row, Wisbech, Cambridgeshire PE13 1EB. Tel. 0945 587084. **T**

South-east Region

Ashford: Enterprise Ashford Ltd, The Enterprise Centre, Old Railway Works, New Town Road, Ashford, Kent TN24 0PD. Tel. 0233 30307. **CIT**

Brighton: Brighton & Hove Business Agency Ltd, 23 Old Steine, Brighton BN1 1EL. Tel. 0273 688882. **WCIT**

Canterbury: The Enterprise Agency of East Kent, 22 St Peter's Street, Canterbury, Kent CT1 2BQ. Tel. 0227 470234; sub-offices: 2 St George's Road, Deal, Kent CT14 6BA. Tel. 0304 367673; 44 Hawley Square, Margate CT9 1PQ. Tel. 0843 290205

Dartford: North-West Kent Enterprise Agency, 2 Hythe Street, Dartford, Kent DA1 1BT. Tel. 0322 91451. **CT**

Eastbourne: Eastbourne and District Enterprise Agency Ltd, c/o Birds Eye Walls Ltd, Lottbridge Drove, Eastbourne, East Sussex BN23 6PS. Tel. 0323 64470; sub-office at Room No. 2, Cortlandt, George Street, Hailsham, East Sussex. Tel. 0323 847923. **CT**

Gravesend: Gravesham Industry Enterprise Agency, 8 Parrock Street, Gravesend, Kent DA12 1ET. Tel. 0474 327118. **WEIT**

Hastings: Hastings Business Ventures, 6 Havelock Road, Hastings, East Sussex TN34 1BP. Tel. 0424 433333. **IT**

Maidstone: Maidstone Enterprise Agency, 25A Pudding Lane, Maidstone, Kent. Tel. 0622 675547. **T**

Medway: Medway Enterprise Agency Ltd, Railway Street, Chatham, Kent ME4 4RR. Tel. 0634 400301. **CEIT**

Surrey: Surrey Business Enterprise (Guildford), Friary Mews, 28 Commercial Road, Guildford, Surrey. Tel. 0483 506969

Surrey: Surrey Business Enterprises (Woking), 19 Vale Farm Road, Woking GU21 1DN. Tel. 04862 28434

Swale: Swale Enterprise Agency, Unit B4, Smeed Dean Centre, Eurolink, Sittingbourne, Kent ME10 3RN. Tel. 0795 27623. **WET**

Tonbridge: Great Weald Enterprise Agency, 34A High Street, Tonbridge, Kent TN9 1EJ. Tel. 0732 360133

West Sussex: West Sussex Area Enterprise Centre Ltd, 69A Chapel Road, Worthing, West Sussex BN11 1BU. Tel. 0903 36499

South Region

Aldershot/Camberley: Blackwater Valley Enterprise Trust, Old Town Hall, Grosvenor Road, Aldershot, Hants. Tel. 0252 319272. **T**

Aylesbury: Aylesbury Vale Business Advice Scheme, 23A Walton Street, Aylesbury HP20 1TZ. Tel. 0296 89055.

Banbury: North Oxfordshire Business Venture Ltd (NORBIS), 2nd Floor, 13 Horsefair, Banbury, Oxon OX16 9AH. Tel. 0295 67900. **T**

Basingstoke: Basingstoke & Andover Enterprise Centre, 9 New Street, Basingstoke RG21 1DF. Tel. 0256 54041

Bedfordshire (Mid. & S. Bucks); BECENTA (Bedfordshire & Chiltern Enterprise Agency), Enterprise House, 7 Gordon Street, Luton LU1 2QP. Tel. 0582 452288. **WCT**

Berkshire (Reading, Maidenhead, Newbury, Slough and Windsor): Berkshire Enterprise Agency, The Old Shire Hall, The Forbury, Reading RG1 3EJ. Tel. 0734 585715. **IT**

East Hampshire: East Hampshire Enterprise Agency Ltd, c/o Bass Brewery (Alton) Ltd, Manor Park, Alton, Hants GU34 2PS. Tel. 0420 87577

Hertford: Stort Valley Enterprise Trust, Vale House, Cowbridge, Hertford, Herts SG14 1PW. Tel. 0279 55261

Isle of Wight: Isle of Wight Enterprise Agency Ltd, 6/7 Town Lane, Newport, Isle of Wight PO30 1NR. Tel. 0983 529 120. **CT**

Letchworth Garden City: Letchworth Garden City Business Centre, Avenue One, Letchworth Garden City, Herts SG6 2HB. Tel. 04626 78272. **WT**

Milton Keynes: Milton Keynes Business Venture, Sentry House, 500 Avebury Boulevard, Saxon Gate West, Central Milton Keynes MK9 2LA. Tel. 0908 660044. **WCI**

Oxford: Thames Business Advice Centre, STEP Centre, Osney Mead, Oxford OX2 0ES. Tel. 0865 249279

Portsmouth: The Portsmouth Area Enterprise, 1st Floor, 27 Guildhall Walk, Portsmouth, Hants. Tel. 0705 833321; branch agencies; 75 High Street, Fareham, Hants. Tel. 0329 282543; Ferry Gardens, Gosport, Hants. Tel. 07017 586621. **IT**

St Albans: (STANTA) Enterprise Agency, 8A Chequer Street, St Albans, Herts AL1 3YZ. Tel. 0727 40563

Southampton: Southampton Enterprise Agency, Solent Business Centre, Millbrook Road West, Southampton SO1 0HW. Tel. 0703 788088. **C**

Stevenage: Stevenage Initiative, Business and Technical Centre, Bessemer Drive, Stevenage, Herts. Tel. 0438 315733. **IT**

Watford: Watford Enterprise Agency Ltd, The Business Centre, Colne Way, Watford, Herts WO2 4ND. Tel. 0923 47373

South-west region

Bath: Bath Enterprise Ltd, Green Park Station, Green Park Road, Bath BA1 1JB. Tel. 0225 338383. **WCIT**

Bristol: Bristol & Avon Enterprise Agency, Cannons Road, Bristol BS1 5UH. Tel. 0272 272222. **IT**

Dorset: Dorset Enterprise, 1 Britannia Road, Parkestone, Poole, Dorset BH14 8AZ. Tel. 0202 748333. CT

East Devon: East Devon Small Industries Group, 115 Border Road, Heath Park, Honiton, Devon EX14 8BT. Tel. 0404 41806

Exeter: Business Enterprise Exeter, Equitable Life House, 31 Southernhay East, Exeter EX1 1NS. Tel. 0392 56060. **WIT**

Frome: Frome Area Management Enterprise (FAME), c/o ARC–South, Garston Road, Frome, Somerset BA11 1RS. Tel. 073 67589. **WT**

Gloucestershire: Gloucestershire Enterprise Agency, 90 Westgate Street, Gloucester GL1 2N2. Tel. 0452 501411. **WT**

Guernsey: Guernsey Enterprise Agency, States Arcade, Market Street, St Peter Port, Guernsey, C.I. Tel. 0481 710043. **C**

Jersey: Jersey Enterprise Agency, Whiteley Chambers, 41 Don Street, St Helier, Jersey, C.I. Tel. St Helier 35578

Kingswood (Bristol): New Work Trust Co Ltd, HQ Avondale Workshops, Woodland Way, Kingswood, Bristol BS15 1QH. Tel. 0272 603871/601106; also at Station Road Workshops, Station Road, Kingswood, Bristol BS15 4PR. Tel. 0272 575577; Small Firms Marketing Centre, London Road, Warmley, Bristol BS15 5JH. Tel. 0272 601109/677807; Business Information Technology Service, Avondale Workshops, Woodland Way, Kingswood, Bristol BS15 1QH. Tel. 0272 603873/4; Vocational Training Services, Avondale Workshops, Woodland Way, Kingswood, Bristol BS15 1QH. Tel. 0272 603872; Bath Control Centre, Unit 1a Bath Riverside Business Park, Lower Bristol Road, Bath BA2 3DW. Tel. 0225 337992/337967. **WCIT**

Mid-Devon: Mid Devon Enterprise Agency, The Factory, Leat Street, Tiverton, Devon EX16 5LL. Tel. 0884 255629. **T**

North Devon: North Devon Enterprise Group, Bridge Chambers, Barnstaple. Devon EX31 1HB. Tel. 0271 76365. **IT**

North Devon: North Devon Manufacturers Association, 95 High Street, Barnstaple, Devon EX3 1HR. Tel. 0271 76427. **CIT**

North and East Cornwall: North & East Cornwall Enterprise Trust (Enterprise TAMAR), The National School, St Thomas Road, Launceston PL15 8BU. Tel. 0566 5632. **WT**

North Dorset: North Dorset Small Industries Group, Emmetts Hay, Hartgrove Orchard, nr Shaftesbury, Dorset. Tel. 0747 811511

Plymouth: Enterprise Plymouth Ltd, Somerset Place, Stoke, Plymouth PL3 4BB. Tel. 0752 59211. **WCI**

Restormel (Mid Cornwall): Restormel Local Enterprise Trust Ltd, Lower Penarwyn, St Blazey, Par, nr St Austell, Cornwall. Tel. 072 681 3079

Somerset: Small Industries Group Somerset, 68 Friarn Street, Bridgwater, Somerset TA6 3LJ. Tel. 0278 424456. **WI**

Swindon: Swindon Enterprise Trust, 54 Victoria Road, Swindon, Wilts SN1 3AY. Tel. 0793 487793. **CIT**

South Dorset: Purbeck Small Industries Group, 4 Streche Road, Swanage, Dorset BH19 1NF. Tel. 0929 425627

Teignbridge: Teignbridge Enterprise Agency, Greenhill, Greenhill Way, Kingsteignton, Newton Abbott TQ12 3BD. Tel. 0626 67534

Totnes/South Hams: South Hams Agency for Rural Enterprise, 4A Leechwell Street, Totnes, Devon. Tel. 0803 864200. **E**

Wansdyke: Wansdyke Enterprise Agency, High Street, Paulton, Bristol BS18 5NW. Tel. 0761 415400

West Cornwall (Kerrier, Penwith and Carrick): West Cornwall Enterprise Trust Ltd, Lloyds Bank Chambers, Market Square, Camborne, Cornwall TR14 8JJ. Tel. 0209 714914

Yeovil: The Enterprise Agency S. Somerset & N. Dorset (SWRPA), 5 St John's House, Church Path, Yeovil, Somerset BA20 1HE. Tel. 0935 21983

London

Brent: Brent Business Venture Ltd, 12 Park Lane (off High Road), Wembley, Middlesex HA9 7RP. Tel. 01-903 7300/7329. **IT**

Bromley: Bromley Enterprise Agency Trust, 7 Palace Grove, Bromley BR1 3HA. Tel. 01-290 6568

Camden: Camden Enterprise Ltd, 57 Pratt Street, Camden Town, London NW1 0DP. Tel. 01-482 2128. **T**

Croydon: Croydon Business Venture Ltd, 26 Barclay Road, Croydon CR0 1JN. Tel. 01-681 8339. **T**

Enfield: Enfield Enterprise Agency, 2-3 Knights Chambers, South Mall, Lower Edmonton, London N9 0TL. Tel. 01-807 5333

Hackney: The Fashion Centre, 46 Great Eastern Street, London EC2A 3LE. Tel. 01-739 8857

Hackney: Hackney Business Venture, 219 Mare Street, Hackney, London E8 3DQ. Tel. 01-986 0529

Hammersmith and Fulham: Hammersmith & Fulham Business Resources Ltd, PO Box 51, Hammersmith Town Hall, King Street, London W6 9JU. Tel. 01-741 7248. **T**

Harrow: Harrow Enterprise Agency, Brush House, Rosslyn Crescent, Harrow, Middlesex HA1 2SE. Tel. 01-427 6188. **CT**

Hillingdon: Hillingdon Enterprise Agency, 'Hilenta', 170A High Street, Ruislip, Middx HA4 8LJ. Tel. Ruislip 39789

Hounslow: Enterprise Hounslow Ltd, 13 Boston Manor Road, Brentford TW8 9DT. Tel. 01 847 3269

Islington: Islington Small Business Counselling Service, 2nd Floor, 49/59 Old Street, London EC1. Tel. 01-251 2752

Islington: *MAGIC*, Manor Gardens Enterprise Centre, 10/18 Manor Gardens, London N7 6JY. Tel. 01-272 3040

Lambeth: Lambeth Business Advisory Service, Courtenay House, 9–15 New Park Road, London SW2 4DU. Tel. 01-674 9844. **WIT**

London: London Enterprise Agency (Lenta), 4 Snow Hill, London EC1A 2BS. Tel. 01-236 3000. **WCEIT**

Merton: Merton Enterprise Agency Ltd, Crown House, 12th Floor, London Road, Merton, Surrey SM4 5DX. Tel. 01-543 2222

Newham: Newham Businesss Advice and Consultancy Service (BACS), London Borough of Newham, The Town Hall, Barking Road, London E6 2RP. Tel. 01-552 5324

North-east Thames: North East Thames Business Advisory Centre, Marshalls Chambers, 80A South Street, Romford, Essex RM1 1RP. Tel. 70 66438

Park Royal (Ealing/Brent): Park Royal Enterprise Trust, Waxlow Road, London NW10 7NU. Tel. 01-961 2717

Richmond: Enterprise Richmond, c/o Richmond Borough, 56 York Street, Twickenham, Middx. Tel. 01-891 0761, ext. 11

Tower Hamlets: Tower Hamlets Centre for Small Businesses Ltd, 99 Leman Street, London E1 8EY. Tel. 01-481 0512, **ET**

Tower Hamlets: Tower Hamlets Clothing Centre Ltd, Europe House, World Trade Centre, East Smithfield, London E1 9AA. Tel. 01-481 2089

Walthamstow: Room 386, Town Hall, Forest Road, Walthamstow, London E17. Tel. 01-527 5544, ext. 4358

Wandsworth (Lenta): Wandsworth Business Resource Service, 140 Battersea Park Road, London SW11 4NB. Tel. 01-720 7053

Westminster: Westminster Enterprise Agency, Beauchamp Lodge, 2 Warwick Crescent, London W2 6NE. Tel. 01-286 1740

Northern Ireland

Carrickfergus: Enterprise Carrickfergus Ltd, Kilroot Park, Lane Road, Carrickfergus, Co. Antrim. Tel. 09603 69528. **ET**

Larne: Larne Enterprise Development Co. (LEDCOM), 3–5 Prince's Gardens, Larne BT40 1RQ. Tel. 0574 70742

Newry: Newry & Mourne Co-operative Society Ltd, 5 Downshire Place, Newry, N. Ireland. Tel. 0693 67011

Northern Ireland: Action Resource Centre – Northern Ireland, 3 Botanic Avenue, Belfast BT7 1JG. Tel. 0232 234504 and 0232 231730. **CEIT**

Northern Ireland: Northern Ireland Small Business Institute (NISBI), University of Ulster, Jordanstown, N.I. Tel. 0231 65131

Wales

Ammanford: Amman Valley Partnership, Amman Valley Business Centre, Margaret Street, Ammanford, Dyfed. Tel. 0296 65131

Cardiff: Cardiff & Vale Enterprise, 5 Mount Stuart Square, Cardiff CF1 6EE. Tel. 0222 494411. **WCIT**

Clwyd: Clwydfro Enterprise Trust, The Shire Hall, Mold, Clywd CH7 6NH. Tel. 0352 2121

Deeside: Deeside Enterprise Trust Ltd, Park House, Deeside Industrial Park, Deeside, Clwyd CH5 2NZ. Tel. 0244 815262/815783. **T**

Delyn: Delyn Enterprise, c/o Courtaulds plc, Greenfields Works, nr Holywell, Clwyd CH8 7HN. Tel. 0352 712151

Llanelli: Llanelli Enterprise Co., 100 Trostre Road, Llanelli, Dyfed SA15 2EA. Tel. 05542 772122. **WIT**

Merthyr Tydfil: Merthyr and Aberdare Development Enterprise (MADE) Ltd, The Enterprise Centre, Pentrebach, Merthyr Tydfil, Mid Glamorgan CF48 4DR. Tel. 0443 692233; also at The Business Centre, 2 High Street, Aberdare, Mid Glamorgan CF44 7AA. Tel. 0685 884335. **WCT**

Ogwr: Ogwr Partnership Trust, The Enterprise Centre, Tondu, Bridgend CF32 9BS. Tel. 0656 724414

Neath: The Neath Development Partnership, 7 Water Street, Neath, West Glamorgan SA11 3EP. Tel. 0639 54111. **WIT**

Newport: Newport Enterprise Agency, Enterprise Way, Off Bolt Street, Newport, Gwent NPT 2AQ. Tel. 0633 54041

Pembrokeshire: Pembrokeshire Business Initiative, Lombard Chambers, 14 High Street, Haverford West, Pembrokeshire, Dyfed SA16 2LD. Tel. 0437 67655/6. **WCT**

Powys: Powys Self Help, The Old Town Hall, Temple Street, Landrindod Wells, Powys. Tel. 0597 4576. **WT**

West Glamorgan: West Glamorgan Enterprise Trust Ltd, 12A St Mary's Square, Swansea, West Glamorgan SA1 3LP. Tel. 0792 475345/475320. **ET**

Scotland

Aberdeen: Aberdeen Enterprise Trust, First Floor, Seaforth Centre, 30 Waterloo Quay, Aberdeen AB2 1BS. Tel. 0224 582599

Airdrie: Monklands Enterprise Trust, Unit Z, 17 Upper Mill Street, Mill Street Industrial Estate, Airdrie ML6 6JJ. Tel. 0236 69255

Alloa: Alloa & Clackmannan Enterprise Trust, 70 Drysdale Street, Alloa, Clackmannanshire FK10 1JA. Tel. 0259 217171

Arbroath: Arbroath Venture Trust, 115 High Street, Arbroath, Angus DD11 1DP. Tel. 0241 70563

Ayr: Ayr Locality Enterprise Resource Trust, 88 Green Street, Ayr, Ayrshire KA8 8BG. Tel. 0292 264181

Bathgate: Bathgate Area Support for Enterprise, 19 North Bridge Street, Bathgate, West Lothian EH48 4PJ. Tel. 0506 634024

Crossgates: South Fife Enterprise Trust Ltd, 6 Main Street, Crossgates, Fife KY4 8AJ. Tel. 0383 515053

Cumbernauld: Cumbernauld & Kilsyth Enterprise Trust, Enterprise Centre, 5 South Muirhead Road, Cumbernauld G67 1AJ. Tel. 02367 39394

Cumnock: Cumnock and Doon Valley Enterprise Trust, 46 Townhead Street, Cumnock, Ayrshire KA18 1LD. Tel. 0290 21159

Cupar: North East Fife Enterprise Trust Ltd, c/o County Buildings, Cupar, Fife KY15 4TA. Tel. 0334 56360

Dalkeith: Midlothian Campaign Ltd, 115 High Street, Dalkeith, Midlothian EH22 1AX. Tel. 031-660 5849

Dumbarton: Dumbarton Enterprise Trust, 2/2 Vale of Leven Industrial Estate, Dumbarton G82 3PD. Tel. 0389 55424

Dumfries: The Enterprise Trust, Heathhall, Dumfries DG1 1TZ. Tel. 0387 56229

Dundee: Dundee Enterprise Trust, Blackness Trading Precinct, West Hendersons Wynd, Dundee DD1 5BY. Tel. 0382 26001.

East Kilbride: East Kilbride Business Centre, PO Box 1, 10th Floor, Plaza Tower, Town Centre, East Kilbride G74 1LU. Tel. 03552 38456.

Edinburgh: Edinburgh Old Town Trust, c/o Arthur Young, 17 Abercromby Place, Edinburgh EH3 6LT. Tel. 031-556 8641

Edinburgh: Edinburgh Venture Enterprise Trust, 2 Canning Street Lane, Edinburgh EH3 8ER. Tel. 031-229 8928

Elgin: Moray Enterprise Trust, c/o A. R. Scott & Partners, 9 North Guildry Street, Elgin IV30 1JR. Tel. 0343 49644

Falkirk: Falkirk Enterprise Action Trust, Suite A, Haypark, Marchmont Avenue, Polmont, Falkirk FK2 0NZ. Tel. 0324 716173

Fraserburgh: Fraserburgh Ltd, Old Station Yard, Dalrymple Street, Fraserburgh AB4 5BH. Tel. 0346 27764

Glasgow: The Barras Enterprise Trust, Trust Office, 244 Galloway, Glasgow G4 0TS. Tel. 041-522 7258

Glasgow: Glasgow Opportunities, 7 West George Street, Glasgow G2 1EQ. Tel. 041-221 0955

Glasgow: Greater Easterhouse Partnership, 16 Shandwick Street, Easterhouse, Glasgow G34 9BP. Tel. 041-771 5591

Glenrothes: Glenrothes Enterprise Trust, North House, North Street, Glenrothes KY7 5NA. Tel. 0592 757903

Greenock: Inverclyde Enterprise Trust, Inverclyde Initiative, 64-66 West Blackhall Street, Greenock PA15 1XG. Tel. 0475 892193

Kilbirnie: Garnock Valley Development Executive, 44 Main Street, Kilbirnie, Ayrshire KA25 7BY. Tel. 0505 685455

Kilmarnock: Kilmarnock Venture, 30 The Foregate, Kilmarnock, Ayrshire KA1 1JH. Tel. 0563 44602

Kirkintilloch: Strathkelvin Enterprise Trust, 10 Rochdale Place, Kirkintilloch, Glasgow G66 1HZ. Tel. 041-777 7171

Leith: Leith Enterprise Trust, 25 Maritime Street, Leith, Edinburgh EH6 5PW. Tel. 031-553 5566

Leven: Levenmouth Enterprise Trust, Hawkslaw Development (Leven) Ltd, Riverside Road, Leven KY8 4LT. Tel. 0333 27905

Motherwell: Motherwell Enterprise Trust, 28 Brandon Parade, Motherwell, Lanarkshire ML1 1UJ. Tel. 0698 69333

Motherwell: Life, Old Town Hall, 1-11 High Road, Motherwell ML1 3HU. Tel. 0698 66622

Newton Stewart: Wigtown Rural Development Company, Royal Bank Building, 44 Victoria Street, Newton Stewart DG8 6BT. Tel. 0671 3434

Paisley: Paisley/Renfrew Enterprise Trust, SITMS, 5 Sandyford Road, Paisley PA3 4HW. Tel. 041 889 0010

Pitlochry: Highland Perthshire Development Company Ltd, 21 Bonnethill Road, Pitlochry PH16 5BS. Tel. 0796 2697

Saltcoats: Ardrossan-Saltcoats-Stevenston Enterprise Trust, 21 Green Street, Saltcoats, Ayrshire KA21 5HQ. Tel. 0294 602515

Stirling: Stirling Enterprise Park, John Player Building, Stirling FK7 7RP. Tel. 0786 63416

The Small Firms Service

The Small Firms Service is a network of centres and counselling offices, run by the Department of Employment. The service provides information and business counselling for owners and managers of small businesses, and advice for people thinking of starting up new businesses. There is no limit to the type of business the service will help.

The Small Firms Service can provide information on any business problem, and can put you in touch with the right people in local authorities, government departments, the professions, chambers of commerce, etc. It also produces a useful series of free booklets on topics such as *Starting your own business – the practical steps*, *Employing people*, *Marketing*, *Selling to large firms* and *How to start exporting*.

If your inquiry is beyond straightforward sources of information, it can be discussed with one of the Small Firms business counsellors who have considerable business experience.

Information from the Small Firms Service is free. For counselling, the first three sessions are free; a modest charge is made for subsequent sessions, if they are needed. The service is available from 13 Small Firms centres and over 100 area counselling offices throughout the country. To contact your nearest regional centre, dial 100 and ask the operator for Freefone Enterprise.

(In Scotland and Wales, the Small Firms Service is operated through the Scottish and Welsh Development Agencies. A similar service in Northern Ireland is operated by the Local Enterprise Development Unit, LEDU House, Upper Galwally, Belfast BT8 4TB (Tel. 0232 691031).)

Rural Development Commission (formerly CoSIRA)

The Rural Development Commission is a government-funded agency whose objective is to stimulate prosperity in the deprived English rural areas by giving assistance to small businesses. This assistance includes a local source of advice backed up by a wide-ranging technical and managerial consultancy service, limited loan facilities and specialized training.

The Commission's services are available to small manufacturing and servicing firms, located in English rural areas or country towns with not more than 10,000 inhabitants. (Agriculture, horticulture and the professions are excluded.) Advice on local matters is free and so, normally, is the first exploratory consultancy or survey visit. Should further advisory or training visits be required, a modest fee is charged, depending on the size of the business.

Further information can be obtained from the Commission's county offices at the following addresses:

North

Darlington: Morton Road, Darlington, Co. Durham DL1 4PT. Tel. 0325 487123 (for Durham, Tyne and Wear, Cleveland)

York: William House, Shipton Road, Skelton, York YO3 6WZ. Tel. 0904 646866/7

Barnsley: 12 Churchfields Court, Barnsley, South Yorks S70 2JT. Tel. 0226 204367

Morpeth: Northumberland Business Centre, Southgate, Morpeth NE61 2EH. Tel. 0670 58807 or 514343 (via Business Centre)

Howden: 14 Market Place, Howden, Goole, N. Humberside DN14 7BT. Tel. 0430 31138

Penrith: Ullswater Road, Penrith, Cumbria CA11 7EH. Tel. 0768 65752/3

Preston: 15 Victoria Road, Fulwood, Preston PR2 4PS. Tel. 0772 713038

East

Bingham: Chancel House, East Street, Bingham, Notts NG13 8DR. Tel. 0949 39222/3 (for Nottingham, Leicester)

Northampton: Hunsbury Hill Centre, Harksome Hill, Northampton NN4 9QX. Tel. 0604 65874

Sleaford: Council Offices, Sleaford, Lincs. Tel. 0529 303241

Cambridge: 24 Brooklands Avenue, Cambridge CB2 2BU. Tel. 0223 354505

Norwich: 13 Unthank Road, Norwich, Norfolk NR2 2PA. Tel. 0603 624498

Ipswich: Bridge Street, Hadleigh, Ipswich, Suffolk 1P7 5AP. Tel. 0473 827893

South-east

Wallingford: The Maltings, St John's Road, Wallingford, Oxon. Tel. 0491 35523 (for Oxon, Bucks and Berks)

Bedford: Agriculture House, 55 Goldington Road, Bedford MK40 3LU. Tel. 0234 61381 (for Beds and Herts)

Braintree: 64A High Street, Braintree, Essex CM7 6ST. Tel. 0376 47623

Maidstone: 8 Romney Place, Maidstone, Kent ME15 6LE. Tel. 0622 65222

Lewes: Sussex House, 212 High Street, Lewes, East Sussex BN7 2NH. Tel. 0273 471399

Winchester: Northgate Place, Staple Gardens, Winchester, Hants SO23 8SR. Tel. 0962 54747

Newport: 6–7 Town Lane, Newport, Isle of Wight. Tel. 0983 528019

South-west

Exeter: 27 Victoria Park Road, Exeter, Devon EX2 4NT. Tel. 0392 52616

Taunton: 1 The Crescent, Taunton, Somerset TA1 4EA. Tel. 0823 276905

Truro: 2nd Floor, Highshore House, New Bridge Street, Truro, Cornwall TR1 1AA. Tel. 0872 73531 or 73281

Bristol: 209 Redland Road, Bristol, Avon BS6 6XU. Tel. 0272 733433

Dorchester: Room 12/13, Wing D, Government Buildings, Prince of Wales Road, Dorchester, Dorset. Tel. 0305 68558 and 69182

Salisbury: 141 Castle Street, Salisbury, Wilts SP1 3TP. Tel. 0722 336255, ext. 252

West

Telford: Strickland House, The Lawns, Park Street, Wellington, Telford, Shropshire TF1 3BX. Tel. 0952 47161/2/3 (for Staffs and Salop)

Wirksworth: Ravenston Road, Wirksworth, Derby DE4 4EY. Tel. 062 982 4848

Malvern: 32 Church Street, Malvern, Worcs WR14 2AZ. Tel. 068 45 64506 (for Gloucester, Hereford and Worcester)

Warwick: The Abbotsford, 10 Market Place, Warwick CV34 4SL. Tel. 0926 499593

Audlem: 6 Shropshire Street, Audlem, Cheshire CW3 0DY. Tel. 0270 812012

Other sources of help

Local authorities

Some local authorities have a department called an 'economic' or 'industrial' development unit, which has responsibility for advising on small business matters and can help very small, new businesses, as well as more established ones. If there is no economic or industrial development unit, then the planning department normally has responsibility for small-business initiatives.

It may be better to contact your local Enterprise Agency first, since it will have information on the help provided by the local authority for small businesses (and many authorities are involved in sponsoring Enterprise Agencies).

Co-operatives

Advice on forming a co-operative can be obtained from: The Co-operative Development Agency, Broadmead House, 21 Panton Street, London SW1Y 4DR. Tel. 01839 2988; in Scotland, The Scottish Co-operatives Development Committee, Templeton Business Centre, Templeton Street, Bridgeton, Glasgow. Tel. 041-554 3797.

Women in Enterprise

This is a voluntary organization which provides information and training on business from a woman's perspective. It also publicizes the achievements of women in business and the issues affecting them, and it carries out research. Further information from the Women in Enterprise National Co-ordinating Office, 26 Bond Street, Wakefield WF1 2QP. Tel. 0924 361789.

The Paul Bogle Foundation

The Foundation is concerned especially with the development of businesses run by people of Afro-Caribbean origin. It offers advice, counselling and training, runs a business club and a magazine, *Wealth*, and has launched an investment fund to provide capital for new and established businesses. For further details contact: The Paul Bogle Foundation Ltd, 189 Kentish Town Road, London NW5 2JU. Tel. 01-267 6476.

And also . . .

- Bank managers
- Accountants
- Graduate Enterprise Programme counsellors (see p. 260)
- Careers officers
- Livewire (see p. 264)
- Project Fullemploy (see p. 261)
- Small-business clubs (see list of Local Enterprise agencies; those marked '**C**' run a small-business club)
- Local chambers of commerce

II Raising finance

Raising money for a very small business usually involves putting up a lot of your own cash and borrowing money from one of the high street banks. There is also another extremely valuable source of support:

The Enterprise Allowance Scheme

The Enterprise Allowance Scheme provides a regular income if you have previously been unemployed and want to start your own business. For up to 52 weeks, you can receive an allowance of £40 a week to supplement the income of the business.

To be eligible for the scheme, you must:

- be receiving unemployment or supplementary benefit yourself or through a member of your family at the time of application;
- have been unemployed and actively seeking work for at least eight weeks (time spent under formal notice or redundancy and on certain MSC schemes – such as the Community Programme – can count towards this qualifying period);
- show that you have at least £1000 available which you are prepared to invest in the business in the first 12 months (this can be in the form of a loan or overdraft);
- be over 18 and under 65;
- agree to work full-time in business.

Also, the business must be new and be suitable for public support (there are certain excluded categories such as nightclubs and gambling establishments).

If you think you are eligible for the scheme, you should ask at your local Jobcentre to be included in an Enterprise Allowance awareness day (this is the first stage in applying to join the scheme).

Other sources of financial help

(1) Special lending schemes for young people under 25 *(see p. 263).*

(2) Financial assistance dependent on locality

Local authorities: some authorities run schemes to help individuals start up in business. They vary widely, but may include loans, grants, guarantees and workshops – or any combination of these. Your Local Enterprise Agency should have further details, or you can approach the local council direct (see Appendix I, p. 235).

The Rural Development Commission (see p. 249) provides grants for the conversion of redundant rural buildings in priority areas of England (such as parts of Cornwall, Devon and Cumbria); the Commission also has a limited loan fund and operates special lending schemes in conjunction with the major banks.

The Scottish and Welsh Development Agencies, the Northern Ireland Local Enterprise Development Unit, and the Highlands and Islands Development Board provide loan facilities and other forms of financial help for small firms. Approach the Small Firms Service or the Local Enterprise Agency initially, to see whether you have a valid case.

There may be other forms of financial support in your particular locality; for instance, in traditional coal-mining areas, loan finance is available from British Coal Enterprise Ltd. Local Enterprise Agencies will be able to provide further information.

Competitions

Prizes from competitions can be a way of boosting your finances, but don't count on them when making your cash-flow projections! Some of the competitions for small businesses are listed below. They are all *likely* to be run on an annual basis, although given their dependence on sponsorship it cannot be stated *definitely* that they will be run every year.

Award for Business Enterprise Competition

A competition for businesses in Scotland employing fewer than 100 people, sponsored by Scottish Business in the Community, the Scottish Enterprise Trusts and major Scottish companies. It has been run on an annual basis since 1985, with several thousand pounds in prize money available each year.

For information on future awards, contact: Scottish Business in the Community, Romano House, 43 Station Road, Corstorphine, Edinburgh EH12 7AF (Tel. 031-334 9876).

Women Mean Business Award

Organized by *Options* Magazine with support from one main sponsor. For women who are sole proprietors, directors or partners in a business. Judges are looking for originality, initiative, management/systems/control, return on investment.

Prizes: holidays and a trophy.

Details from the Editor, *Options* Magazine, 25 Newman Street, London W1P 3HA (Tel. 01-631 3939).

She Magazine Small Business Competition

Organized by 'She' Magazine, with sponsorship.

Annual competition for people intending to start their own businesses and those who have been trading for less than two years. Competitors submit a written entry of up to 1,500 words, describing their product or service, the market for it, how they propose to sell it, their resources, finances, skills and background. In 1986 the first prize was £3,000 cash, £1,000-worth of office furniture, a photocopier, £500-worth of stationery, an answering machine, dictation equipment, PR advice, business books, an MSC training course and Small Firms Service advice.

Further details from: the Competitions Editor, *She*, National Magazine House, 72 Broadwick Street, London W1V 2BP (Tel. 01-439 7144).

Livewire

See p. 264.

III *Premises*

Science Parks

Science parks act as seed beds for innovation, providing premises for high-tech businesses close to, or on the campuses of, universities and polytechnics. This proximity can have tremendous benefits in terms of 'technology transfer'; access to the expertise of the 'parent' educational institution and scientific and technological support facilities.

The following are members of the UK Science Park Association:

Aberystwyth Science Park, Mid-Wales Development, Ladywell House, Newton, Powys SY16 1JB. Contact: Conrad Jenkins. Tel. 0686 26965. *Or* Industrial Liaison Office, The University College of Wales, Aberystwyth SY23 3DD. Contact: Russell Jones. Tel. 0970 3111

Antrim Technology Park, Industrial Development Board for Northern Ireland, Thomas Street, Ballymena, Co. Antrim, Northern Ireland BT43 6BA. Contact: George Dillon. Tel. 0266 3655

Aston Science Park, Aston Triangle, Love Lane, Birmingham B7 4BJ. Contact: Harry Nicholls. Tel. 021-359 0981

Bolton Technology Exchange, Unit 4, Queensbrook, off Spa Road, Bolton, Lancs BL1 4AY. Contact: David Bromley. Tel. 0204 361708

Brunel Science Park, Brunel University, Uxbridge, Middlesex UB8 3PH. Contact: Peter Russell. Tel. 0895 72192

Cambridge Science Park, Bidwells, Trumpington Road, Cambridge CB2 2LD. Contact: Henry Bennett. Tel. 0223 841841

Cardiff Technology Centre, County of South Glamorgan, County HQ, Newport Road, Cardiff CF2 1XA. Contact: Jeff Andrews. Tel. 0222 499022

Chilworth Research Centre, Chilworth Manor, Chilworth, Southampton SO9 1XB. Contact: Shirley Smith. Tel. 0703 767420

Heriot-Watt Research Park, Room 201, Department of Mechanical Engineering, Heriot-Watt University, Riccarton, Edinburgh EH14 4AS. Contact: Ian Dalton. Tel. 031-449 5111

Highfields Science Park, City of Nottingham, Department of Technical Services, Lawrence House, Clarendon Street, Nottingham NG1 5NT. Contact: Tony Edwards. Tel. 0602 418561. *Or* Industrial and Business Liaison Officer, University of Nottingham, University Park, Nottingham NG7 2RD. Contact: John Webb. Tel. 0602 506101

Listerhills High Technology Development, University of Bradford, Bradford BD7 1DP. Contact: Lawrence West. Tel. 0274 733466

Loughborough Technology Centre, Department of Planning and Transportation, County Hall, Glenfield, Leicester LE3 8RJ. Contact: Michael Gwilliam. Tel. 0533 871313. *Or* Pro-Vice Chancellor, University of Technology, Loughborough, Leicestershire LE11 3TD. Contact: F. D. Hales. Tel. 0509 263171

Manchester Science Park, Enterprise House, Lloyd Street North, Manchester M15 4EN. Contact: Tom Broadhurst. Tel. 061-226 1000

Menai Technology Enterprise Centre, Fford Deiniol, Bangor, Gwynedd LL57 2UP. Contact: Dafydd Jones. Tel. 0248 354103

Merseyside Innovation Centre, 131 Mount Pleasant, Liverpool L3 5TF. Contact: Arthur Rimmer. Tel. 051-708 0123

Mountjoy Research Centre, South Road, Durham DH1 3LE. Contact: John Turner. Tel. 0385 44173. *Or* Industrial Research Laboratories, Science Laboratories, South Road, Durham DH1 3LE. Contact: Eric Howells. Tel. 0385 64971

Newlands Centre, Industrial and Commercial Development Agency, University of Hull, Cottingham Road, Hull HU6 7RX. Contact: David Geekie. Tel. 0482 46311

Newtech (Clywd) Limited, Newtech Square, First Avenue, Deeside Industrial Park, Deeside, Clywd CH5 2NU. Contact: John Allen. Tel. 0244 822881

Portsmouth Advanced Technology Centre, Portsmouth Polytechnic, Anglesea Road, Portsmouth PO1 3DJ. Contact: Terry Duggan. Tel. 0705 827681

St John's Innovation Park, The Bursary, St John's College, Cambridge CB2 1TP. Contact: Chris Johnson. Tel. 0223 338627

Salford University Business Services Ltd, Salbec House, Salford M6 6GS. Contact: Geoff Mortimer. Tel. 061-736 8921

Sheffield Science Park, Sheffield City Council, Department of Employment & Economic Development, Palatine Chambers, Pinstone Street, Sheffield S1 2HN. Contact: Bridget Pemberton. Tel. 0742 766755. *Or* Sheffield City Polytechnic, Pond Street, Sheffield S1 1WB. Contact: Jack Hobbs. Tel. 0742 20911

South Bank Technopark, 90 London Road, London SE1 6LN. Contact: Jeffe Jeffers. Tel. 01-928 2900.

Surrey Research Park, PO Box 112, Guildford, Surrey GU2 5XL. Contact: Malcolm Parry. Tel. 0483 579693

The Bart's Centre, Medical College of St Bartholemew's Hospital, West Smithfield, London EC1A 7BE. Contact: Madeleine Craggs. Tel. 01-606 7404

University of Birmingham Research Park, Birmingham Research and Development Ltd, Institute of Research and Development, Vincent Drive, Birmingham B15 2SQ. Contact: Derek Burr. Tel. 021-471 7977

University of East Anglia Science Park, University Village, Wilberforce Road, Norwich NR4 7TJ. Tel. 0603 56161

University of Reading Science Park, Earley Gate, Whiteknights, Reading RG6 2AH. Contact: Tony Giles. Tel. 0734 875123

University College of Swansea, Innovation Centre, Singleton Park, Swansea SA2 8PP. Contact: Sidney Brailsford. Tel. 0792 205678

University of Warwick Science Park, Barclays Venture Centre, University of Warwick, Coventry CV4 7EZ. Contact: David Rowe. Tel. 0203 418535

West of Scotland Science Park, 1.01 Kelvin Campus, Glasgow G20 0SP. Contact: Alasdair McNicoll. Tel. 041-946 7161

Managed workspaces

Perhaps the most imaginative response to the needs of small-scale entrepreneurs who lack the resources or do not need to rent premises of their own has been the emergence of local community workspaces, where a variety of small businesses share office facilities and common business services. These offer two distinct advantages:

- Because facilities are shared, the cost to individual business people or running their enterprise is far less than if they were operating on their own.
- Because many people operate better in a social atmosphere, and do not like the isolation starting a business can bring, shared workspaces offer a place where you can literally (in the words of the sales brochure) 'work on your own where you are not alone'.

Information on local managed-workspace schemes should be available from your local Enterprise Agency. There is also a national organization for such projects: the National Managed Workspace Group, c/o Richard Allsop, Magazine Business Centre, 11 Newarke Street, Leicester LE1 5SS (Tel. 0533 559711).

Other means of finding business premises:

- Through the Rural Development Commission.
- Through local Enterprise Agencies.
- Through local estate agents and specialist business transfer agents.
- Some local authorities maintain registers of vacant industrial and commercial premises.

IV Small-business training

Many institutions now run training courses for people who would like to set up their own businesses. Research has shown that taking some form of small business training can significantly reduce the risks involved in establishing any kind of new enterprise, so it is well worth taking advantage of the opportunities available for improving one's business skills.

In general terms, the courses available fall into the following categories:

Manpower Services Commission (MSC) – Training for Enterprise (TFE)

There are three main training programmes provided by the MSC. All of them are free, and you may attend if you are unemployed, employed or recently self-employed.

Business Enterprise Programme (BEP)

This is for people who plan to be self-employed or to run a small business. Anyone who has only recently set up in business will also find it useful. BEP lasts for seven days, but, as it is a part-time course, it takes about five weeks to complete it. This gives you the chance to develop your business idea and do some practical research. The first day describes the realities of self-employment. The next six days are run in three equal blocks and cover basic business-management skills such as cash flow, sales forecasting and marketing. You will also be given help to prepare your business plan, which will help you bring everything together.

For local information on BEP, contact the nearest MSC Training Group Area Office (the address and telephone number should be in the telephone directory under Manpower Services Commission) or your Jobcentre.

Firmstart

This is aimed at those whose businesses are likely to expand considerably and employ about ten people after about a year. It is, therefore, highly selective. It is a part-time programme which lasts about six months. Most of the training takes place at weekends. The training is intensive, and there are regular review sessions with a panel of experts and ample opportunity to research the business thoroughly. The timescale of the programme makes it ideal for anyone who has already started his or her business.

Firmstarts are run in several centres around the country. You can get more information from ATP4, W441, MSC, Moorfoot, Sheffield, S1 4PQ (Tel. 0742 703531).

The New Enterprise Programme (NEP)

This is the full-time version of Firmstart. It lasts sixteen weeks: there are four weeks of intensive training (residential) and twelve weeks of market research and business development, during which progress is regularly supervised. If you are unemployed when you attend the programme, you may be entitled to various weekly allowances and expenses.

You can get more information on the NEP from ATP4, W441, MSC, Moorfoot, Sheffield, S1 4PQ (Tel. 0742 703531).

Graduate Enterprise Programme

If you are still at university, polytechnic or college (or have recently graduated), you should investigate the Graduate Enterprise Programme (GEP). Its aim is to promote and stimulate the idea of setting up your own business as a viable career choice for graduates, and to provide a package of intensive training and support for a limited number of potential graduate entrepreneurs. The GEP is a good starting point for any undergraduate or recent graduate who is thinking of starting a business, because (although the number of places for full-time training is limited and entry is competitive) the local counselling networks established as part of the programme can refer you to other sources of local training and small-business advice, such as Enterprise Agencies and MSC training schemes, should you not gain a place on the GEP itself.

From 1988 the programme will be available at various centres in England, Scotland, Wales and Northern Ireland. The features of the GEP are:

- introductory awareness sessions around the country;
- individual counselling and a selection process to choose those with the most viable business ideas for intensive training;
- for selected candidates, an intensive package of training and financial support (a training allowance, market research grant and enterprise allowance), as well as business advice in the first months of trading.

Further information is available from university, polytechnic and college careers services, or (in Great Britain) from the Manpower Services Commission, ATP4, Room 441, Moorfoot, Sheffield S1 4PQ. Details of the Northern Ireland Graduate Enterprise Programme may be obtained from the

Northern Ireland Small Business Institute, University of Ulster, Jordanstown, Co. Antrim BT37 0QB.

Project Fullemploy

Project Fullemploy is a national organization which aims to promote more effective involvement of minority ethnic communities in the economic life of the UK.

It is a registered charity, providing training and advice on self-employment for anyone over the age of 18 through its six enterprise centres in Bradford, Manchester, Sandwell, Bristol, Clerkenwell and Deptford.

Flexible, part-time training courses are provided by means of group sessions, tutorials, visiting professionals and practical research. Resource centres, adjoining the training centres, offer drop-in advice. Participants are helped to test the viability of their business idea, to develop and compile a business plan and to make applications to funding bodies.

For more information contact the Enterprise Development Manager at Fullemploy's Central Office, 102 Park Village East, London NW1 3SP (Tel. 01-387 1222).

Small business training for specific trades and industries

Hotels and Catering: the Hotel and Catering Training Board runs a series of linked courses for people interested in setting up their own hotel and catering businesses. Further information is available from: The Hotel and Catering Training Board, International House, High Street, Ealing, London W5 5DB. Tel. 01-579 2400

Art and design: Lenta (the London Enterprise Agency), together with the Manpower Services Commission, runs a fourteen-week Design Enterprise Programme for art and design graduates under 30. Further information from the London Enterprise Agency, 4 Snow Hill, London EC1A 2BS. Tel. 01-236 3000

Village shops: the Rural Development Commission (see p. 249) runs a range of specialist courses throughout England for both potential and experienced shopkeepers.

Other training courses

Many local Enterprise Agencies provide, or have access to, small-business training. Refer to the list of local Enterprise Agencies on pp. 235–49; those coded 'T' provide training.

Some university and polytechnic careers services run one-day introductory courses for undergraduates who are thinking about starting their own businesses. Ask for further details of these and the Graduate Enterprise Programme at your careers service.

Adult education institutes and colleges of further education may provide part-time courses on setting up a small business.

The Open University runs a home study course, *Start Up Your Own Business*. For further information contact: Associate Student Central Office, Open University, PO Box 76, Milton Keynes MK7 6AN.

Open Learning for Small Businesses

A new and practical way to improve management skills and staff performance. These specially developed self-help training packages enable the user to learn individually, at their own convenience and at their own pace. The subjects include management, marketing, finance and other vital business skills. Details are available from Open Learning for Small Businesses, Standard House, 15 High Street, Baldock, Herts ST7 6AZ (Tel. 0462 895544).

V Schemes for young people

(In most cases, 'young' is defined as being under 25.)

Business Finance

The Prince's Youth Business Trust

The Prince's Youth Business Trust (PYBT) has been formed by the merger, in 1987, of the Youth Enterprise Scheme and the Youth Business Initiative. Established as a charitable trust, PYBT provides a comprehensive range of start-up finance, business advice and information, enterprise training and marketing support.

Training bursaries of up to £1000 may be provided for young unemployed people, under 25, who want to start their own businesses. The money may not be used as working capital or for rent, raw materials or stock but can be spent on tools and equipment, transport, fees, insurance or training.

Those who receive training bursaries must produce a realistic plan and accept continuing advice and support from a local nominee of the Trust and two advisers (normally a bank manager or someone with a financial background and a representative from the proposed type of business).

Loans of up to £5,000 are available, and applicants must submit a business plan and be referred through an enterprise agency or other relevant advisory organization. Where possible, they should make a personal contribution to their enterprise.

Both unemployed young people and those who have just started a business may apply.

For further information contact: the National Co-ordinator, PYBT, 8 Jockey's Fields, London WC1R 4TJ (Tel. 01-430 0521).

Enterprise Allowance

See p. 235.

Legal and General Young Entrepreneurs' Scheme

The scheme provides loans of £500–£2,500 for people between 16 and 25 to enable them to start up in business. All participants must accept ongoing support and advice from a business adviser – usually via their local Enterprise Agency. Applicants for the scheme submit a comprehensive business plan and cash-flow forecast to Legal & General.

Further information from Enterprise Agencies or from: Maureen Howe, Community Affairs Adviser, Legal and General Group PLC, 11 Queen Victoria Street, London EC4N 4TP (Tel. 01-248 9678).

Other schemes

Livewire

Livewire is a scheme to provide business advice and counselling for anyone between 16 and 25 with an idea for self-employment. It is also an awards scheme, with cash awards at local and national level for the most promising ideas.

Entries can be from private businesses, co-operative or collective ventures or projects of benefit to the community. Part-time businesses can also be entered, enabling young people who are still in full-time education to benefit.

Applicants for the scheme are put in contact with their county co-ordinators and, through them, with local advisers who can help them to put their plans into practice.

Registration forms for the Livewire scheme are available from Jobcentres, libraries, youth organizations, schools and colleges, or by writing to: Peter Westgarth, UK Director, Livewire, Freepost, Newcastle NE1 1BR (Tel. 091-261 5584).

Instant Muscle

Instant Muscle is a registered charity, which helps young people (particularly those who are unemployed or disadvantaged) to set themselves up in business.

It operates in seven regions: Scotland, the North-West, Tyne/Tees, Yorkshire, London, South Wales and Central. Each region has business advisers who help participants to indentify their skills, evaluate the commercial possibilities of those skills, prepare a business plan and cash-flow forecast, find the necessary resources to start trading, survive and, hopefully, expand. In suitable cases Instant Muscle can provide short-term, interest-free loans of £1 000 to enable participants to qualify for the Enterprise Allowance Scheme.

Unemployed young people are generally introduced to Instant Muscle's business advisers by Jobcentres, by the Careers or Probation Services, by Youth Clubs, by Enterprise Agencies or – best of all – by their friends. Information can also be obtained from: the Central Office, Instant Muscle, The Haymill Centre, 11 Burnham Lane, Burnham, Slough SL1 6LZ (Tel. 06286 63926).

Head Start

Head Start is a scheme which helps young people between 18 and 25 to become self-employed or to set up their own small businesses. It offers one-day information and 'awareness-raising' workshops and, with voluntary support from the local business community, runs eight-week training programmes in business skills. In 1987 the scheme was operating in twenty-one locations throughout the UK.

Further information from: The Enterprise Unit, The Industrial Society, Peter Runge House, 3 Carlton House Terrace, London SW1Y 5DG (Tel. 01-839 4300).

Local Projects

There are also many local projects to assist young people to set up in business, providing business advice, training and (sometimes) financial assistance in the form of loans or grants. Enterprise Agencies are the best source of information on the schemes available locally.

One example of a local project is the Newcastle Youth Enterprise Centre (at 25 Low Friar Street, Newcastle upon Tyne, Tel. 091 261 6009), which provides workspace, business information and training. Another, in certain areas of Scotland, is a scheme called Enterprise Funds for Youth, administered by three Enterprise Trusts: Ardrossan-Saltcoats-Stevenston Enterprise Trust, Bathgate Area Support for Enterprise and Glasgow Opportunities. (For addresses, see under 'Enterprise Agencies', p. 235.) The scheme is sponsored by the Scottish Development Agency and aims to encourage young people aged 16 to 25 to start or develop their own small businesses by making low-interest loans of up to £3000.

Other schemes that may be of particular interest to young people include Graduate Enterprise Programme (p. 260), and Project Fullemploy (p. 261).

Further Reading

Books

(1) *Books on starting up and running a small business:*

These titles embrace running a small business in *general* terms: they typically cover areas such as: investigating the market, raising capital, marketing and selling, professional advisers, premises, accounts, taxation and employing people.

Clegg, Gillian and Colin Barrow: *How to start and run your own business*, 1984, Macmillan.
A very full and detailed guide to the subject. Recommended.

Daily Telegraph: *How to set up and run your own business*, 5th edn 1986, Daily Telegraph.
A basic introduction to most topics – finding premises, marketing and sales, raising finance, tax, recruitment and employment law, export.

Edwards, Richard: *Running your own business*, 2nd edn 1983, Oyez Longman.
For the older, more established reader (for instance, the author suggests selling one's house and moving to a smaller one to raise capital).

Golzen, Godfrey: *Working for Yourself*, 9th edn 1987, Kogan Page.
Part 1 covers running your own business; Part 2, businesses requiring capital; Part 3 is a directory of low-investment, part-time opportunities for the self-employed; Part 4, freelance work. One of the classic guides, with something in it for everyone.

Lundberg, T.: *Starting in Business*, 1985, Woodhead-Faulkner. A detailed guide, especially to the financial aspects of setting up a small business.

Mogano, M.: *How to start and run your own business*, 5th edn 1985, Graham & Trotman.
Topics such as investigating the market, start-up funds, professional advice, planning and financial control, sales and marketing, export.

Morris, M. J.: *Starting a Successful Small Business*, 1985, Kogan Page.
A step-by-step guide to setting up a business.

Rosthorn, John, Andrew Haldane, Edward Blackwell and John Wholey: *The Small Business Action Kit*, 1986, Kogan Page.
A series of checklists, worksheets, flow charts and summaries covering essential aspects of starting and running a small business.

Rudinger, Edith (ed.): *Starting your own business*, rev. edn 1986, Consumers' Association and Hodder & Stoughton.
Clearly presented guide to the main aspects of starting a business.

Watkins, D. S. *et al.*: *Be Your Own Boss*, 1982, National Extension College.
A kit to help people decide on their suitability for self-employment and their capacity for running a small business, to work out whether a real opportunity exists and to assess their business ideas. Useful checklists, questionnaires, etc.

Woodcock, Clive (ed.): *The Guardian Guide to Running a Small Business*, 6th edn 1987, Kogan Page.
Covers topics such as sources of finance, marketing, tax, employing people. Based on articles which have appeared in the 'Small Business Page' of the *Guardian*.

(2) *Books on self-employment*

Most of these titles cover the basic aspects of running a business (usually in less detail than those in the first category), and then analyse different opportunities, e.g. catering, furniture restoring, minicab driving, etc. Case-study examples of people who have successfully made a go of self-employment are often included.

Attwood, Tony: *Creating your own job: how to survive the recession*, 1982, Hamilton House Publishing.
Ideas for people in the 'shoestring' category.

Crow, John (ed.): *Setting up a Workshop*, 1983, Crafts Council.
For students at art colleges and craftspeople – advice on setting up a craft workshop.

Golzen, Godfrey: *Going Freelance*, 1985, Grafton Books.
Useful if you are intending to work for other organizations on a sub-contract basis, rather than running your own business *per se*.

Mason, Micheline: *Creating your own work*, rev. edn 1983, Gresham Books.
A book to read *before* you become self-employed. Not a 'how to set up a business' guide, more 'why set up a business?' Well researched and includes some interesting case-studies.

Partons, Chris and Angela Neustatter: *Work for Yourself*, 1980, Pan.
Illustrated by a wide range of case-studies. Insubstantial but very readable.

Pettit, Rosemary: *Occupation: self-employed*, 2nd edn 1981, Wildwood House.
Entirely the case-study approach. The author interviewed some 60-odd self-employed people in 1976, following up their careers in 1980. Interesting and well written.

Prentis, Nigel: *The Self-Employment Fact Book*, 1983, Great Ouse Press.
Basic, easy-to-read information. Includes a glossary of business terms.

(3) *Books on home-based or part-time opportunities*

Farrell, Peter: *Spare-time Income*, 1982, Kogan Page.
General information and directory of opportunities.

Fowler, Alan and Deborah: *Making Money Part Time*, 1986, Sphere.
General background information and a directory of part-time, home-based opportunities.

Franklin, Olga: *A practical guide to making money at home*, latest edn 1983, Macdonald & Janes.
A directory of home-based opportunities – some interesting ideas, e.g. genealogist, goat-keeper, french polisher.

Gray, Marianne: *Working from home*, 1982, Judy Piatkus (Publishers).
Over 200 ideas for home-based businesses.

Rundinger, Edith (ed.): *Earning money at home*, rev. edn 1986, Consumers' Association.
Topics such as organizing domestic life, accounts, tax, selling, plus list of opportunities.

(4) *Key source books*

These books are useful as sources of information, both for small-business proprietors and for business advisers.

Barrow, Colin: *The Small Business Guide*, 2nd edn 1984, BBC.
Covers the hundreds of organizations and publications providing information for small businesses.

Bollard, Alan: *Just for starters: a handbook of small-scale business opportunities*, Intermediate Technology Publications, 1984.
A guide for small business and employment support agencies; also useful for those considering starting their own businesses. Reviews the success and failure of typical new ventures, considering potential barriers to new start-ups. Also profiles 33 industries where small enterprises could be profitable.

Croner's Reference Book for the Self-Employed and Smaller Business, Croner Publications.
A loose-leaf reference book on all legislation affecting the self-employed.

The publishers supply amendments on a monthly basis, so the book can be continually kept up to date.

(5) *For young people*

Hall, Paddy: *Work for yourself: a guide for young people*, 1983, National Extension College.
Lively and well written – with quizzes, checklists, charts, cartoons and photographs.

Phillips, Gary: *Down to Business*, 1983, COIC.
Basic information for business starters, written in a simple, readable style.

Rickard, Graham: *Working for yourself*, 1984, Wayland.
The 'case-study' approach, with illustrations. Written in the first person, but the style of each case-study is unmistakably that of the author. Aimed at school-leavers.

Stewart, Judith: *Working in Self-Employment*, 1986, COIC.
Outlines the main business formats, with supporting profiles. Includes list of information sources and suggested reading.

Watts, Alan S.: *Be Your Own Boss at 16*, 1986, Kogan Page.
General business information, discussion of the pros and cons of working for yourself, ideas and case-studies.

(6) *Co-operatives*

Cockerton, Peter and Anne Whyatt: *The Workers' Co-operative Handbook*, rev. edn 1986, ICOM Publications.
A practical guide to setting up a worker's co-op, illustrated by several short case-studies. Rather academic in tone.

How to set up a Co-operative Business, 1985, Co-operative Development Agency.
A detailed guide to setting up a co-operative business, including advice on co-operative organization, the various model legal structures, comprehensive lists of support organizations and resource material.

Pearce, John: *Running your own co-operative*, 1984, Kogan Page.
Basic introductory information for those thinking of setting up a co-op.

(7) *Books on specific aspects of running a small business*

Bland, Michael: *Be Your Own PR Man*, rev. edn 1983, Kogan Page.
A public relations guide for the small business.

Chaplin, Paul: *Choosing and Using Professional Advisers*, rev. edn 1986, Kogan Page.
A guide to choosing an accountant, bank manager, solicitor or other specialist.

Clayton, Patricia: *Law for the Small Business*, 5th edn 1986, Kogan Page.

Farrell, Peter: *How to Buy a Business*, 1983, Kogan Page.

Harries, John: *Your Business and the Law*, 2nd edn 1983, Oyez Longman.
A clear, readable guide to the legal side of running a business.

Patten, Dave: *Successful Marketing for the Small Business*, 1985, Kogan Page.

St John Price, A.: *Understand Your Accounts*, 2nd edn 1986, Kogan Page.
Finance for the non-accountant.

Woodcock, Clive: *Raising Finance: The Guardian Guide for the Small Business*, 5th edn 1986, Kogan Page.
A comprehensive guide to sources of finance. Rather hard going, but useful even for the 'shoestring' entrepreneur.

(8) Opportunities in specific trades and industries

Cox, Roger: *Running Your Own Shop*, 1985, Kogan Page.

Garner, Ursula and Judy Ridgway: *Running Your Own Catering Business*, 1984, Kogan Page.

Hosking, Sarah: *Working for Yourself in the Arts and Crafts*, 1986, Kogan Page.

Hotel and Catering Training Board: *Small Business Information Pack*, 6th edn 1986.
A directory of services for small businesses in the hotel and catering industry.

Hotel and Catering Training Board: *Starting up your own business*, 1982.

Levene, P.: *How to Start and Run Your own Shop*, 1985, Graham & Trotman.

Linton, Ian: *Writing for a Living*, 1985, Kogan Page.

Ludman, Kim: *Running Your Own Building Business*, 1986, Kogan Page.

Ridgway, Judy: *Home Cooking for Money*, rev. edn 1986, Judy Piatkus (Publishers).

Riley, Noel and Godfrey Golzen: *Running Your Own Antiques Business*, 1984, Kogan Page.

Rose, John and Linda Hankin: *Running Your Own Photographic Business*, 1985, Kogan Page.

Rowland, Tom: *Selling Antiques from Home*, 1982, Pelham Books.

Stacey, Nigel: *Running Your Own Driving School*, 1984, Kogan Page.

Vellacott, Audrey, and Liz Christmas: *Doing Bed and Breakfast*, rev. edn 1987, David and Charles.

Newspapers

The *Guardian* has regular small-business features on Fridays, *The Times* on Fridays, and the *Financial Times* on Tuesdays.

Periodicals

Business Opportunities Digest, monthly, published by Chartsearch Publications in association with the Institute of Small Business, 57–61 Mortimer Street, London W1N 7TD.
Analyses at least 25 business opportunities in each issue.

Business Success (incorporating *What Finance*), monthly, published by Parkway Publications Ltd, Beechmore House, 7 Broadhurst Gardens, London NW6 3QX (Tel. 01-328 3344).
Encouragement and information for small businesses – 'to make their enterprising ideas take off and succeed'.

Small Business Confidential, a subscription magazine published by Stonehart Publications Ltd, 57/61 Mortimer Street, London W1N 7JD (Tel. 01-637 4383).

Your Business, fortnightly, published by Your Business Magazine Ltd, 50 Poland Street, London W1V 4AX (Tel. 01-437 5678).

Free (or almost free) publications

General

A useful guide to free publications (although the book itself costs £5.95) is *Sources of Free Business Information*, by Michael J. Brooks, 1986, Kogan Page.

AGCAS Career Information Booklet: *Alternative Work Styles* (*including Self-Employment*) free from university and polytechnic careers services, or £1.25 (including postage) from Central Services Unit, Crawford House, Precinct Centre, Manchester M13 9EP.

Barclays Bank: *Starting Your Own Business*, *Financial Control in the Smaller Business*, *Financial Planning in the Smaller Business*.

Department of Health and Social Security: *National Insurance Guide for the*

Self-employed. Free leaflet from local offices of the DHSS. (There are also other DHSS leaflets which may be relevant, such as *National Insurance contributions for people with small earnings from self-employment* and *Class 4 NI contributions*.)

Health and Safety Executive: *The law on health and safety at work: essential facts for small businesses and the self employed*. Free from local Health and Safety Executive offices.

Inland Revenue: *Starting in Business*, free from the local Inspector of Taxes. A guide to taxation.

Lloyds Bank: *Starting Your Business, Expanding Your Business, Services to Business*. Free booklets.

London Enterprise Agency (Lenta) and Good Housekeeping: *Good Housekeeping Guide to Starting Your Own Business*.
A very useful introductory guide. Send 35p plus a large s.a.e. to Good Housekeeping Money, 72 Broadwick Street, London W1V 2BP.

London Enterprise Agency (Lenta): *Running a market stand*, free booklet. Particularly useful for the London area.

Midland Bank: *Building a Successful Business*, pack of four free booklets.

National Westmister Bank: *Start up and go with Natwest, Know Your Own Business*. Free booklets.

The Small Firms Service produce a series of free booklets on aspects of starting a small business. To contact the service, dial 100 and ask for Freefone Enterprise.

Free periodicals

Executive Post, a free executive job-hunters' newspaper published weekly by Professional and Executive Recruitment (Moorfoot, Sheffield S1 4PQ) has regular small-business features. Recent graduates who register with Professional and Executive Recruitment are sent free copies of a similar publication, *Graduate Post*, which also sometimes carries articles on small-business topics. (Copies are also available on a subscription basis from Newpoint Publishing, Newpoint House, St James Lane, London N10 3DF.)

In Business Now, bi-monthly newspaper published by the Department of Trade and Industry, available free to small businesses in the UK. Write to: In Business Now, Freepost, London SW1P 4BR.

National Westminster Bank Small Business Digest. Free from any branch of the Natwest. The digest covers topics of interest and relevance to small businesses.